PORNLAND

How Porn Has Hijacked
Our Sexuality

Gail Dines

BEACON PRESS
BOSTON

Beacon Press
25 Beacon Street
Boston, Massachusetts 02108-2892
www.beacon.org

Beacon Press books
are published under the auspices of
the Unitarian Universalist Association of Congregations.

14 13 12 11   8 7 6 5 4 3 2 1

This book is printed on acid-free paper that meets the uncoated paper
ANSI/NISO specifications for permanence as revised in 1992.

Design and composition by Wilsted & Taylor Publishing Services

Library of Congress Cataloging-in-Publication Data
Dines, Gail.
  Pornland : how porn has hijacked our sexuality / Gail Dines.
    p. cm.
  Includes bibliographical references and index.
  ISBN 978-0-8070-0154-7 (paperback : alk. paper) 1. Pornography.
2. Pornography—Social aspects. 3. Sex. 4. Sex—Social aspects. I. Title.
  HQ471.D549 2010
  363.4'70973—dc22   2009046250

For David and T,
the loves of my life

CONTENTS

PREFACE

Howard Stern regularly features porn on his show, and for this he was the second-highest paid celebrity in the world in 2006; Hugh Hefner's life, with his blonde, young, and embarrassingly naive "girlfriends," is the topic of the hugely popular *The Girls Next Door* on E! Entertainment; retired mega–porn star Jenna Jameson has written a bestselling book and appears in numerous popular celebrity magazines, and Sasha Grey, the new, more hard-core Jenna Jameson, is featured in a four-page article in *Rolling Stone* in May 2009 and appears in a Steven Soderbergh movie. Kevin Smith's movie *Zack and Miri Make a Porno* is warmly received by movie critics; pole dancing is a widely popular form of exercise; students at the University of Maryland show a porn movie on campus; and Indiana University invites pornographer Joanna Angel to address a human sexuality class. I could go on, but these examples illustrate how porn has seeped into our everyday world and is fast becoming such a normal part of our lives that it barely warrants a mention. The big question is, What are the consequences of this saturation for our culture, sexuality, gender identity, and relationships? The answer is that we don't know for sure. One thing is certain: we are in the midst of a massive social experiment, only the laboratory here is our world and the effects will be played out on people who never agreed to participate.

The architects of the experiment are the pornographers, a group of (mostly) men who are out to maximize their profits: to create markets, find products that sell, invest in R & D, and develop long-term business plans. In short, and as this book will show, they are businessmen from start to finish, not innovators committed to our sexual freedom.

Porn is now so deeply embedded in our culture that it has become synonymous with sex to such a point that to criticize porn is to get slapped with the label anti-sex. As I travel the country giving lectures on the effects of porn, the insults thrown at me by some people are telling: they range from uptight prude to uncool, old-time man-hating, sex-policing feminist—the type of feminist who supposedly screams rape every time a woman and man have sex, the kind of feminist who has been derisively referred to as a "victim-feminist" because she supposedly sees all women as sexual victims incapable of enjoying sex.

But what if you are a feminist who is pro-sex in the real sense of the word, pro that wonderful, fun, and deliciously creative force that bathes the body in delight and pleasure, and what you are actually against is porn sex? A kind of sex that is debased, dehumanized, formulaic, and generic, a kind of sex based not on individual fantasy, play, or imagination, but one that is the result of an industrial product created by those who get excited not by bodily contact but by market penetration and profits. Where, then, do you fit in the pro-sex, anti-sex dichotomy when pro-porn equals pro-sex?

To appreciate just how bizarre it is to collapse a critique of pornography into a critique of sex, think for a minute if this were a book that criticizes McDonald's for its exploitive labor practices, its destruction of the environment, and its impact on our diet and health. Would anyone accuse the author of being anti-eating or anti-food? I suspect that most readers would separate the industry (McDonald's) and the industrial product (hamburgers) from the act of eating, understanding that the critique was focused on the large-scale impact of the fast-food industry and not the human need to eat and the pleasure the experience of eating yields. So, why, when I talk about pornography, is it difficult for some to understand that one can be a feminist who is unabashedly pro-sex but against the commodification and industrialization of a human desire? The answer, of course, is that pornographers have done an incredible job of selling their product as being all about sex, and not about a particular constructed version of sex that is developed within a profit-driven setting.

I want to make clear that when I talk about "porn," I am referring mainly to "gonzo"—that genre which is all over the Internet and is today one of the biggest moneymakers for the industry—which depicts hard-core, body-punishing sex in which women are demeaned and debased. As someone who has lectured on college campuses for over twenty years, I have witnessed a seismic change in the way porn has come to shape young adults' sexuality. Before the advent of the Internet, it used to be that some men sporadically "used" porn when growing up; it was the more soft-core type of porn, and they often had to steal it from older males, most likely their fathers. Increasingly, what I hear from students is that men today regularly (often daily) use the gonzo type of porn, and many have now become accustomed to its hard-core scenes. What seems contradictory is that for all their increased porn use, men today are also generally more responsive and interested in engaging in thoughtful discussion and reflection after my lectures.

In these conversations, I hear something I never used to—concern and anxiety from young men. These guys have just heard a lecture on the effects of porn, complete with an explicit slide show, and they are beginning to recognize how porn has shaped how they think about sex. While past generations of men who used porn had limited access to the material, this generation has unlimited access to gonzo porn. Nowadays the average age for first viewing porn is just eleven years. This means that, unlike before, porn is actually being encoded into a boy's sexual identity so that an authentic sexuality—one that develops organically out of life experiences, one's peer group, personality traits, family and community affiliations—is replaced by a generic porn sexuality limited in creativity and lacking any sense of love, respect, or connection to another human being. Many times I feel profoundly sad after speaking to these young men.

I have a college-aged son, and I couldn't stand for the pornographers to set up camp in his sexual identity. When he was entering his teenage years, we talked candidly about the use of porn and its potential effects. I told him that as he was getting older, he would most likely come across some porn, and he had a choice to look or not to look. I said that should he decide to use porn, then he was going to hand over his sexuality—a sexuality that he had yet to grow into, that made sense for who he was and who he was going to be—to someone else. Why, I asked him, would you give anyone something so valuable and precious, something that ultimately is yours, not theirs? When I look out at the men in the lecture hall, they remind me of my son, and I feel outraged that they are caught in the crosshairs of this predatory industry, one that has a huge financial stake in habituating them to a product that dehumanizes all involved.

While men tell me their stories of porn use, women have stories of their own. Most college-aged women I speak with have never seen gonzo, but their sexuality is increasingly shaped by it as the men they partner with want to play out porn sex on their bodies. Whether their sexual partners pressure them into anal sex, want to ejaculate on their face, or use porn as a sex aid, these women are on the frontlines of the porn culture. Some capitulate, some negotiate, and many are confused as to why the men they hook up with, date, or marry are always trying to push the sexual envelope.

But even if a woman stays away from men who use porn—no easy task given its widespread usage—she can't insulate herself from it. Women's magazines, fashion ads, TV, music videos, and box office movies bombard women with images that would have, a decade ago, been defined as soft-core porn. Whether the case is Britney Spears writhing around almost naked or *Cosmopolitan* magazine informing readers that porn could spice up their lives, women are increasingly being socialized in a culture that is hypersexualized, and at the center of this is the image of the young, toned, hairless, (often) blonde white woman gazing seductively at the camera.

This hypersexualization has put pressure on women to look and act like they just tumbled out of the pages of *Maxim* or *Cosmopolitan*. Whether it be thongs peeping out of low-slung jeans, revealing their "tramp stamp," their waxed pubic area, or their desire to give the best blow job ever to the latest hookup, young women and girls, it seems, are increasingly celebrating their "empowering" sexual freedom by trying to look and act the part of a porn star.

While such a shift is toasted by mainstream magazines, the porn industry, and even some feminists as an indicator of society becoming more sexually free, many female students I speak to aren't joining in the celebration. They feel pressured, manipulated, and coerced into conformity. Men they hook up with expect porn sex: anonymous, disconnected, and devoid of intimacy, and if they don't get it, then they move on. And even if the women deliver, the men still move on because in a porn culture, one woman is much the same as the next, as long as she meets, to some degree, the conventional standards of "hotness."

Although I have been studying the porn industry for over two decades, nothing prepared me for how quickly hard-core, cruel porn would come to dominate the Internet. I could see the images getting harder and harder core over the years, but they were still a long way from the brutality that is now commonplace in gonzo. The Internet caused a revolution in porn, but in my travels across the country, I find that there are many people, especially women and older generations, who are completely unaware of what is going on. This is why I've decided to include in this book at times detailed and explicit descriptions of what is now considered mainstream porn. In some cases it is simply not possible to describe the images without using the language of porn. Such language is used sparingly and only when it is necessary to convey the harsh reality of the images and their messages.

It is impossible to do the work I do and not be deeply affected. I am affected as a mother, a feminist, a teacher, and an activist. This is my attempt to invite you into the dialogue and to bring to public consciousness a problem that, I believe, is a serious public health issue. I hope you'll consider and debate what I've found and, by the final chapter, perhaps you'll understand why I believe that pornographers have hijacked our sexuality, and why it's about time we wrested it back.

Porn and the Industrialization of Sex

Don't Come Here Looking for Love
—Ad for Im Live, a porn Web site

It is January 2008 and I am in a cavernous convention hall surrounded by hard-core porn images of women being anally, vaginally, and orally penetrated. I am trying to have a conversation with Patricia, a middle-aged African American woman who is a security guard working for slightly more than minimum wage, but we both have difficulty hearing as our voices are drowned out by the orgasmic sounds coming from the movies being shown all around us. Patricia is distinguished from the other women in the hall not only by her age and race but by the fact that she is fully clothed. Most other women here are wearing only thongs and pasties, in stark contrast to the thousands of dressed men milling around them. Some men stand in long lines waiting to have their picture taken with scantily clad women, while others wander from booth to booth, looking for the latest movie. I am at the Adult Entertainment Expo, the pornographers' annual trade show in Las Vegas.

Patricia has a bad crick in her neck from trying to avoid looking at the porn that is being projected onto the screens. Needless to say, this is no easy feat. She expresses her frustration about being forced to work this detail, as she has never before seen porn. Divorced for many years, Patricia tells me that after doing this job for a few days, she now knows why she "can't find a good man to settle down with." As we talk, one of the very few African American porn performers in the hall walks past us, dressed in the usual porn garb of high-heeled shoes and not much more. Patricia taps me on the shoulder and says, "Go and tell her that it is not good for her to be doing this stuff." At that very moment a fan goes over to the porn performer and puts his hand on her crotch; his friends take a picture. Patricia groans.

As someone who studies porn, I am accustomed to these kinds of images, but Patricia is new to them, and it is through her eyes that I see this situation for what it really is: a parallel universe where the complexity of humans, the multiple pleasures of life, and the deep connections that nourish and sustain us vanish. In their place are blow jobs, erect penises, shaved vulvae, surgically enhanced breasts, distended anuses, and a limitless supply of semen. Patricia and I are in the middle of a world that reduces humans to orifices and body parts, bled dry of soul, personality, history, and future, as life in the porn world is only about the here and now, where penetrating someone or being penetrated is all humans exist for. As I am writing notes for my book, Patricia starts to plot her future far away from Las Vegas.

As I wander around the hall, talking to pornographers, it becomes very clear that they are not particularly interested in sex. What turns these people on is making money. The only time they seem excited is when they are discussing market shares, niche products, or direct marketing versus bulk mailing in one of the many business seminars that accompany the trade show. Many of the porn producers I interview freely acknowledge that they are in the business to make money, not to further our sexual empowerment or creativity. They see themselves as caught up in a business that, thanks to the growth of the Internet, is like a runaway train. What they will admit is that porn is becoming more extreme, and their success depends on finding some new, edgy sex act that will draw in users always on the lookout for that extra bit of sexual charge. Not one of the men I talk to seems particularly interested in how these new extremes will be played out on real women's bodies, bodies that are already being pushed to the brink of their physical limits. No, these men want their piece of the pie, and their single-minded focus on the bottom line is evident.

Making money in the porn industry is not as easy as it was during the early days of the Internet; the explosion in recent years of the number of films and Web sites has produced a glut of products. Paul Fishbein, founder of *Adult Video News* (*AVN*), an industry trade publication, has stated that "the laws of supply and demand have been turned upside down. We're on par to put out 15,000 new releases this year, which is just insane."[1] The other problem Fishbein points to is the enormous amount of pirated or free material on the Internet. Everyone I spoke to at the Expo was worried about this highly competitive market, and many shared the feelings of one producer who told me that "this is an industry running out of ideas." As we spoke, the latest film from this person's company played on a screen in the booth; it featured a young woman being anally penetrated as she knelt in a coffin.

In fact, images today have now become so extreme that what used to be considered hard-core is now mainstream pornography. Acts that are now commonplace in much of online porn were almost nonexistent a couple of decades ago. As the market becomes saturated and consumers become increasingly bored and desensitized, pornographers are avidly searching for ways to differentiate their products from others.

This shift in both quantity and quality has had profound implications for the ways boys and men experience porn.[2] To begin to understand the changes, consider how young men and boys were introduced to porn in pre-Internet days. Hormones raging, boys would most likely discover their father's *Playboy* or *Penthouse* to masturbate to. These magazines, with their soft-core, soft-focus pictures of naked women, taught boys and men that women existed to be looked at, objectified, used, and put away until the next time. Their future supply of porn was dependent on what they or their friends could pilfer from their father's stash or maybe from the local convenience store. The sexism of these images was bad enough, but compared to porn today, the porn of yesterday seems almost quaint.

Rather than sporadic trips into a world of coy smiles, provocative poses, and glimpses of semi-shaved female genitalia, youth today, especially boys, are catapulted into a never-ending universe of ravaged anuses, distended vaginas, and semen-smeared faces. When they masturbate to the stories, acts, and narratives of such porn in a heightened state of arousal, a cornucopia of messages about women, men, relationships, and sex are sent to the brain. The questions that need to be asked here are, What is the content of these images? and What do they say to ever-younger and more impressionable consumers about sex, love, and intimacy?

MAKING HATE:
PORN SEX AND THE DESTRUCTION OF INTIMACY

Through my experience lecturing on pornography for over two decades, I have found that most women and some men have an idea of pornography that is twenty years out of date; what comes to mind is often simply a *Playboy* centerfold. It's crucial to be aware of the images that are now considered ordinary in mainstream Internet pornography. The usual way I show my audience how hard-core the industry has become is through a PowerPoint presentation featuring snapshots from well-traveled sites. I use words rather than pictures here, but I need to add that however extreme the scenes I describe sound, my descriptions are nothing compared to actually viewing porn.

Because commercially produced Internet porn is mainstream, easily accessible, and cheaply available, I have decided to focus on it here. As the Internet has become the dominant distribution system, it is now the main channel by which most men, especially young men, access porn.[3] To ensure that this is an accurate reflection of all porn available on the Internet, and not one that focuses on only the most excessive, I started my search by typing "porn" into Google and clicked on some of the sites that appeared on the first page.[4] After clicking around for a few seconds I was directed to hundreds of sites that offered a whole range of sex acts, many of which show one woman and multiple men. Some of the most popular acts advertised and depicted during my quick search are

- vaginal, anal, and oral penetration of a woman by three or more men at the same time;
- double anal, in which a woman is penetrated anally by two men at the same time;
- double vagina, in which a woman is penetrated vaginally by two men at the same time;
- gagging, in which a woman has a penis thrust so far down her throat she gags (or, in the more extreme cases, vomits);

- ass-to-mouth, in which a penis goes from a woman's anus to her mouth without washing; and
- bukkake, in which any number of men ejaculate, often at the same time, onto a woman's body, face, hair, eyes, ears, or mouth. In some of these movies, the men ejaculate into a cup, and the "money shot" is the woman drinking the semen mixture.[5]

To discern what a curious user would find if he wanted to look at porn without paying for site membership, I randomly selected some images to click on and stayed only at Web sites offering a free tour or sample video. I started by clicking on OnlyBestSex.com, which advertised itself as having a free porn search engine for "Sex Videos and Hot XXX sites." On that site was an ad for Gag Me Then Fuck Me, featuring image after image of women being orally, anally, and vaginally penetrated by from one to three men. The introductory text on the site reads: "Do you know what we say to things like romance and foreplay? We say fuck off! This is not another site with half-erect weenies trying to impress bold sluts. We take gorgeous young bitches and do what every man would REALLY like to do. We make them gag till their makeup starts running, and then they get all other holes sore—vaginal, anal, double penetrations, anything brutal involving a cock and an orifice. And then we give them the sticky bath!"[6] Viewers can click onto any number of sample videos, which act as teasers for longer movies. The one advertising "Laura" tells the reader: "The last thing we needed here was a vomiting girl—but this time it was close. Stopping is not our style, so she was grabbed by the head and facefucked as if there was no tomorrow. She tried hard to swallow, but there was too much muck, and the bitch had no real choice but to take it all. And of course her love tunnel looked like a train passed through!"

A few more clicks and I was at GagFactor.com owned by JM Productions, a much-talked-about site in the porn trade magazines. When I clicked on it I was invited to "Join us now to Access Complete Degradation." On the site are hundreds of pictures of young women with penises thrust deep into their throat. Some are gagging, others crying, and virtually all have faces, especially their eyes, covered in semen. The user is bombarded with images of mascara running, hair being pulled, throats in a vicelike grip, nostrils being pinched so the women can't breathe as the penis fills the mouth, and mouths that are distended by either hands pulling the lips apart or penises inserted sideways. Below each set of pictures are "quotes" by the male porn performers. Some examples are

- "Watching the transition from civilian to cumbucket is an amazing thing to watch."
- "Stupid, stupid whores. Gotta love 'em!"
- "I love turnin' the screws on these dumb whores!"
- "It's true, getting throatfucked keeps you skinny cuz all that snot that comes out of your face burns calories."
- "I'm not sure what's wrong with these girls but I am thankfull [*sic*] for their existence."

As a way to promote its movies, Gag Factor provides twenty- to thirty-second free clips. One of the trailers I clicked on listed the following biographical details of the woman:

NAME: Scarlett
AGE: 24
STATUS: Long Since Vanished

"Scarlett" is blonde, dressed in revealing Victoria's Secret–type underwear, and has a viselike contraption digging into her neck and head. The short clip opens with Scarlett sitting on a toilet having a penis thrust down her throat while the man attached to the penis manipulates her head back and forward using the handles on the vise. He drags her off the toilet onto her knees while he continues to thrust viciously into her mouth. You watch Scarlett from above begin to gag, eyes bulging, and as she tries to pull away to breathe, the man pulls the vise toward his penis with greater force so she can't move. As all this is going on he is screaming at her: "Get off the fucking toilet, get your ass on your knees, right motherfucking now.... I am a fucking psychotic motherfucking bitch...fucking you till your fucking mama comes from the grave."[7] The intensity of the images and words made these twenty seconds of video feel like twenty minutes to me.

After a few more clicks I was at the Anal Suffering site, which promises, "Every week, we'll bring you a new Suffering Slut. Weak, Destroyed, Agonizing in Anal Pain and Totally Fucked Up right in her ass. And you'll have all the glory of watching them."[8] The pictures and free clips do indeed show women grimacing in pain as they are being forcefully anally penetrated by one man, and often vaginally by another at the same time. Other similar sites show close-up images of women's red and swollen anuses, allowing the viewer to linger on the damage. On one site advertising the movie *Anally Ripped Whores*, the text reads: "We at Pure Filth know exactly what you want and we're giving it to you. Chicks being ass fucked till their sphincters are pink, puffy and totally blown out. Adult diapers just might be in store for these whores when their work is done."[9]

From there I moved into the teen porn genre, which lists movie titles such as *Teen Hitchhikers, Teens for Cash, Teen Dirty Slut, Soaped Pink Teen Pussy*, and *Petite Teen Hard Fuck* as well as the whole subgenre of babysitter porn, which includes *Banged Babysitters, Cute Babysitter Riding Cock, Fuck the Babysitter*, and *Gag the Babysitter*. Predictably, there are hundreds and hundreds of images of young-looking women with small breasts and shaved vulvae, wearing adolescent markers such as school uniforms, braids, and bobby socks while hugging stuffed animals or sucking popsicles. The text on the Fuck the Babysitter site reads, "Naughty Babysitter Knows What She's Good for: sucking cock and drinking cum." Many of the free sample films show the "teen" being initiated by a much older man into what is supposedly her first sexual experience.

This is just a smattering of what's available online to any person who is minimally computer literate.[10] As noted, boys see their first porn on average at eleven years of age, and by then most have computer skills sophisticated enough that they can access any of the sites described above.[11] For the uninitiated, the scenes I have just described might seem like outliers from the extreme end of the industry, but unfortunately these images are all too representative of what is out there on the Internet and in mass-produced movies. In one of the few studies that have been conducted on the content of contemporary porn, it was found that the majority of scenes from fifty of the top-rented porn movies contained both physical and verbal abuse of the female performers.[12] Physical aggression, which included spanking, open-hand slapping, and gagging, occurred in over 88 percent of scenes, while expressions of verbal aggression, calling the woman names such as bitch or slut, were found in 48 percent of the scenes. The researchers concluded that "if we combine both physical and verbal aggression, our findings indicate that nearly 90% of scenes contained at least one aggressive act, with an average of nearly 12 acts of aggression per scene."[13]

Even some in the porn industry are beginning to critique the violent and degrading images that are now part of mainstream Internet porn. For example, veteran porn producer Holly Randall, one of the few women producers in the industry who has had some success, wrote: "With high-end productions pushed to the side to make way for amateurish, extreme content, we created a market for what I call the Porn Olympics.... Now it was a question of how far you could push the envelope: how many men can you have sex with in one film, how many dicks can you fit in your orifices, how many ways can you eat cum? In the attempt to one-up the last guy, scenarios I couldn't even dream up became, well, somewhat normal."[14] Most of the acts Randall is talking about are found in a subgenre of porn called *gonzo* by the industry.[15] Often referred to as *wall-to-wall* because it contains sex scene after sex scene with no attempt at a plot or story line, this type of porn is, according to a 2005 article in *AVN*, "the overwhelmingly dominant porn genre since it's less expensive to produce than plot-orientated features." The features also sell well, but what makes gonzo so profitable is that it is, according to the same *AVN* article, "the fare for the solo stroking consumer who merely wants to cut to the chase, get off on the good stuff."[16]

The *AVN* article itself cuts to the chase, as getting off is, after all, what porn is all about. But what it ignores, and for good reason, is the range of messages men imbibe as they masturbate. Porn, like all other images, tells stories about the world, but these stories are of the most intimate nature, as they are about sexuality and sexual relationships. When men turn to porn to experience sexual arousal and orgasm, they come away with a lot more than just an ejaculation because the stories seep into the very core of their sexual identity. To suggest otherwise would be to see sex as just a biological urge, removed from the social context within which it is developed, understood, and enacted in the real world. No biological urge exists in a pure form, devoid of cultural meaning or expression, and in American society, porn is probably the most visible, accessible, and articulate teller of sexual stories to men.

PORN STORIES

For all of its millions of images, themes, and pseudo-plotlines, the story gonzo porn tells about women, men, and sex is amazingly consistent. This is because porn images are produced by an industry and are hence scripted, formulaic, and genre-bound representations. As much as pornographers would like us to think that they are just capturing people having sex, in reality, the images are carefully crafted and choreographed. Consumers of porn have certain expectations as to how the story will unfold, and the more a movie, television show, or indeed any text follows a set pattern, the less ambiguity there is in the storytelling. This in turn means that the consumer is more likely to come away with the messages that the producer intended, and less likely to decode the story in some idiosyncratic way. So what are the stories porn tells the user?

The messages that porn disseminates about women can be boiled down to a few essential characteristics: they are always ready for sex and are enthusiastic to do whatever men want, irrespective of how painful, humiliating, or harmful the act is. The word "no" is glaringly absent from porn women's vocabulary. These women seem eager to have their orifices stretched to full capacity and sometimes beyond, and indeed, the more bizarre and degrading the act, the greater the supposed sexual arousal for her. The women who wander through this world are, whether they know it or not, all whores by nature, as they all have a price, often as low as a few bucks (as in "Every bitch will suck cock for a few dollars" or "This slut will do anything for rent money"). Even though these women love to be fucked, they seem to have no sexual imagination of their own: what they want always mirrors what the man wants. This may explain why women in porn spend enormous amounts of time giving men oral sex, yet they rarely expect or demand reciprocity. Actually, the only demands they seem to make involve asking the man to thrust harder and harder.

In the porn world, women are never concerned about pregnancy,

STDs, or damage to their bodies, and are astonishingly immune to being called cunts, whores, cumdumpsters, sluts, bitches, hot slits, fuck-tubes, squirty skanks, and stupid hoes. They seem comfortable with the idea that their partner(s) views their sexuality as something unclean (as in "dirty cunt," "filthy little whore," or "nasty cumdumpster") and often refer to themselves in these ways. Indeed, women of the porn world seem to enjoy having sex with men who express nothing but contempt and hatred for them, and often the greater the insults, the better the orgasm for all involved. This is an uncomplicated world where women don't need equal pay, health care, day care, retirement plans, good schools for their children, or safe housing. It is a world filled with one-dimensional women who are nothing more than collections of holes.

The story pornography tells about men is actually much simpler. Men in porn are depicted as soulless, unfeeling, amoral life-support systems for erect penises who are entitled to use women in any way they want. These men demonstrate zero empathy, respect, or love for the women they have sex with, no matter how uncomfortable or in pain these woman look. Probably the most peculiar thing about porn-world men is that they even lack the ability to express arousal, because no matter how erect their penises are, they exhibit none of the signs we normally associate with sexual excitement. The only time the men moan, grunt, or writhe is when they are about to ejaculate; the rest of the time they methodically thrust their penis into the woman's orifices with a look of deep concentration on their faces. This can get very bizarre, especially in an oral sex scene where a stoic man gags a woman by thrusting his penis deep in her mouth, yet she is the only one having orgasmic responses. And when porn men are done, they are really done—there is not the slightest show of postcoital intimacy with the woman they have just ejaculated onto.

In a world populated by women who are robotic "sluts" and men who are robotic studs, the sex is going to be predictably devoid of any intimacy. Porn sex is not about making love, as the feelings and emotions we normally associate with such an act—connection, empathy, tenderness, caring, affection—are replaced by those more often connected with hate—fear, disgust, anger, loathing, and contempt. In porn the man makes hate to the woman, as each sex act is designed to deliver the maximum amount of degradation. Whether the man is choking her with a penis or pounding away at her anus until it is red raw, the goal of porn sex is to illustrate how much power he has over her. It is what he wants when, where, and how he wants it, because he controls the pace, the timing, and the nature of the acts.

The power that men have over women in porn sex is encoded into the sex acts and the physical and verbal abuse that accompanies them. Oral sex is more often than not played out with him standing up and her on her knees; in this superior position he can control the pace of thrusting by holding onto her face and/or neck in a viselike grip. When a woman pulls away from the penis in an attempt to catch her breath, he intensifies the thrusting, causing her to gag even more. Vaginal and anal penetration often take place with her lying on a bed, sofa, or table while he again stands above her, a good position to look her in the face and tell her just what a disgusting whore she really is. If he has his hands on her body, they are not there to caress or fondle, but to either hold her down or stretch an orifice so that her body becomes that much more accessible and vulnerable. That she is a mere object is clear in many scenes where men will suddenly grab a woman and pull her down on a sofa or to the floor so he can position his body above hers as he ejaculates onto her face or into her mouth. In some cases this is so rough that she lands on the floor with a thud and has to quickly rearrange her body so the viewer gets a bird's-eye shot of the semen being squirted on her.

What seems surprising at first about gonzo porn is how few scenes there are with multiple women and one man, especially as for many men, having sex with more than one woman is a time-worn fantasy. When there are multiple performers it is usually one woman with any number of men. If porn is indeed about dominance and degradation, then it makes sense that the woman will be outnumbered since multiple men penetrating her suggests powerlessness. Should the tables be turned and there be more women than men in the scene, then there is always the possibility that the women, outnumbering the man, are the ones who hold the power.

Scenes where a woman is multiply penetrated also reveal the way in which much of gonzo porn is about seeing just how far you can push a woman's body before it is injured. A vagina or anus that has two penises in it is vulnerable to tearing and prolapse. A penis thrust deep into the throat can also cause damage, as can a penis thrust in sideways so the woman's mouth is stretched to almost inhuman proportions. The volume of porn produced today means that a frenzied competition has begun, as producers not only push the sexual envelope but place their women actors at higher and higher levels of risk in the process. In this race to the bottom, the fantasy cruelty of porn spills over into the real world.

One of the most degrading acts in porn is called the "money shot," where the man ejaculates on the face or body of the woman. This usually marks the end of a scene and is central to the construction and marketing of the porn movie. While this has been a staple of porn for many years, recently it has taken a new turn in gonzo: the woman either drinks the collective ejaculate of any number of men (bukkake) or holds it in her mouth and the camera lingers on the ejaculate dribbling down her chin. Another relatively new twist is "cum swapping," where a woman passes the semen into the mouth of another woman. There are now porn movies that specifically focus on this, as *Cum Swapping Bitches* and *Cum Swapping Cheerleader*, as well as movies that promise to show women swallowing the semen.

The ejaculate also marks the woman as used goods, as owned by the man or men who just penetrated her. Veteran porn actor and producer Bill Margold explained the money shot like this: "I'd like to really show what I believe the men want to see: violence against women. I firmly believe that we serve a purpose by showing that. The most violent we can get is the cum shot in the face. Men get off behind that, because they get even with the women they can't have. We try to inundate the world with orgasms in the face."[17] That viewers enjoy money shots is evident by the postings on the Adult DVD Talk forum, a Web site for porn fans.[18] Here fans talk about their favorite money shot at length, often giving a detailed account of the scene. Jim 2, for example, tells his virtual friends that "I consider gangbang scenes memorable that end with the girl a total mess, having a huge amount of cum on her face and tits,"[19] while The The likes to see "the gag reflex kicking in."[20] Some of the posters make clear that for them, pleasure comes in watching a woman really suffer: "Kaci Starr starts retching/gagging as soon as the first drop of sperm hits her tongue—it's so great. The best scene for this (and for Kaci getting totally overwhelmed in general) is her amazing scene in *Throat Gaggers #10*. She actually starts throwing up the cum (and some of whatever she had for lunch! lol) during the cumswallowing portion of the scene. She starts tearing up as she struggles to keep it all down. Wonderful stuff."[21] The money shot would seem a succinct way to deliver multiple messages about the way sex can be used as a vehicle to mark the feminine as all-powerless and the masculine as all-powerful.

I daresay that the sexual acts I have described above are not ones that most women seek out in the real world, nor ones that most men feel comfortable asking their partner to engage in. Conversely, acts that are part of many people's sexual experience, such as kissing, caressing, cuddling, and fondling, are noticeably absent in pornography. This forces us to ask why men who view porn are so attracted to images that depict types of behavior so at odds with the real world. One obvious answer could be that men go to porn as a way to play out a fantasy, a way to conjure up mental images that are not real but nonetheless pleasurable. But if it were as simple as this, then why isn't there an equal amount of porn that depicts women and men having great sex that involves deep connection and intimacy, with women having fabulous orgasms brought about by a highly skilled male lover who has an intuitive understanding of women's bodies? This, too, would be a fantasy for many viewers, but it is clearly not one that porn chooses to represent with any regularity. Instead porn plays out "fantasy" sex that looks more like sexual assault than making love.

Some may argue that assault is too strong a word, but if we analyze what is actually going on in a gonzo scene in a way that speaks to the experiences of the woman in the movie, then we get some insight into what is happening to her as a human being. A living, breathing person is being penetrated in every orifice by any number of men—men she most likely has no real emotional connection with. Their penises are often longer and thicker than average, and they are sometimes fortified with Viagra, since penetration without ejaculation has to go on for some time.[22] Her body, like ours, has real physical limits, yet the goal of the movie is to see just how far these limits can be pushed. At some point during all the pounding, her vagina will become sore, her anus raw and swollen, and her mouth will ache from having large penises thrust in and out for an extended amount of time. As this is occurring, she is being called every vile name under the sun. During this bodily assault, which even the industry admits is taking its toll on the bodies of the women,[23] she has to look like she is enjoying it, she has to tell the men penetrating her that she loves their big cock or whatever, and finally she has to lick the semen as if she loves the taste.

When the movie is done, she will get up from the bed or floor, go to the bathroom to wash off the sticky substance and check her orifices to see if any damage has been done. She also will need to ensure that she does not have any of the diseases or ailments for which she is now high risk, given what her body has just been through. These include, according to the Adult Industry Medical Health Care Foundation, the following: HIV; rectal gonorrhea; tears in the throat, vagina, and anus; chlamydia of the eye; and gonorrhea of the throat.[24] And she will endure all this again and again until she is either too worn out to continue or is disregarded by the industry in favor of "fresh meat," of which, it seems, there is never any shortage.

Men who go looking for porn are often already aroused as they anticipate their soon-to-be-had orgasm. Clearly, in this state they are not in any mood to start doing a critical deconstruction of how the woman is being treated, but it truly doesn't take much observation to notice that her body is being used in ways that appear to be painful and degrading. Few of the women are seasoned actresses, and many are not able to conceal their discomfort and pain as they are being penetrated by multiple penises. Some of the women look exhausted and defeated by the end of the scene.

As porn becomes more extreme, and the woman's body is treated in harsher ways, one wonders how users manage to sustain an erection. No doubt there are some who enjoy watching women suffer, but I honestly do not believe that the average man is a woman-hating sadist. This is indeed the image of men the pornographers generate, but it is one that, ironically, given our man-hating reputation, feminists reject since we have never believed that men are born misogynists. And those of us who have male children refuse to accept that the little boy we birthed, fed, bathed, nurtured, and love came out of the womb with a homing device for GagFactor.com.

If we refuse to accept the easy answer that men have a natural predisposition to get off on hurting women, then we have to look to the culture for answers as to why some men seek out and enjoy gonzo. We have to ask, What is it about male socialization and masculinity that helps prepare them—or, I would say, groom them—into seeking out and masturbating to such images? The answers do not lie within individual men; rather, they are found in the culture that we all live in. Porn is not something that stands outside of us: it is deeply embedded in our structures, identities, and relationships. This did not happen overnight, and there is a story to tell about how we got to the point that mainstream Internet porn has become so hateful and cruel.

We begin the investigation with a history of the porn industry that focuses on the ways that *Playboy, Penthouse,* and *Hustler* provided the economic and cultural space for today's hard-core porn. Chapter 1 specifically looks at how the competition among the three magazines pushed the envelope on what was considered "acceptable" mainstream porn in the 1970s and '80s. Today, there is a whole new range of agents pushing porn into the mainstream, and chapter 2 takes a look at some of the major individuals and companies that have succeeded in sanitizing porn.

Arguing that porn is mainstream goes beyond noting the way the images have infiltrated our lives to include an analysis of how porn has seamlessly been woven into mainstream capitalism. Chapter 3 takes a close look at what it means for the porn industry to be part of a wider corporate structure and how many mainstream industries such as hotels, banks, and cable operators make large sums of money from the porn industry. The need to create markets and offer consumers something different explains in part why porn is always on the lookout for some new bizarre sex act. What it doesn't explain is how men can be aroused by such images of women being dehumanized and debased. Chapter 4 argues that to answer this we need to look at the ways that men are socialized by the culture and the porn industry, since both have an image of men as aggressive, unfeeling, and disconnected from their emotions and from other people.

What happens to men who use porn? This is without doubt the most hotly debated issue in the discussion of porn. Rather than rehash the whole debate or delve into the numerous studies by psychologists, in chapter 5 I look at how images affect the way we perceive reality and why, given what we know about media effects, it is incorrect to argue that men walk away from porn unchanged.

Men are not the only group to be changed by the porn culture. Girls and women, while not major consumers of porn, are inundated with pop culture images that just a decade ago would have been seen as softcore. Chapter 6 looks at how the image of femininity thrown at girls and women has become increasingly narrow, to the point that a "hot" body is the only one that meets very strict cultural standards. Some groups have celebrated this hypersexualization as empowering for women, but I argue that this is pseudo-empowerment since it is a poor substitute for what real power looks like—economic, social, sexual, and political equality that give women power to control those institutions that affect our lives.

Pornographers, always trying to add extra sizzle to gonzo sex, have developed a number of niche markets. One very lucrative niche features people of color, the topic of chapter 7. Not a genre known for its subtlety, porn produces and reproduces some of the worst racist stereotypes of past and present. Given that most of these films are made for a white male audience, the question here is, How do sexualized racist images shape the way users think about race? Another niche that is popular is called pseudo-child porn because although it uses women who are eighteen or over, they are actually made to look much younger. Chapter 8 illustrates how by using the props of childhood—socks, school uniforms, teddy bears—pornographers invite the user into a world where the sexualization of children is normalized.

The conclusion asks what is to be done about this pornographization of our culture. No easy answers jump out as obvious since this is a problem that has deep roots in the way our society is structured. Ultimately, to fight this juggernaut we will need collective action. Individual solutions are important, but social change never happens on the individual level. The pornographers did a kind of stealth attack on our culture, hijacking our sexuality and then selling it back to us, often in forms that look very little like sex but a lot like cruelty. The only solution to this is a movement that is fierce in its critique of sexual exploitation and steadfast in its determination to fight for what is rightfully ours.

ONE

Playboy, Penthouse, and Hustler

Paving the Way for Today's Porn Industry

> Porn has entered the mature years.... It's no longer naughty,
> underground. It's an up-front, in-your-face business, as much
> a part of the pop culture as anything else. We're in a different
> phase of our pop culture.
> —Paul Fishbein, publisher of *Adult Video News*

The *Playboy* bunny is everywhere, on pencils, watches, handbags, lingerie, sunglasses, socks, and even hot-water bottles. It is without doubt one of the most highly recognized logos in the Western world and has made Hugh Hefner and *Playboy* household names. While *Playboy* did not invent porn, it did bring it out of the backstreet onto Main Street; for this it holds a central place in the story of how porn became entrenched in our culture.[1] Hugh Hefner presented himself to the public as a playboy partial to wearing pajamas, but he was actually an incredibly savvy businessman with a knack for tapping into and exploiting the cultural themes of post–World War II America.

Before *Playboy*, pornographic magazines were not circulated through mainstream channels of distribution, so access to them was limited. Post *Playboy*, it was a very different world after Hefner eroded the cultural, economic, and legal barriers to mass production and distribution of porn. Just one step behind Hefner came Bob Guccione, founder and publisher of *Penthouse* magazine, who pushed the envelope even further. However, it was a strip club owner from Kentucky who mapped out just how far a pornographer could go and still have access to mainstream channels of distribution. Larry Flynt, a skilled businessman, made *Hustler* magazine a household name in the 1970s. Although their inaugural products now seem tame by comparison, through their battle to outdo one another, Hefner, Guccione, and Flynt groomed Americans into accepting today's hard-core Internet porn.

BUILDING A PORN INDUSTRY

Playboy was an overnight success story, with circulation growing from 53,991 in its first month (December 1953) to 175,000 by its first anniversary issue. By 1959 *Playboy* had a monthly circulation of 1 million. In its heyday of the late 1960s and early 1970s, Playboy was an enormous company, with sales of over $200 million and more than five thousand employees.[2] Clearly, as Michael Kimmel argues, "*Playboy* struck a nerve with American men," and many books have attempted to describe exactly what that nerve was.[3] To explore the *Playboy* phenomenon and the magazine's role in laying the groundwork for the contemporary porn industry, the magazine has to be historically located in the economic and cultural trends at work during the 1950s, which at different times and to varying degrees contributed to *Playboy* becoming the lifestyle-pornographic magazine of choice for the upwardly mobile, white American male in the postwar years.

Historians agree that the 1950s were a time of enormous change in the United States, both economically and culturally. They point to the economic boom, the baby boom, the growth of suburbia, the pressure to marry at an early age, and the push toward consumption as a way of life as trends that, while not being specific to the 1950s, were nonetheless magnified in that decade.[4] *Playboy* occupied an ambivalent place in relation to these trends—it celebrated some as good for the country while condemning others as harmful to American men. It was its uncanny ability to pick and choose among these trends that made *Playboy* a success not only with readers but also, eventually, with advertisers.

Hefner was clear about his target audience from the very beginning. He wrote in the first issue of *Playboy*, published in December 1953: "If you are a man between 18 and 80, *Playboy* is meant for you.... We want to make it clear from the start, we aren't a 'family' magazine. If you are somebody's sister, wife or mother-in-law and picked us up by mistake, please pass us along to the man in your life and get back to the *Ladies' Home Companion*."[5] For a magazine to clearly state that it was not "a family magazine" in the 1950s was close to heresy. According to social historian Stephanie Coontz, it was during this period that there was an unprecedented rise in the marriage rate, the age for marriage and motherhood fell, fertility increased, and divorce rates declined. From family restaurants to the family car, "the family was everywhere hailed as the most basic institution in society."[6]

The mass media played a pivotal role in legitimizing and celebrating this "pro-family" ideology by selling idealized images of family life in sitcoms and women's magazines, while demonizing those who chose to stay single as either homosexual or pathological. The most celebrated sitcoms of the period were *Leave It to Beaver, Father Knows Best,* and *The Adventures of Ozzie and Harriet.* The ideal family was white and upper middle class, with a male breadwinner whose salary supported a wife and children as well as a large home in the suburbs. The primary roles for men and women were seen as spouses and as parents, and the result was a well-run household populated by smart, well-adjusted kids.

The print media also got in on the act, carrying stories about the supposed awfulness of being single. *Reader's Digest* ran a story entitled "You Don't Know How Lucky You Are to Be Married," which focused on the "harrowing situation of single life."[7] One writer went so far as to suggest that "except for the sick, the badly crippled, the deformed, the emotionally warped and the mentally defective, almost everyone has an opportunity to marry."[8] In the 1950s, "emotionally warped" was a coded way of saying homosexual, and indeed many single people were investigated as potential homosexuals and by extension Communists, since the two were often linked during the McCarthy years.[9]

This pressure on men to conform not only to the dictates of domestic life but also to the growing demands of corporate America had its critics in the popular media. Some writers pointed to the conformist male as a "mechanized, robotized caricature of humanity...a slave in mind and body."[10] According to Barbara Ehrenreich, magazines like *Life, Look,* and the *Reader's Digest* carried stories suggesting that "Gary Gray" (the conformist in the gray flannel suit) was robbing men of their masculinity, freedom, and sense of individuality.

While pop psychologists criticized the corporate world for reducing American males to "little men,"[11] it was women in their roles of wives and mothers who were essentially singled out as the cripplers of American masculinity. As Ehrenreich has argued, because "the corporate captains were out of the bounds of legitimate criticism in Cold War America," women were the more acceptable and accessible villains.[12] Described as greedy, manipulative, and lazy, American women were accused of emasculating men by overdomesticating them.[13]

Probably one of the most woman-hating books of the time was Philip Wylie's *Generation of Vipers*, first published in 1942 and reprinted after World War II. For Wylie, wives were the cause of men's problems because they controlled the home with an iron fist and worked their spouses to death in order to enjoy a life of leisure. As Wylie so eloquently put it, "It is her man who worries about where to acquire the money while she worries about how to spend it, so he has the ulcers and she has the guts of a bear."[14]

It was during these woman-hating, pro-family years that *Playboy* hit the newsstands. Picking up on the themes of the 1950s, *Playboy* editors, from the very first issue, defined single women as menaces to the *Playboy* reader since they were out to trap him into marriage and bleed him financially. Indeed, the first major article in the first issue of *Playboy* was called "Miss Gold-Digger of 1953." Bemoaning the good old days when alimony was reserved for "little floosies," *Playboy* editors wrote, "When a modern day marriage ends, it doesn't matter who's to blame—it's always the guy who pays and pays and pays and pays." Echoing Wylie's assertion that women had taken over America, the article continued, "A couple of generations ago, this was a man's world, nothing could be further from the truth in 1953."[15]

This was a theme that *Playboy* was to express repeatedly in its early years. Burt Zollo, writing in the June 1954 issue, told *Playboy* readers to "take a good look at the sorry, regimented husbands trudging down every woman-dominated street in this woman-dominated land. Check what they're doing when you're out on the town with a different dish every night." For those men who had been lucky enough to escape marriage, Zollo warned them to beware of June, the marriage month, since "woman becomes more heated, more desperate, more dangerous."[16]

Dangerous women were also the focus of Wylie's article "The Womanization of America," published in *Playboy* in September 1958.

Starting from now-familiar themes, Wylie accused American women of taking over the business world, the arts, and, of course, the home. It was the home, according to Wylie, where men especially ceased to be men: the "American home, in short, is becoming a boudoir-kitchen-nursery, dreamed up for women by women, and as if males did not exist as males."[17] According to *Playboy*, the position of American men continued to deteriorate; by 1963, an article in the magazine claimed that the American man was being worked so hard by his wife that he was "day after day, week after week…invited to attend his own funeral." This state of affairs could not continue, according to the writer, William Iversen, because "neither double eyelashes nor the blindness of night or day can obscure the glaring fact that American marriage can no longer be accepted as an estate in which the sexes shall live half-slave and half-free."[18]

While the anti-woman ideology of *Playboy* was not new, what was new was the way it was tied in to an anti-marriage position; American wives were beyond salvation, they had been given too much power and the only solution was to refuse to conform to the ideal of domesticity. However, simply telling men not to conform by staying single would not have been enough in the 1950s, since nonconformity was taken as a sign of either homosexuality or social pathology. What was needed was an alternative to "Gary Gray," an image of a man who refused to conform but was still considered a man. This man worked hard, but for himself, not for his family; he was actively heterosexual, but with lots of young, beautiful women (just like the ones that populated the magazine), not with a wife. Such a man, Zollo informed readers in the June 1954 issue of *Playboy*, did indeed exist and he was the "true playboy": the well-dressed, sophisticated guy who could "enjoy the pleasures the female has to offer without becoming emotionally involved."[19] *Playboy* was to become the manual for men who aspired to be playboys, and these men, born and raised in a time of material deprivation (the Great Depression and then the Second World War) and sexual conservatism, needed all the help they could get to learn how to become a big-spending, upmarket consumer of goods and women.

Part of *Playboy's* overnight success can be explained by the lack of competition, since the men's magazine industry was dominated by magazines that specialized in what was referred to as "blood, guts and fighting."[20] After the war, this industry enjoyed record-breaking profits, with sales increasing 62 percent from 1945 to 1952.[21] At the time there was some concern over the increasingly violent content of these magazines. Naomi Barko, for example, writing in 1953, complained that men's magazines were dominated by "war, big-game hunting, women, speed sports and crime," a world in which "jobs, families, careers, education and civic problems are never mentioned."[22] What these magazines offered, Weyr argues, was an escape from suburban life, but one based on danger and adventure, rather than sex.[23]

The print pornography market at the time was dominated by cheap, under-the-counter pinup magazines, the type that few men would feel comfortable displaying on their coffee table. Hefner was well aware that the financial potential of such magazines was limited in the 1950s, and, moreover, he did not want to create just a "porn" magazine; rather, he wanted to develop an upmarket lifestyle magazine that would have the pornographic pinup as its centerpiece. This was the core of the magazine, but unlike the other porn magazines of the time, this pinup would be delivered to the readers in a package that celebrated the upper-middle-class bachelor life, the type of life that the 1950s male dreamed of leading, be he a college student, a married man living in the suburbs, or an upwardly mobile corporate male.[24]

SELLING *PLAYBOY* TO THE PLAYBOY

Hefner's desire to create a pornographic lifestyle magazine with mainstream distribution, readership, and status meant he had to carefully construct a public image of *Playboy* as a quality lifestyle magazine that had "tasteful" pictures of women, rather than as a pornographic magazine that carried articles on consumer items and current events. The fact that *Playboy* was in the business of constructing and reconstructing its image is apparent in the way it marketed itself to various target groups. Hefner's initial marketing strategy was to sell *Playboy* as a softcore pornography magazine to the potential distributors and as a lifestyle "men's" magazine to the targeted audience. In April 1953, eight months before the first copy of *Playboy* hit the stands, Hefner sent a letter to twenty-five of the largest newsstand wholesalers throughout the country inquiring about potential interest in the magazine, which was originally to be called *Stag Party*.[25] The letter read:

> Dear Friend,
>   STAG PARTY—a brand new magazine for men—will be out this fall—and it will be one of the best sellers you have ever handled.... It will include male pleasing figure studies, making it a sure hit from the very start. But here's the really BIG news! The first issue of STAG PARTY will include the famous calendar picture of Marilyn Monroe—in full color! In fact every issue of STAG PARTY will have a beautiful full page, male pleasing nude study—in full natural color. Now you know what I mean when I say that this is going to be one of the best sellers you have ever handled.[26]

While the pictorials were emphasized in the letter to wholesalers, it was the lifestyle section of the magazine that was promoted to readers. In the first edition of *Playboy*, Hefner told his readers:

> Within the pages of *Playboy* you will find articles, fiction, pictures, stories, cartoons, humor and special features...to form a pleasure-primer styled to the masculine taste....We plan spending most of our time inside.
>   We like our apartment. We enjoy mixing up cocktails and an hors-d'oeuvre or two, putting a little mood music on the phonograph and inviting in a female acquaintance for a quiet discussion on Picasso, Nietzsche, Jazz, Sex.[27]

Notice that when the editors addressed the reader, the pictures were just one of many attractions, rather than *the* attraction. The reader was invited not to masturbate to the centerfold but rather to enter the world of the cultural elite, to discuss philosophy and consume food associated with the upper middle class. To sell the magazine primarily in terms of its pictorials—how it was marketed to distributors—would have constructed a very different image for the reader to identify with. The markers of upper-class life, which appear causally thrown in as afterthoughts (cocktails, hors d'oeuvres, and Picasso), were deliberately

placed to cloak the magazine in an aura of upper-middle-class respectability.

The centerfolds seem very tame by today's standards, with their
carefully concealed pubic hair and coy gazes at the camera. However, in
the 1950s, they were considered risqué and some in publishing believed
that Hefner was headed for jail. These centerfolds were, however, the
selling point of the magazine. As one *Playboy* editor, Ray Russell, com-
mented in an interview: "We could have all the Nabokovs in the world
and the best articles on correct attire without attracting readers. They
bought the magazine for the girls. We couldn't take the sex out. The
magazine would die like a dog."[28] But, given the time period, Russell
would have been equally correct if he had reversed the order and said
that the magazine would die like a dog if they'd taken the articles out.
These were crucial in providing a cover and giving permission to the
self-defined middle-class American male to indulge in consuming porn,
an activity that had previously been defined as "low class."

One effective technique that Hefner employed to give *Playboy* an
upmarket image was to develop the literary side of the magazine. For
the first few years *Playboy*'s literary content was chosen, usually, from
the public domain, given the magazine's limited cash reserves. However,
as sales increased toward the end of 1956, Hefner employed Auguste
Comte Spectorsky, formerly an editor at the *New Yorker*, to develop the
literary side of the magazine. While Spectorsky did turn *Playboy* into
a magazine that attracted the most respected of American writers, he
constantly butted heads with Hefner as he became increasingly uncomfortable with the sexual content of the magazine, urging Hefner to put
more money and effort into building the literary and lifestyle features.
It seems that Spectorsky was not aware of the role that the literary side
was to play in legitimizing *Playboy* and mistakenly assumed that Hefner's
main interest was in creating more of a literary magazine than a pornographic one.

While the two factions fought over the content of the magazine,
they were careful to construct in the magazine an ideal reader who
bought *Playboy* for the articles, interviews, humor, and advice columns.
If Spectorsky can be faulted, it is for believing in the image of the
ideal reader that *Playboy* constructed. This ideal reader was, of course,

the playboy. Although articles and editorials often made reference to the playboy who read *Playboy*, it was in the April 1956 issue that Hefner most clearly laid out his image of the ideal *Playboy* reader. "What is a playboy? Is he simply a wastrel, a ne'er-do-well, a fashionable bum? Far from it. He can be a sharp minded young business executive, a worker in the arts, a university professor, an architect or an engineer. He can be many things, provided he possesses a certain kind of view. He must see life not as a vale of tears, but as a happy time, he must take joy in his work, without regarding it as the end of all living; he must be an alert man, a man of taste, a man sensitive to pleasure, a man who—without acquiring the stigma of voluptuary or dilettante—can live life to the hilt. This is the sort of man we mean when we use the word playboy."[29]

The actual *Playboy* reader of the 1950s looked nothing like the playboy described above. As for being men of taste, most of the readers had grown up during a time of material deprivation and were not accustomed to high-level consumption. Thus, these men needed to be schooled in the ways of living "life to the hilt" and especially in how to spend money. Clearly, given the experiences of the older generation, these young men could not turn to their parents for guidance on how to spend their discretionary income. A new, modern teacher was needed and Hefner was only too willing to comply, providing an image to men of what constitutes a *Playboy* lifestyle. This meant the products offered by the magazine were to be of the highest quality: the short stories, the interviews with famous people, the cars, the alcohol, the clothes, the food, the advice about consumer items to buy—and, of course, the women.

From the very first issue, pages and pages of editorial comment set out to "teach" readers what products to buy in order to become a playboy. In the early years, mainstream advertisers kept a distance from *Playboy* because of its pornographic content, so the products were discussed in articles rather than shown in advertisements. For example, the first issue presented a special feature on desk designs to inform the reader which desks made the best impressions. Arguing that big desks and heavy cabinets were depressing and old-fashioned, the editors suggest that the new, more sleek-looking desks told clients that "this executive and his firm are as up-to-date as tomorrow, know where they are going and will use the most modern methods to get there."[30] The comparison of the old with the "modern" was a standard theme in the early years of *Playboy*, and the reader was consistently told that a real playboy bought only modern lampshades, ties, clothes, and ice buckets (the Fiberg ice bucket being the one to "please any playboy").[31]

Playboy was not the only media product to sell the 1950s young adult an ideology of consumption. According to historian George Lipsitz, the main function of television in the 1950s was to provide "legitimation for transformations in values initiated by the new economic imperatives of postwar America."[32] One way to do this, according to Ernest Dichter, the marketing guru of the 1950s, was to demonstrate "that the hedonistic approach to life is a moral one, not an immoral one."[33] While *Playboy* was one of many media corporations to employ Dichter, it was one of a few whose clear aim was to turn the male into a consumer. Elaine May has argued that the 1950s was in general the period of the "expert," where increasing numbers of people turned to professionals for advice on just about every aspect of life, from what to buy to how to prepare for a nuclear war.[34] *Playboy* editors certainly played the role of expert, telling readers "what to wear, eat, drink, read and drive, how to furnish their homes and listen to music, which nightclubs, restaurants, plays and films to attend, what equipment to own."[35]

However, as with all advertising, the actual product on offer was not the commodity being advertised but rather the fantasy of transformation that this product promised to bring to the consumer's life. The high-quality products shown in *Playboy* would transform the reader into a "playboy" who could then have the real prize: all the high-quality women he wanted—just like the ones who populated the magazine. The women in the *Playboy* pictorials were designed to be "teasers," demonstrating to the reader what he could have if he adopted the *Playboy* lifestyle of high-level consumption. In an interview, Hefner revealed this strategy of sexualizing consumption when he explained: "*Playboy* is a combination of sex...and status...the sex actually includes not only the Playmate and the cartoons and the jokes which describe boy-girl situations, but goes right down in all the service features."[36]

Hefner, by sexualizing consumption, provided an extremely hospitable environment for advertisers looking to expand markets in the postwar boom. By the end of 1955, advertisers had overcome their initial fear of advertising in a "men's entertainment" magazine and were, according to Weyr, "clamoring to buy."[37] During the 1950s and 1960s, *Playboy* continued to increase its readership and its advertising revenue, and by the late 1960s the circulation figures reached an all-time high of 4.5 million. An article in *Business Week* in 1969 entitled *"Playboy* Puts a Glint in the Admen's Eyes" discussed the enormous popularity of *Playboy* magazine with advertisers, quoting a media man at J. Walter Thompson Company, the world's largest advertising agency at the time, saying that years ago none of their clients would have touched *Playboy* but "today, it's a routine buy." The magazine then informed its readers that "last year JWT expenditure in the magazine increased 70%."[38]

Despite the increased advertising revenue that *Playboy* enjoyed well into the 1960s, its relationship with advertisers was stormy. The main reason for this was *Playboy*'s somewhat split personality as both a lifestyle magazine and a porn publication. According to Weyr, the advertisers liked *Playboy*'s readership (mostly white, college-educated, upwardly mobile men) yet disliked its sexual content for fear of being associated with a sleazy porn magazine. In the early years, Hefner and his major associates regularly flew to New York for emergency meetings with advertisers whose clients felt that the pictorials or stories had become too explicit.[39] Many of these meetings ended in a promise from the *Playboy* staff to limit the overt sexual content and no revenue was lost. One such battle occurred over a story by Calder Willingham that appeared in the July 1962 issue. Called "Bus Story," it focuses on the rape of a seventeen-year-old girl by an older man. However, as in much of pornography, the story is written in a way that sexualizes the brutality: "There are times to be tender and times to be just a little rough. This was a time to be just a little rough. Left forearm heavily across her breasts and left hand gripping her shoulder so hard she winced, Harry used his knees like a wedge, grey eyes hypnotic above her. 'Open your legs,' he said in a cold, hard and vicious tone. Lips apart and eyes empty with shock, the girl did as she was told. A moment later, hands limp on his shoulders, a gasp came from her. Then another gasp."[40] According to Weyr, a number of companies, including Ford Motor, threatened to cancel contracts with *Playboy* and a number of newsstand wholesalers refused to carry the July issue. Fear of losing the advertisers prompted Hefner to write a letter of apology to all the major corporations who advertised in the July issue, and he offered to meet personally with their representatives.[41] This kind of economic power meant that advertisers policed (and continue to police) the sexual content of *Playboy*. Thus, built into the magazine was a conflict between the need to attract advertising revenue and the need to keep readers interested by publishing sexual content.

When there was no competition from other magazines, keeping readers was relatively easy since their only other option was the poorly produced, down-market variety of pornography, which certainly did not offer the reader a "playboy" image of himself. However, as the pornography market began to develop, other magazines adopted the *Playboy* formula. Chief among these competitors was *Penthouse*, a magazine that specifically aimed to replace *Playboy* as the best-selling pornography magazine in the country. The competition between *Playboy* and *Penthouse* that took place in the early 1970s not only hurt *Playboy* financially, it also changed the mainstream print pornography industry by pushing the limits of what was deemed acceptable, both legally and culturally.

PLAYBOY, PENTHOUSE, AND HUSTLER GO TO WAR

The first hint that *Playboy* had some serious competition came in 1969 when full-page ads appeared in the *New York Times*, the *Chicago Tribune*, and the *Los Angeles Times* showing the *Playboy* bunny caught in the crosshairs of a rifle. The caption read, "We're going rabbit hunting." The ads were for *Penthouse* magazine, which would be on the newsstands later that year. According to Miller, the news was at first greeted with some amusement by the *Playboy* staff, since by then the magazine's circulation had reached 4,500,000 a month.[42]

Bob Guccione, editor-publisher of *Penthouse* magazine, aimed to compete with *Playboy* by copying its format of offering both a literary and lifestyle side while making the pictorials more sexually explicit. He did this by forgoing advertising revenue in the short term, planning to draw in the advertisers after he had put *Playboy* out of business. In a *Newsweek* article on *Penthouse*, London-based Guccione was quoted as saying, "I'm not coming to America to be number No. 2 ... in five years, *Playboy* and *Penthouse* will be locked in a toe-to-toe competition."[43]

Penthouse started with a circulation of 350,000. By February 1970 this figure had grown to 500,000. Miller argues that one major reason for the increase was that *Penthouse* photos were more explicit, especially in their willingness to reveal pubic hair.[44] *Playboy*, meanwhile, resisted pubic hair by focusing instead on what they called the "girl next door look." The more explicit imagery in *Penthouse* was the focus of a number of articles in mainstream magazines, from *Forbes* to *Business Week* to *Time*, all commenting on the willingness of *Penthouse* to go beyond *Playboy*'s levels of explicitness. *Forbes* described *Penthouse* as being "much bolder. Whereas *Playboy* bared breasts in the mid-fifties, now *Penthouse* has introduced pubic hair ... and kinky letters to the editor on subjects like caning and slave parties."[45] Such articles could be seen as free advertising for *Penthouse* since they often discussed the competition in a tongue-in-cheek manner, with no analysis of how this publishing war, with its battleground being the female body, could have consequences for the way women's bodies were represented in mainstream pornography and media. Rather, the articles gave titillating accounts of Guccione's *Penthouse* ("his girls look less airbrushed—and hence sexier —than *Playboy*'s and the copy in *Penthouse* is more bluntly erotic") and gave quotes as teasers from *Penthouse* magazine stories ("Her eyes sparkled. 'We are in a birchwood. Perhaps you want to birch me. Yes?'").[46] The only topic that was treated with any seriousness in these articles was the impact that this war was having on the financial health of the magazines.

By the end of 1970, *Penthouse*'s circulation had reached 1,500,000. Hefner decided that he could no longer ignore Guccione and there "began a contest between Hefner and Guccione to see who could produce the raunchier magazine."[47] In August 1971, *Penthouse* carried its first full-frontal centerfold and in January 1972, *Playboy* did the same. The change in policy was successful; by September 1972, *Playboy*'s circulation had risen to 7 million, but by 1973, it began to decline, while *Penthouse*'s increased to 4 million. To make matters worse for *Playboy*, the magazine's advertisers were beginning to complain again about the explicit nature of the pictorials, and high-level executives had to fly to New York to placate them. Eventually, due to the combined pressure of advertisers, internal battles with editors, and the appearance of competitors such as *Gallery* and *Hustler*, which captured the more hard-core market, Hefner capitulated to *Penthouse*, sending a memo to all the department editors informing them that *Playboy* would cease to cater to those readers interested in looking at the more hard-core images. He would instead return to the magazine's previous standards.[48]

Circulation figures from the 1990s suggest that Hefner made the right decision. In 1995, *Playboy* had a monthly circulation of nearly 3.5 million, while *Penthouse* reported just over 1 million. One possible explanation for this is that *Playboy*, in staking out its terrain as the respectable soft-core, lifestyle magazine, still had no real competitor. Indeed, in its promotional material aimed at potential advertisers, *Playboy* compared itself to *Sports Illustrated, Rolling Stone, Esquire, GQ*, and *Details*, and described itself as being about "the way men live in the nineties.... Entertainment, fashion, cars, sports, the issues, the scene, the people who make waves, the women men idealize."[49] What is clearly absent from *Playboy*'s list of competitors is its real major competitor, *Penthouse*, and what is thus rendered invisible in its promotional description is the pornographic content that sells the magazine.

Penthouse, on the other hand, because it tended to be more explicit in its focus on women's genitals, simulated sexual intercourse, sexual violence, and group sex, had only one foot in the acceptable "soft-core" market, with the other in the more "hard-core" market. This was probably the worst of both worlds because the magazine couldn't compete with either. It couldn't attract the writers or interview subjects that provided *Playboy* with its markers of respectability and thus its advertising revenue; nor could it attract readers away from the hard-core magazines by being even more explicit, for fear of offending the advertisers it already had.

The magazine that was largely responsible for drawing readers away from both *Playboy* and *Penthouse* with the promise of delivering real pornography was the more hard-core *Hustler*. Within three and a half years of its inception, *Hustler* reached a circulation of over 3 million, and after four years was showing a profit of over $13 million. It is no coincidence that Flynt published the first issue of *Hustler* in 1974 because one of the results of the battle between *Playboy* and *Penthouse* was a growing acceptance in the mainstream porn market of more explicit imagery, which opened the way for mass distribution of more hard-core materials. Without a doubt, Flynt has had to fight many legal battles, but the groundwork laid by *Playboy* and *Penthouse* facilitated his aim of creating the "first nationally distributed magazine to show pink."[50]

Understanding the pivotal role that product differentiation plays in capitalism, Flynt wrote in the first issue of *Hustler*, "Anyone can be a playboy and have a penthouse, but it takes a man to be a Hustler."[51] Flynt repeatedly wrote in *Hustler* that his target audience was "the average American" whose income made it impossible for him to identify with the high-level consumption and lifestyle associated with *Playboy* and *Penthouse*. Taking shots at both competitors for being too upmarket, for taking themselves too seriously, and for masquerading the "pornography as art by wrapping it in articles purporting to have socially redeeming values," *Hustler* carved out a role for itself in a glutted market as a no-holds-barred magazine that told it like it was, "unaffected by the sacred cows of advertising."[52] From the very first issue, Flynt limited advertising in his magazine mainly to those companies involved in the sex industry (phone sex, vibrators, and penis enlargers being the main wares advertised).

The decision to sacrifice advertising revenue and instead rely largely on subscription-financed revenue paid off—*Hustler* is the most successful hard-core magazine in the history of the pornography industry and Flynt is a multimillionaire today. Moreover, given the type of magazine Flynt wanted to produce, he had no choice; it seems unlikely that even the most daring of advertisers would select *Hustler* as the place to market its products. Flynt created a magazine that looks different from *Playboy* and *Penthouse* in its print and image content. The first few pages of the magazine are often given over to advertisements from the sex industry, with very explicit pictures of women's genitals and men's penises. While *Penthouse* may have published shots of women's internal genitalia, leaking or ejaculating penises were strictly taboo in any section of *Playboy* and *Penthouse*. Within the first ten pages of *Hustler* is a regular feature called "Asshole of the Month," whose centerpiece is a photograph of a male bending over, testicles in full view, and the picture of a politician or celebrity superimposed onto the anal opening.

Although *Hustler*'s key marketing strategy has been its claim to be the most "outrageous and provocative" sex magazine on the shelves, its centerfolds and pictorials in the early years tended to adopt the more soft-core codes and conventions (young, big-breasted women bending over to give a clear view of their genitals and breasts) rather than the hard-core ones specializing in explicit sexual penetration. *Hustler* was careful not to alienate its mainstream distributors with pictorials that might be considered too hard-core and thus find itself relegated to the porn shops, a move that would have severely limited sales (*Hustler*'s success was mainly due to its ability to gain access to mass-distribution outlets in the United States and Europe).

However, *Hustler* also had to keep its promise to be more hard-core or else it would have lost its readership to the more glossy, expensively produced soft-core *Playboy* or to the more hard-core pornography sold in "adult bookstores." One way that *Hustler* negotiated this built-in conflict was to use cartoons as the place to make good on its promise to its readers to be "bolder in every direction than other publications."[53] Cartoons, because of their claim to humor, thus allowed *Hustler* to depict "outrageous and provocative" scenarios such as torture, murder, and child molestation that might, in a less humorous form such as pictorials, have denied the magazine access to the mass-distribution channels.

One recurring theme in *Hustler* was the construction of the reader as a man who likes "tasteless" humor and no-frills pornography, and lacks the financial ability to live like a playboy and own a penthouse. This image trades on the most classist of stereotypes, one that *Hustler* has worked hard to promote both in and out of the magazine. In the 1970s, *Hustler* regularly ran a full-page picture of an overweight, middle-aged white male wearing shabby-looking clothes leaning on a bar, his beer gut spilling over his worn jeans and a glass of beer in his hand. The caption underneath read, "What Sort of Man Reads *Hustler*?" The answer, of course, is a fat, unkempt, working-class male who drinks beer all day. Flynt told *Newsweek* in 1976 that *Hustler* was more interested in attracting truck drivers than professors, and that "we sell to the Archie Bunkers of America."[54]

This implied reader of *Hustler* was as accurate a description of *Hustler*'s readers as the playboy was of *Playboy*'s readers. While both constructions were marketing ploys, they worked in very different ways. *Playboy* is an advertising-driven magazine, and like all such magazines, has to present an "image...for potential readers to desire, identify with, and expect to attain through consuming the magazine."[55] Thus, while *Playboy* continued to sell an image of the reader as an upper-middle-class executive, the median income for *Playboy* readers (less than 50 percent of whom have a college degree) in the mid-1990s was $26,000 a year for single men and $41,000 for married men.[56] This was hardly a salary that allowed a man to play at the level depicted in *Playboy*.

On the flip side, the *Hustler* reader's median income in 1995 was $38,500, putting him squarely in the middle-income bracket of the *Playboy* reader.[57] Despite *Hustler*'s caricatured image of working-class men, few if any actual subscribers, then, would have seen themselves as belonging to the same class as the "Archie Bunker" beer-swigging hustler. One possible reason for *Hustler*'s unusual marketing strategy of presenting the "ideal reader" in anything but ideal terms was to allow the real reader to *not* see himself as the intended reader. This enabled the reader to buy *Hustler* while at the same time distancing himself from this "outrageous" magazine, filled with cartoon images of semen, feces, child molesters, and women with leaking vaginas. For the duration of the reading and masturbation, he is slumming in the world of "white trash," an observer to the workings of a social class that is not his own.

Hustler seems to have been successful in its marketing ploy because mainstream publications and academics have bought into the image of the *Hustler* reader. *Newsweek* referred to *Hustler* as appealing to "beer-belly macho," while *Time* defined it as being the most "vulgar" of sex magazines.[58] In an article on *Hustler*, Laura Kipnis suggests that neither she nor the reader of her article (printed in a scholarly collection on cultural studies, targeted to academics), are *Hustler*'s "implied reader."[59] Rather than shedding light on who actually buys the magazine, Kipnis is actually reinforcing the marketing strategy of *Hustler* since no one is meant to see himself as the "implied reader." The "implied reader" constructed in *Hustler* is someone to be either avoided or ridiculed, certainly not someone to identify with.

However, in *Hustler*'s advertising promotional material, the reader was defined as the "hard-working middle-class American Male" who "makes substantial purchases through mail-order services."[60] It would seem that while *Hustler* publicly called its readers "Archie Bunkers," it wanted to assure its advertisers that they nonetheless had disposable income by writing "middle-class" on the first line of the promotional material as well as prominently displaying the median income ($38,500) in the reader profile box situated in the center of the sheet. Always the savvy businessman, Flynt is well aware that the image of the reader he constructs *for* the reader would not attract advertisers, so not only does he redefine the reader when looking to sell advertising space, he also provides a more accurate description.

THE PLAYBOY AND THE HUSTLER:
MARKETING HEFNER AND FLYNT

Hugh Hefner is probably the first pornographer in America to have achieved mainstream celebrity status. Like his magazine itself, Hefner was marketed as an upscale, high-quality commodity in order to reduce the sleaze factor normally associated with pornographers. Articles on Hefner rarely picture him outside of his opulent surroundings; they are nearly always accompanied by photographs of him lounging on his famous round bed surrounded by "bunnies" or "girlfriends," flying in his customized plane, or dancing the night away in the fully staffed Playboy mansion. Writers have gone into great detail about Hefner's daily life, praising the gourmet food and excellent service at the mansion, which "has a staff of twelve which functions around the clock," the kidney-shaped pool "with [the] inviting nook called Woo Grotto," and his "rotating round bed."[61] Hefner's life is cast as the playboy American dream come true: he is a man who works hard, plays hard, and has achieved the ultimate goals in life. A *Forbes* article on Hefner's success even ran the heading "Hugh Hefner Found Complete Happiness Living the *Playboy* Life."[62]

Hefner is presented as the all-American businessman who is "modern, trustworthy, clean, respectable" and is not afraid of hard work, since, according to *Newsweek*, "he works as much as 72 hours at a stretch."[63] In the late 1950s and early 1960s, most of the major newspapers and news magazines carried articles on Hefner the businessman rather than Hefner the pornographer. In these articles the centerfolds were backgrounded and the business success of *Playboy* and Hefner foregrounded. Part of this "playboy" image also involved him being a patron of liberal organizations such as the ACLU (American Civil Liberties Union) and NORML (National Organization for the Reform of Marijuana Laws). *Playboy* magazine has often run stories on Hefner's attendance at parties held in honor of his financial contributions to various causes.

Flynt, on the other hand, is presented as a working-class pervert who carries his poor Kentucky background with him wherever he goes. He is portrayed as low class, uneducated, and vulgar and, unlike Hefner, he has been demonized by the press as a sleazy pornographer. Many of the articles on Flynt highlight his poor beginnings as a way to link his class background with his sexual tastes. *Time*, for example, in an article on the 1978 shooting of Flynt, told its readers that "ever since Flynt came out of the Kentucky mountains to escape the poverty of his sharecropper family, he has led an aggressive life. He quit school in the eighth grade, entered the army at 14, worked nights at a General Motors assembly plant, whizzed through two marriages, two divorces and a bankruptcy by age 21 and finally opened eight 'Hustler' go-go bars around Ohio."[64]

In a similar vein, *People* magazine referred to Flynt as "a nightmare version of the American dream come true. Born into an impoverished Kentucky family, he never completed high school."[65] Whereas Hefner is represented as a man who has a playboy sex life (good, clean heterosexual sex with young, attractive females), Flynt is cast as a pervert who at the age of eight "lost his virginity to a chicken on his grandmother's farm" and now runs the "most vulgar of the leading sex magazines."[66] Flynt's late wife Althea is described as an ex-go-go dancer who was "brazenly debauched," drug addicted, and destroyed by AIDS.[67] While Hefner has been involved with women who were either murdered (Dorothy Stratten) or committed suicide (Bobbie Arnstein), he is the "Teflon pornographer" in that his reputation as a fine, upstanding American citizen remains intact to this day.

This celebration of Hefner and demonization of Flynt helped to obfuscate the connections between *Playboy* and *Hustler* as the two magazines that staked out the parameters of the once hugely successful mass-distributed pornography magazine industry. The success of these magazines is measurable not only in terms of past sales and advertising revenue but also by the role they played in laying the economic, cultural, and legal foundations for the contemporary multibillion-dollar-a-year porn market. *Playboy* was especially important for today's high-end feature studios since it helped create the idea that porn could be both classy and tasteful. For the more gonzo type of porn, *Hustler* helped build a taste for images that overtly degraded women.

PLAYBOY, PENTHOUSE, AND *HUSTLER* TODAY

Times have indeed changed for the three magazines, as the Internet has taken over as a major source of porn delivery, and the porn magazine business is struggling to stay alive. Guccione has come a long way from when *Forbes*, in 1985, put him on its Rich List, estimating his fortune to be about $200 million. According to *Forbes*, by 2003, *Penthouse* had a circulation of only 320,000 and was losing $6 million a year.[68] Guccione's company went bankrupt and *Penthouse* was bought by Marc Bell Capital Partners.[69] While the magazine is no longer a moneymaker (*Penthouse* had only twelve pages of ads in the March 2008 issue), *Forbes* reported in 2008 that the Penthouse Media Group is the world's largest adult entertainment company owing to "a racy collection of 27 social-networking Web sites that Marc Bell and Daniel Staton, company chairman, bought late last year for $500 million in cash and stock."[70] Guccione himself was in deep financial trouble and in 2003 he had to sell off his famous collection of paintings and his thirty-something-room house in Manhattan.

Even though it is a huge business concern, *Penthouse* is not a major brand in today's pop culture. Bell was even quoted as saying, "*Penthouse* is just another Web site. We are in the social-networking business. We are not in the business of *Penthouse*."[71] The largest networking site it owns is AdultFriendFinder, a site where people can find sex partners. With 22 million active members, it is, according to *Newsweek*, one of the most highly traveled Web sites in the world.[72] *Penthouse*, through its various acquisitions, has now developed synergy among its different product lines: "*Penthouse* Pets make guest appearances in nine *Penthouse*

Executive Clubs, which bring in $4 million in licensing fees a year. Ads in *Penthouse* magazine tout AdultFriendFinder. Members of that site will soon be able to subscribe to an online version of the magazine, which will be delivered as a pdf file, for $1 a month."[73]

Penthouse is not the only porn magazine to branch out into other areas that are more profitable than magazines. Hustler has built a large business empire and Flynt now has a number of Internet sites, the most profitable being Hustler.com and Barely Legal, which specializes in women who look more like adolescents than adults. Some of his more successful businesses include a Hustler Casino in Los Angeles, a chain of sex shops, his adult video productions, and a distribution company. In an interview in 2004, Flynt revealed that the magazine was 80 percent of his business in the 1980s but in 2004, it accounted for only 20 percent, with the rest Internet and video.[74] Flynt is thought to be a billionaire by some in the industry, but whatever his wealth, he has been extremely successful in diversifying his business interests.

Of the three magazines, *Playboy* is the most visual brand in pop culture. According to an article in *Multichannel News,* "The overall *Playboy* image remains a potent brand in magazines, television and the Internet, not just in America but around the globe." Although Playboy Enterprises has been losing money for some time—in March 2009 it reported a losing quarter, with net losses of $13.7 million—its consumer product division continues to do very well. This is because the Playboy brand has penetrated the mainstream like no other pornographic product. Playboy licenses a whole range of products, including underwear, socks, notebooks, pens, watches, and sunglasses, and is always on the lookout for new items. Bob Meyers, president of Playboy media, is quoted as saying, "Our brand is unique in that we have this certain aura."[75]

Playboy launched a cable station in 1982—the Playboy Channel, later renamed Playboy TV—and it quickly made its way into 750,000 homes through 450 cable stations. In 1994, *Playboy* became the first magazine to have a Web site and by the mid-1990s, Playboy launched Adultvision and bought up a number of the "Spice Channels," as well as Club Jenna, which was originally started by porn star Jenna Jameson. Some of these channels carry hard-core porn, but Playboy has been careful to keep a distance from these ventures so as not to tarnish its soft-core image. Recently Playboy has been strategizing how to get into the mobile phone porn business, and in 2008 the company "signed a deal with THQ Wireless to develop Playboy-branded lifestyle-themed mobile games, which will not have nudity."[76] Playboy is also going into casinos and what they call "Playboy concept Boutiques" that carry only Playboy-branded products. According to Chris Napolitano, *Playboy's* editorial director, "The whole licensed products business now generates in excess of $800 million in global retails sales in more than 150 countries."[77]

One way that Playboy has recently gained increased public visibility is through *The Girls Next Door*, a popular reality show on E! Entertainment, which supposedly documents Hefner's life with his young "girlfriends." The show, launched in 2005, provides a sanitized version of life at the Playboy mansion, never showing the reality of the experience for the young women who live and sleep with eighty-three-year-old Hefner. In *Bunny Tales*, Izabella St. James, an ex-"girlfriend" of Hefner's, writes about what really went on at the mansion; how Hefner would have unprotected sex with a number of women, one after the other, but regardless of how many women he penetrated, he could orgasm only by masturbating to pornography. St. James discloses that many of the young women didn't want to have sex with Hefner but "it was part of the unspoken rules. It was almost as if we had to do it in return for all the things we had."[78] Needless to say, this is not the image the show depicts.

All three companies have had to retool in order to stay afloat in the contemporary porn market. The industry now looks very different from when they began, with men today demanding harder and harder porn. The question is whether they keep up with this demand and move into more hard-core porn or whether they've sowed the seeds of their own destruction by helping to create an appetite for such porn. While the future remains unclear, what we do know is that without these three magazines and publishers, the porn industry would not be where it is today. Each publisher was willing to push the boundaries and in so doing, made pornography increasingly visible in mainstream pop culture. The more Flynt and Guccione pushed the envelope, the more acceptable *Playboy* looked, and the more *Playboy* penetrated the mainstream, the more latitude *Hustler* and *Penthouse* were given to move hard-core. This symbiotic relationship meant that by the time the Internet was introduced into homes, the culture had been well groomed to accept pornography as a part of everyday life rather than as an industry that produces a system of images that debases and dehumanizes women and men.

TWO

Pop Goes the Porn Culture

Mainstreaming Porn

> Pornography has become the media's darling topic these days.
> Right now there is invariably *something* about the business and/
> or pleasure of pornography staring at you from a newspaper
> column, cable TV show, local news report or magazine article.
> —Tripp Daniels, *Adult Video News*

We have come a long way from the days when porn was thought of as dirty pictures for seedy men who couldn't get a real woman. Today porn is being celebrated everywhere, from Howard Stern's popular TV and radio broadcasts showcasing rising porn stars to one of the most successful cable TV shows ever, *Sex and the City*, which regularly features porn as a fun addition to a woman's sex life. Even Oprah Winfrey got in on the act, with *O Magazine* carrying pro-porn articles by "sex educator" Violet Blue, who encourages women to use porn as a sex aid. An article in the *LA Times* in 2008 titled "Porn Stars Are the New Crossover Artists" focused on how porn has become an integral part of mainstream pop culture: "Once largely shunned as pariahs by the entertainment industry, porn stars are turning up with increasing regularity on shopping-mall movie screens and in prime-time television shows, underscoring pornography's steady migration over the last three decades from the pop-culture margins to the mainstream."[1] How did this shift to the mainstream happen? The answer is simple: by design. What we see today is the result of years of careful strategizing and marketing by the porn industry to sanitize its products by stripping away the "dirt" factor and reconstituting porn as fun, edgy, chic, sexy, and hot.

The more sanitized the industry became, the more it seeped into the pop culture and into our collective consciousness.

While there is a long list of sanitizing agents, I have selected for discussion some that are more contemporary and have had a major impact on our cultural shift. Chief among these is the *Girls Gone Wild* franchise owned by Joe Francis, a man many liken to Hugh Hefner in his public persona as a jet-setting playboy. Just as Hefner acted as a bridge between the two worlds, so too does Joe Francis, since his product has been whitewashed as belonging to the world of pop culture, not porn. In this chapter's discussion of the links between pop culture and porn, what becomes clear is that the lines are increasingly blurring and we are seeing a mingling of the two forms to the point that our pop culture resembles the soft-core pornography of ten years ago.

GIRLS GONE WILD

> I'm not selling Bibles, you know…at the end of the day, I'm selling naked girls. People want to buy naked girls.
>
> —Joe Francis, creator and owner, *Girls Gone Wild*

Girls, often drunk, are the commodity that Joe Francis sells to consumers. Famous for getting girls to "go wild" for the camera, Francis is today a multimillionaire businessman who owns what is often seen as a fun, young, hip company that spontaneously captures young women undressing and flashing in public.[2] In most of the media articles on Francis, it is mistakenly assumed that *Girls Gone Wild* (*GGW*) is merely a show where inebriated college girls flash their breasts, while in reality much of the footage, especially on its Web site, is explicit sex, ranging from woman-on-woman sex to solo women inserting dildos into their (shaved or waxed) vaginas. Francis set out to deliberately and carefully craft an image of *GGW* not as a porn product, but rather as hot, sexy fun that pushes the envelope of mainstream pop culture. The more visibility *GGW* has in pop culture, the bigger the potential market. That this was a successful marketing scheme is evident in the $40 million a year *GGW* does in sales.[3]

Francis's business plan to develop a brand that stood out from other mainstream porn videos by giving it a more soft-core-focus gloss worked, since he has created what he (correctly) defines as "one of the most widely recognized entertainment and lifestyle brands in the US. This one-time pop culture phenomenon has become a part of the fabric of America and is synonymous with youth culture."[4] But for all his claims that his show firmly belongs in pop culture, in reality *GGW* is closely tied to the pornography industry and its distribution channels. One of the most telling business deals that Francis recently brokered is with WebQuest, a California-based interactive services firm whose client list is 95 percent pornographers, including Vivid and Hustler, two of the largest and most successful pornography corporations in the world. According to *XBIZ*, WebQuest built "the *GGW* Cash members area, constructing new tours and preparing to launch the program as a continuation of the *Girls Gone Wild* video line of flesh-flashing co-eds."[5]

On the *GGW* Web site, the usual warning posted on pornography sites flashes on the screen: "GirlsGoneWild.com (the website) is an 'adult-oriented' site containing images and text of a sexual nature. Only adults at least 18 years of age are permitted to enter." A "bonus" offered by the Web site is free access to other pornography Web sites, including Lipstick Lesbos, a pornography site run by the hard-core company Hustler. The ad for Lipstick Lesbos on the *GGW* site reads, "Hustler proudly presents their top selling XXX Lesbian Video Series. You get a front row seat to see what goes down when the boys are away and pussy comes out to play."[6] The links to these pornography sites illustrate how Francis actually sees *GGW* because it is standard practice to host links only to those businesses that are directly related to the corporate positioning of the company's site. It is also noteworthy that the *GGW* site does not have even one link to any pop culture site that is also known to push the sexual limits of mainstream media (for example, *MTV, Maxim,* or *FHM*).

Another sign of how *GGW* is positioned is its visible presence at porn trade conventions that showcase the porn industry's wares. At a 2007 three-day pornography consumer trade show in Los Angeles called Adultcon, models from *GGW* wore scanty clothing and posed with fans who wanted to take their pictures. This was clearly a marketing strategy to promote *GGW* DVDs; over forty are listed for sale on the wholly pornographic Adultcom Web site. In the promotional copy accompanying the DVDs, the products are pitched in ways that will appeal to porn consumers. The copy for *GGW Sexiest Moments Ever* reads: "At *Girls Gone Wild*, hot and sexy college girls are our business, and business is booming! This volume is loaded with girls from all over the country, getting wild for our cameras, and for you. We've truly outdone ourselves with this mind-blowing edition of sexy and steamy moments."[7]

The largest pornography convention in the world is run by *Adult Video News* every January in Las Vegas. In January 2007, IVD (one of the major distributors of pornography in the world) hosted a party for *GGW* that was described as one of the most exclusive parties held during the convention. According to *AVN:* "Mainstream models and party-girls mingled with hardcore starlets, suits groped sluts, and it wasn't long before the girl-girl smooches began amid the inevitable 'Woo-hoo!' mating call of genus *Whoranicus Americana....* Spotted in the throng of revelers [was] *Girls Gone Wild* mogul Joe Francis."[8]

Probably the most succinct description of the way *GGW* links pop culture to porn is WebQuest president Bruce Benevento's use of the word "bridge" when describing how *GGW*'s image will help place pornography products in the mainstream market. WebQuest's other major pornography client is Hustler, and when comparing the two companies, Benevento is quoted as saying: "Larry Flynt has been branding for 30 plus years, but if you say *Girls Gone Wild*, everybody knows exactly what you are talking about.... *GGW* is a socially acceptable adult product because it conjures up images of young college kids having fun, frolicking on the beach—it seems very innocent. And while the Hustler brand has tremendous power, there are some markets that are closed to it. You don't see Hustler.com at night on television like you do *Girls Gone Wild....* This is a unique opportunity to bridge markets."[9] What separates *Hustler* from *GGW* is, in Benevento's opinion, not that *Hustler* is pornography and *GGW* is pop culture, but that *GGW* is, *unlike Hustler,* a pornography product that can be marketed as pop culture.

The success of *GGW* is largely due to the way that the porn industry has shifted toward the more hard-core. As body-punishing gonzo sex became the norm, it crowded out the softer porn. Francis filled the resulting void with *GGW.* It never shows male-female sexual relations so there is no intercourse, erect penises, or ejaculate—all markers of hard-core porn. Instead all we see are young women, lots and lots of them in various stages of undress and sexual activity. These women are indeed the selling point of *GGW*, and not just because they are young and conventionally attractive but because they are what Francis calls "real." All over the *GGW* Web site are phrases such as "real girls," "all real," and "raw, real and uncut." Francis argues that it is, in fact, authenticity that distinguishes *GGW* from other porn products:

> There really was never anything like it in the mass market before. You didn't ever get to choose real girls.... What *Girls Gone Wild* doesn't have in sexual desire, it makes up for in its voyeuristic realism. One can compensate for the other without seeing full male female penetration sex. It's so compelling; it doesn't have to be harder. I think what a lot of adult companies do is they just keep getting harder and harder and harder and dirtier and dirtier and dirtier, that's how they feel it needs to go. But you can be more compelling without having to do peeing or those different fetish things. What makes it compelling is it's real. Those are real girls doing these things.[10]

What appears to be so important about "real" is that the *GGW* images are perceived by users as a documentation of reality rather than a representation of it.[11] In place of the scripted and carefully crafted scenes of hard-core porn, the user supposedly gets to witness a real woman doing porn for the first time in her life. By using "real" women, *GGW* socializes users, suggesting that everyday women are sexually available. These are women the user can imagine hooking up with for the very reason that they are not professional porn performers. This brings the porn story of "all women are sluts" right into the center of pop culture and subsequently the lives of men. Like reality TV, the viewer can insert him- or herself into the action by believing that what he or she is watching is actually real and not staged.

What makes *GGW* look real is the women's lack of sophistication, which is evident in their nervous giggles, their sometimes clumsy moves, and their need to be coached by the cameramen on how to perform.

They look more like girls than women. In the more explicit *GGW* videos, the unexpected sometimes happens; clothes get tangled up, dildos aren't inserted properly, women collapse in a heap of laughter, and orgasms—whether real or fake—take a long time to happen, and when they do, they appear to be authentic. Real seems to be what the viewers want, and while many porn sites advertise that their women are real women (rather than porn performers), few can actually deliver on the promise because they use women who are often recognizable to seasoned users.

The voyeuristic thrill men get from *GGW* with its "real" girls—after all, it's not called *Women Gone Wild*—would seem to be akin to watching a female lose her virginity, as this is the first time the girl has performed sex on camera. What she also loses is her "good girl" status as she shifts from being the girl next door to the girl who is just as slutty as the other women in porn. That *GGW* particularly goes after the "good girl" is evident in the comment made by former *GGW* production manager Mia Leist that the camera crew hones in on "the ones you wouldn't expect to do it."[12] This adds a kind of authenticity to *GGW* that is missing in the more formulaic, scripted type of porn. In *GGW* it is not always clear just how far the cameramen can push the girl. Will she stop at flashing or can they get her to go all the way?

Many of the people I speak to when lecturing are baffled as to why young women agree to appear in *GGW* at all—after all, they get only a tank top or a hat for doing so. From the Web site and videos, it seems that literally thousands of girls are ready and willing to throw themselves at Joe Francis. There are a number of reasons for this, some of which are connected to the sophisticated recruiting machinery of *GGW* and some as simple as the fact that nearly all the young women are in late adolescence—a time of special vulnerability to cultural messages. After speaking with young women who appeared on *GGW*, what has become clear to me is that Francis and his team are experts in manipulating these women into becoming the raw material of his product. The important point to remember is that these women have already been seasoned by the culture to see themselves as sex objects, and Francis and his team build on this by overwhelming them with compliments about how hot and beautiful they are and what beautiful bodies they have.

Given its visibility in pop culture, young people tend to associate *GGW* with celebrity culture. Beyond the appeal of celebrity cachet, though, the party culture message associated with *GGW* is that everyone featured is having fun. By editing out those women who refuse to cooperate, *GGW* creates a closed world where everybody seems only too willing to perform sexually for the camera. The public image of *GGW* itself then becomes a recruitment tool as it draws in young people looking to do something adventurous and edgy.

As soon as the *GGW* bus pulls into a vacation resort, the staff creates a party atmosphere, whether it be on the beach or in a nightclub. Francis's team members are typically in their twenties and early thirties, attractive, casually dressed, and bathed in celebratory status by virtue of their connection to *GGW*. These men shoehorn their way into student peer groups by using their "cool" status to ingratiate themselves with the women, and they adopt a "fun-loving" persona as they begin to scout for potential recruits. In this way, they work their way into a group of women who are most likely (at least) ten years their junior.

The team is coached to always be on the lookout for a "10," which translates into a young, white, blonde, blue-eyed female with big breasts and a toned body. The cameramen even get bonuses for finding and filming such women.[13] Women of color, especially black women, appear to be completely off-limits. For example, in one painful scene from *GGW*'s *Sex Starved College Girls 3*, the cameraman homes in on three girls, two white and one black. All three look excited to be on *GGW*, but it is the white women who get all the attention. As they begin to kiss, the camera focuses on the white women. The black woman stands perfectly still, not knowing what to do with herself as her two friends get into a heavy make-out session. As the scene continues, the camera blocks out the black woman completely. This exclusion of women of color from *GGW* suggests that the targeted audience is white men, because there is a general belief in the porn industry that men on the whole prefer to watch porn that features women of their own racial group.[14]

If you watch enough of these videos, you'll spot a pattern: the *GGW* team targets a woman who is surrounded by male and female peers. The cameramen then proceed to encourage the surrounding students to nag the woman to flash. Some of the women agree quickly while others take a lot of convincing. Because many of the young women are in the developmental stage where peer acceptance is all-important, it is not surprising that they cave in. If Francis and his team were themselves to be seen to pester a woman into flashing, then they would appear as adult predators of adolescent girls. Instead, they cleverly manipulate the peers of these girls to do their "dirty work."

The *GGW* team, by setting up camp in student-dominated places, is actually infiltrating the private space of these students. Spring break (or similar times when students get together on vacation) is typically a time when young adults congregate without older adult supervision. There is an expectation on the part of the students that while on vacation with peers, they will be able to experiment sexually with minimal consequences. According to one study:

> Activities on spring break…were described as exceptions to every-day experience, outside of usual standards, expectations, norms. Students used phrases such as "what happens in Daytona, stays in Daytona," "nothing that happens here comes home" and "nothing counts." They portrayed an atmosphere in which the usual rules and moral codes did not apply. Students provided detailed descriptions of how some had behaved "totally out of character" or in ways that "they never would at home." These illustrations and the results of the statistical analysis support the picture of spring break as the environment in which personal codes are temporarily suspended.[15]

This sense of having a "pass" to experiment sexually on vacation with unforeseeable long-term consequences is precisely what Francis exploits as a way to recruit young women. The alcohol-soaked, sexually charged, no-holds-barred atmosphere of spring break provides a perfect atmosphere for the *GGW* team to manipulate the girls into behaving in ways that would normally be outside their repertoire of behavior.

The videos in which the girls are seen actually performing sexually (this is usually masturbation, girl-on-girl sex, and/or inserting dildos into the vagina and sometimes anus) show just how predatory the *GGW* team is. The first scene often reveals the cameraman walking into a room and approaching a woman or a group of women, who giggle as he begins dishing out the compliments. He then, in a gentle voice, starts to give them instructions on how to undress and what to do with each other. He will say things like "Why don't you touch her tits?" "Give her a slap," "Open your legs wide," and so on. If we consider the power imbalance in the room at that moment, then it becomes easy to understand why it's so difficult for a woman to change her mind once a scene has been set in motion. The cameraman is older, has celebrity status, and, most important, is clothed. She, on the other hand, is a late adolescent, most likely drunk, and naked in front of men she does not know.

Adolescents, by definition, are trying on identities to see which one fits. They are seeking out ways of being in the world that make sense for who they are and who they want to be. Since the most visible identity on offer for a young woman is one that emphasizes her as a sexual being to the exclusion of anything else, then performing sex on camera becomes one more way to express who you are.

One of the major problems associated with being on *GGW* is that the young women's behavior is forever frozen in time on tape; they can't take it back, hide it, or deny that they did it. For some of the young women I have spoken with, the aftermath of appearing in *GGW* was devastating. One young woman who flashed for *GGW* told me that she felt like the image would follow her for the rest of her life. She said that she had agreed to flash "because I was drunk and it seemed like fun. Well, it isn't fun now because what people always seem to find out about me is that I was on *GGW*." While they might have thought sexually performing for the camera was fun at the time, their families, communities, and peer group turned against them once they found out what they had done, labeling them as sluts, a label that they carry with them wherever they go. These young women grew up in a media culture where women such as Paris Hilton, Pamela Anderson, and Kim Kardashian seemed to have benefited from having sex tapes of them in public circulation. What these young women find out after performing for *GGW* is that while celebrities can get away with such sexual performance on camera, the average female stripped of wealth and glamour gets treated not as a Paris Hilton wannabe but as a "slutty" girl who deserves to be ridiculed and shunned.

For many of the young women I have spoken with, life changed dramatically after an appearance on *GGW*, and some even suffer symptoms similar to post-traumatic stress disorder. One woman told me that after she had girl-on-girl sex with her friend, she felt like "a stupid whore and I can't stop people watching me. All the guys at school watch me and I feel horrible." Their moment of recklessness has been captured on film, and they feel that it will define them for the rest of their lives, overriding all other parts of their identity. For some of these young women, wherever they go, be it a new school or job, their *GGW* images dog them. Some drop out of school, others become depressed, and many carry a deep sense of shame. What I found was that their lives had been derailed as plans for school or careers were dropped. Ellen started college with the hope of being a business major but after the tape of her having sex with her friend was shown at a frat party during the first semester, she dropped out of school. In Ellen's case, as in that of others I interviewed, depression prevented her from even leaving the house. Trisha told me that "my life will never be the same. I had so many plans and look at me now, a dropout with no future."

As these women struggle to rebuild their lives, Joe Francis gets richer and richer. He has hit on a winning idea and in spite of the many legal cases against him—he has been accused of racketeering, drug trafficking, child pornography, bribery, possession of a controlled substance, and introducing contraband into a Florida jail—his company continues to grow. By developing a brilliant marketing campaign and brand, he has helped to make the culture more porn-friendly and by so doing, he has further blurred the line between pop culture and pornography.

JENNA JAMESON

> Her breasts are scarred from having her breast implants removed, her face looks like it collapsed, and she still has her silicone injected lips! Not to mention her puss and ass are probably as big as a car garage.... It is a good thing she retired because this is one old slut that needs to be put down.
>
> —Blog post

Jenna Jameson achieved what seemed like the impossible just a generation ago—she became the first-ever real porn star. She managed to break through the porn barrier by moving seamlessly between the porn world and mainstream media. In the past, porn performers couldn't shake the sleaze factor and were hence considered untouchable by most mainstream pop culture industries. Jameson changed all this as she became a household name, thanks in part to the many stories on her life in celebrity magazines such as *People* and *US*, her best-selling book *How to Make Love Like a Porn Star*, shows about her that appeared on VH1, E! Entertainment, and HBO, and her appearances in ads for companies such as Abercrombie & Fitch and Pony. That no other woman in porn has ever penetrated the mainstream to such a degree is not lost on the porn industry. *Playboy* in its January 2009 issue named Jameson the first porn performer to "become a mainstream icon." The Adult Movie Awards run by *Adult Video News* has a category called Jenna Jameson Crossover Star of the Year, in which female porn performers compete to see who has come closest to emulating Jameson's mainstream status.

The story told by the media of how Jameson became a porn star is one that highlights just how carefully the porn industry crafts its image as fun, chic, and hot while ignoring the reality of what happens to most women in the industry. In interviews she often says that she got into the industry because she is a very sexual person and pornography was an obvious career choice. Interviewers take this at face value, buying into an image of a highly sexual woman who luckily finds her niche in porn. Numerous stories underscore how she is in control of her own life and how she is a living example of the way a woman can make a successful career in the porn industry. In these accounts, porn is cleansed of its sleaziness and Jameson, a white, blonde woman with an all-American look, becomes the walking (wholesome) image of the industry, rather than the men who own and control much of the porn or the many women who end up poor with damaged bodies and STDs, working the streets to pay the rent.

Missing from most media accounts of Jameson is the real story of her life, which is much less glamorous than her public image. In *How to Make Love Like a Porn Star*, she gives a detailed account of a childhood and early adulthood marred by neglect and abuse. Her mother died when she was two and her early life was chaotic, not least because she was at times neglected by her father. As a teenager, she was gang-raped,

beaten, and left for dead and later raped by her abusive boyfriend's un-
cle. When she was sixteen, her father threw her out, so she went to live
with her boyfriend, who encouraged her to start stripping. She was so
desperate that in order to get her first gig, she removed her braces with
a pair of pliers. Later on she became addicted to a cocktail of drugs and
nearly died.

While articles occasionally mention the abuse, they gloss over the
actual amount and the ways that such experience shapes choices and
decisions in later life. The story of a neglected teenager being turned
out of her home by her father and encouraged to become a stripper by
her boyfriend is much more seedy and unlikely to paint the porn industry in a positive light. Most of these articles instead focus on her
wealthy lifestyle and the way she has built a one-woman porn empire. Indeed, she made many millions from her films, from her Web site, called
Club Jenna (now owned by Playboy), from selling computer games in
which the user gets to masturbate Jameson as well as have "sex" with
her, from her sex toys, T-shirts, mugs, action figures, and ring tones
that feature her moaning. She even has an anatomically accurate model
of her vagina and buttocks molded in soft plastic. An article in *Forbes*
on Jameson demonstrates the way that mainstream media cleanse the
porn industry by focusing only on her success. It summarizes her life as
follows:

> By day Jameson posed for nudie magazine covers, and at 19 she quit
> stripping to act in adult films—mainly to retaliate against her beau,
> who had been cheating on her, as she tells it. She shot her first scene
> in 1993 and a year later landed a contract with Wicked Pictures,
> which paid her $6,000 a month to perform in eight to ten feature
> films a year, doing three or four scenes in each. Even better money
> came in from a return to the brass pole: "After I became famous, I
> made sick money stripping," she says with a laugh. At her peak she
> got $5,000 a show, typically did four shows a night and made extra
> cash posing for Polaroids with panting patrons ($40 per), selling her
> latest movie ($50) and gouging gawkers for tips. She claims she of-
> ten made $50,000 a week.[16]

Nowhere does this article, or most of the other ones, point out the physical and emotional cost that the industry extracts. For example, in a particularly vacuous interview with Jameson, Anderson Cooper (he calls her "the reigning queen" of porn) says, "You know, as you say, I think, in the book, [pornography] can be very demeaning to women." Jameson responds with, "Well, it can be. I think that nowadays, the American public, they're much more accepting of the adult industry, and it goes to show that we should give the American public much more credit than we do." Jameson clearly avoids answering the question and Cooper, rather than pursuing what is a crucial issue, moves on to another topic.[17]

Were these interviewers to delve more deeply, they would find that Jameson's relationship to the porn industry is complex and vacillating—she insists that she loved her work and yet at times her anger at men and at the industry shows through. This was most clearly demonstrated at the Adult Video News Awards in 2008, when she stated in an angry voice, "I will never, ever ever spread my legs for this industry again. Ever." What was surprising was that the golden girl of the porn industry was booed by her colleagues, possibly because she hinted that she, the woman who made more money from performing in porn than any other woman in the world, was negatively affected by the industry. In some interviews Jameson tells the truth of her life, and in so doing, shows just how much the industry uses up women. One particularly instructive interview Jameson did was with publisher Judith Regan. Asked what her experiences have taught her about men, Jameson replies, "You start to hate men a little bit cuz you see them in a really awful light. They're drunk, they're, you know, rude, they're out of control. You put some alcohol in them and it gets ugly." She continues by saying that her work as a stripper "showed me what they [men] are capable of." When Regan asks, "Which is?" she replies, "Total degradation." What follows is a startling admission by Jameson. When she is asked by Regan if she felt degraded she replies, "Yes, when you are young you are not able to rationalize exactly what is going on. I had a few troubles with it but then, you know, you grow up quickly and I understood what it took to do what I did." But rather than taking this any further, Jameson quickly turns the interview on its head by saying that "I wasn't being objectified,

I was being empowered."[18] It is difficult to fathom how being degraded is empowering, but it is important to remember that Jameson is on the job when she is being interviewed and thus she can only go so far with her criticisms.

The usual mantra from the porn industry is that women are empowered by doing porn, and this is one way to claim one's sexuality. Digging a little deeper into Jameson's life actually illustrates just how disempowered she has felt while making porn. In her book she describes her first photo shoot: "Spreading my legs was the worst. I had no idea it would be so intimidating to sit spread-eagled under bright lights in a room full of clothed people. The photographer keeps shouting 'wider!' Now 'show me pink!'...Though I really wanted to please him, I couldn't...exposing my insides to strangers was so daunting that, instead of spreading my lips with my fingers, I kept trying to cover them up."[19] This does not sound like a woman who ended up in porn because she loves her body and is a "very sexual being," but rather a scared and embarrassed teenager who was in way above her head. Her account of stripping in her book also illustrates the physical harms these women endure. These include whacking their head on the pole, catching a nipple piercing in their hair or somewhere else, ruptured breast implants from landing/rolling/hitting the pole wrong, bunions, corns, bone spurs, constant sprained ankles, swelled knees, shin splints, lower back pain, degenerative muscle tissue on the pads of feet, neck problems (bulged or degenerative discs) from whipping the head around, joint problems from constant bending and unnatural positions, rotator cuff injuries, a swollen sacrum, hearing problems from loud music, and "bruises on the ass from guys pinching it."[20]

But probably the most damning statement on the sex industry is her description of how women are treated in porn: "Most girls get their first experience in gonzo films—in which they're taken to a crappy studio apartment in Mission Hills and penetrated in every hole possible by some abusive asshole who thinks her name is Bitch. And these girls...go home afterward and pledge never to do it again because it was such a terrible experience. But, unfortunately, they can't take that experience back, so they live the rest of their days in fear that their relatives, their co-workers, or their children will find out, which they inevitably do."[21] This is a very different Jenna Jameson to the one showcased on E! Entertainment or interviewed by Howard Stern. On a show in 2008 Jameson was asked by Stern if her boyfriend likes to "bukkake" (ejaculate) on her face. Playing along, Jameson laughs and says that her boyfriend likes it so much that she's requested bejeweled goggles for Valentine's Day. This is the more common public face of Jameson, not surprisingly, as she still makes money from her movies, toys, and gadgets and were she to be angry or truthful most of the time, her fan base might well decline.

But for all of her popularity, there are many porn users who actively dislike Jameson because they think she is too sanitized and that the sex she was willing to do is considered "vanilla" by the porn fans that post on the Adult DVD Talk discussion board. Chief among their complaints is her unwillingness to do anal scenes. Gonzo 420 puts it best when he says, "NEWSFLASH to all you Jenna Jameson fans... SHE SUCKS AND IS OVERRATED!! Thank god she retired from the business. Now people can focus on whores that actually like sex and like being a whore. When did Jenna Jameson ever do anal? Oh thats [sic] right she didn't, because she's not a good whore at all."[22] An example of how these users are obsessed by anal sex is the thread that discusses a scene in one of her movies that looks like she was anally penetrated. Sam W starts the discussion with the following observation: "I know other than dildos Jenna didn't do any anal scenes. However, I got in a Jenna mood the other day and put in 'Jenna Ink,' and watched the last scene (the Army scene). I noticed that when she is taking it from behind while kind of just bending over, the guy was going in and completely out of her. Anyway, one time he went to go back in her he actually 'misses' and goes into her ass. Jenna pushes him off and says something I think and has a smile on her face. I slowed it down and he definitely goes into her ass."[23] There follows a spirited discussion of the scene, with most fans agreeing that for a short time she was indeed anally penetrated. That this is important to users speaks volumes about the role of anal sex in porn since the act is often used to thoroughly subordinate the woman, and that Jameson has reached mega status without being used in this way irks many users.

The way many of the users feel about Jameson is summed up by Bornyo when he writes: "I think it's become pretty clear that she had no real impotance [*sic*]. I'm sure *Playboy* will tell you she is worthless. Porn is a revolving door or a conveyor belt if you will. Her flavor of the month has long expired and it was only thru shrewd marketing that she was able to keep herself afloat as long as she did. Her performances are lacking when compared to her peers and there are fresher and better girls coming along every day."[24] Eye Balls a Bleeding agrees, as he comments that Jameson's porn star status is a "lot of hype over nothing. There is nothing really to distinguish her from any other porn chick." He goes on to say, however, that she does deserve praise for the fact that "she is idolized by hundreds and hundreds of lazy young girls who rush into porn thinking that they are going to be the next Jenna Jameson and make millions. Thus ensuring a never ending supply of 18 year olds hopping on a bus and heading to Chatsworth."[25]

If we look beyond the inherent misogyny in Eye Balls a Bleeding's post (all women, or rather, "porn chicks," are interchangeable), it is interesting to see that he has identified one of Jameson's biggest contributions to pornography—her ability to act as a recruitment tool. Before Jameson there was no woman in porn who had a lifestyle that was in any way desirable. The sleaze factor, together with the low pay and abusive work conditions, did not seem very enviable, but today, as the culture becomes more pornographized, and as well-paid jobs become a thing of the past for many working-class women, Jameson's life does indeed look inviting. Because the mainstream media largely ignore what actually happens to women in porn, the acts they need to perform, their short shelf life, and the ongoing risk of STDs, and instead use Jameson as a porn mascot, then more and more women facing a life of minimum-wage labor are likely to be attracted to the sex industry.[26]

Jameson has also opened the door for other porn performers to enter the mainstream. The one who seems the most likely to succeed is Sasha Grey, a woman whom one porn producer at the Adult Entertainment Expo in Las Vegas described as "willing to do any sex necessary to be a star." In 2008 she was offered the lead part in a Steven Soderbergh movie, and that same year *XBIZ News* reported that "Sasha Grey continues her move into the mainstream with a racy appearance in an ad for the American Apparel clothing line."[27] Sasha Grey is now poised to become as big if not bigger than Jameson, and her rise to fame will no doubt help pave the way for more women to become celebrity porn stars.

VIVID ENTERTAINMENT

> This is a business, and we treat it like a business.
> —Steve Hirsch, founder of Vivid Entertainment

No discussion of porn going mainstream would be complete without mentioning Vivid Entertainment, the biggest and most successful porn studio in the world. Launched in 1984 by Steve Hirsch, the studio produces high-end Hollywood-film-like features as opposed to cheaply made gonzo movies. With an estimated revenue of $100 million, Vivid dominates the feature market and has virtually become a household name. With its high-tech, upmarket movies, this studio has become the acceptable face of porn, especially when compared to the more body-punishing, cheaply made gonzo.

The company's promotional copy describes Steve Hirsch as a "creative visionary who saw the potential for a company to grow beyond the confines of the adult entertainment industry."[28] Vivid releases over sixty videos a year, the movies distributed through a range of platforms such as DVD, pay-per-view, video-on-demand cable and satellite television, and the Internet. In addition to porn movies, Vivid also promotes such products as snowboards, calendars, and condoms.

Famous for its conventionally attractive stars, Vivid uses the old Hollywood-type contract system, in which the performers sign on to do a number of movies. These women have become known as the "Vivid Girls" and are often featured on Howard Stern and in men's magazines such as *Maxim*. When Hirsch explains why he uses the contract system, it is apparent how he treats these women as commodities: "If I was going to put a girl into a movie and I am going to spend a bunch of money promoting and marketing this movie then the next time a guy wants to see a

movie with her I want him to come back to me. I don't want to be spending my money to promote and market a girl that's in another guy's movie
next week or next month or next year."[29] There are usually ten to twelve
women signed with Vivid at a time, and the majority is white because
the goal is to promote these women as the public face of porn as well as
to have them serve as ambassadors for Vivid in the mainstream media.
While the company may have a few "ethnically ambiguous" women, it
mostly doesn't hire African American women, who are still on the lowest
level of the porn industry.

Hirsch has stated in interviews that he wanted to make porn mainstream, and given his appearances in the mainstream media (E! Entertainment, Fox, MSNBC), he has become somewhat successful. I
appeared on *Rita Cosby: Live and Direct* with him on December 14, 2005,
and the show was a perfect example of how the corporate media mainstream porn. Cosby began the show by saying:

> Tonight, we're going to take you into the epicenter of the multi-
> billion-dollar porn industry that is booming in the digital age in
> ways that you may not even know. We'll show you why the person
> next to you looking at their cell phone or iPod may really be watch-
> ing porn.
>
> We want to emphasize tonight that, like any industry, there are
> good and bad elements. We're not passing judgment on the merits
> of porn tonight...that's a whole other topic—but instead, we're re-
> porting to you on just how pervasive it is becoming in our modern-
> day society.

The stage was set for a "nonjudgmental" show that in the end turned
out to be an hour's advertisement for the porn industry. Making no attempt to explore the range of genres in porn, Cosby focused only on
the feature side, and for the first fifty minutes most of the people she
interviewed were connected to Vivid. I appeared in the last ten minutes
but was quickly silenced when I said that the show was an example of
shoddy journalism as it promoted only a positive image of the porn industry. *Adult Video News* wrote the following commentary: "It was called

'Rita Cosby: Live & Direct,' but on Wednesday evening, the more appropriate title would have been 'The Vivid Show.' The company was described during the telecast as 'the largest adult film company in the world.' Until the last 10 minutes, every guest was either a Vivid owner, a Vivid employee or a Vivid contractor, and nearly every location shot was on a Vivid set, or featured a Vivid contract girl doing a Web-cam show. What can we say but, 'Kudos to Vivid's publicity department!'"[30] Kudos indeed! What was missing from the story is that for all its gloss and upmarket chic, Vivid produces pornography that exploits women. The sex in the videos is hard-core, with anal, vaginal, and oral penetration. While the acts are not as rough as those in gonzo, acts such as gagging, slapping, putting the penis in sideways so the woman's mouth is stretched, and rough anal penetration, which are typical in gonzo, are filtering down into Vivid movies. The movies, like all porn movies, are penis-centered: the job of the women is to arouse the man, keep him erect, and bring him to orgasm. Female sexual pleasure is nothing more than a reflection of what the man wants, as she is there to please him. However glossed up the movies are, they are still pornographic in their depiction of women and men and the stories they tell about relationships, sexuality, and intimacy.

In my interviews with porn producers, I have discovered that the sense in the industry is that this is the type of porn made for couples. Some of the producers I spoke to at the Adult Entertainment Expo told me that men buy this porn because it provides women with a gentle introduction to porn; it is a way for men to encourage their partners to perform certain acts they may not be interested in doing. In addition, the glossy style, the conventionally attractive porn performers, and the "story line" make it more woman-friendly.

Even though Vivid is a leader in producing feature porn, in 2007 the company experienced a 35 percent drop in DVD sales, which *AVN* describes as disheartening, "considering Vivid is one of the largest, most respected adult content producers in the world."[31] However, this decline in sales did not signal an overall downward trend for Vivid but rather a move away from DVDs to other forms of technology, especially Vivid's Web sites and pay-per-view services on television and online. By developing its Internet presence, Vivid is able to both drive and harness the new cutting-edge technologies, as porn has been a leading innovator in developing and popularizing new technologies.

The examples of *GGW,* Jameson, and Vivid were selected because they clearly show how pornography is infiltrating the mainstream culture. Added to these are numerous other people, media genres, movies, and companies that have further brought porn into pop culture. Music videos, for example, with their soft-core images of barely clothed young women writhing around on the floor, look like much of porn did a decade or so ago. In his documentary on music videos, *Dreamworlds,* Sut Jhally highlights the various ways that women's bodies are represented for male consumption.[32] He specifically talks about the methods used to segment the body into bits and pieces, such that the women become merely a collection of interchangeable body parts. Jhally also points out that female artists themselves must conform to these strict codes of representation. Britney Spears's video *Womanizer* is a good example of how a female performer must look like a sex object. Lying naked on a bench, she writhes around looking semi-orgasmic. Jhally makes the point that one of the main reasons for this mode of representation is that the videos are geared to an adolescent male consumer.

Men's magazines such as *Maxim*—called "lad mags" in Britain because of their crass and adolescent-type content—similarly cater to a young adult male audience. With their pinup-type images and articles on sex, alcohol, and sports, these magazines construct a world of male fantasy where women exist solely as sex objects. The tone of the magazines is probably best described by Sean Thomas, a founding member of *Maxim:* "Magazines like *Maxim* are not in the business of news reporting—there are papers and TV stations for that. No, the purpose of the lad mag is to tell guys that it is OK to be guys—to drink beer, play darts, and look at girls. When we started *Maxim* we consciously felt that we were leading a fight-back against the excesses of sneering feminism. I believe we succeeded."[33] Part of the anti-feminist stance that *Maxim* so proudly adopts is the way it constructs masculinity as predatory and aggressive. Sex in *Maxim* is what men want from women, and articles abound on how to please her, not for her sake, but as a way for him to manipulate her into having more sex.[34] Issues relating to intimacy and relationship building are rarely discussed in *Maxim* or any of the other lad mags, as the sex is presented as casual and male-oriented. In his study of the content of men's magazines, Laramie Taylor found that "these magazines offer little in the way of sexual information that is different from the broad, stereotypical perceptions of sex as androcentric and men's sexuality as focused on variety."[35]

Because these magazines and their Web sites are not classed as pornography, they are available to males of any age and are often the reading material of choice for men in public places such as trains and planes. They are powerful vehicles for disseminating a pro-porn ideology without actually getting the label porn thrown at them. As feminist scholar Matt Ezzell has argued, "The ideology of the lad mags, which constructs masculinity as sexually aggressive, competitive, and consumerist, is virtually indistinguishable from that of the mainstream pornography industry."[36]

Probably the biggest "lad" in pop culture is Howard Stern. Known for his incessant chatter about porn and porn stars, he has been described by Vivid owner Steve Hirsch as a key player in the mainstreaming of porn. According to Hirsch, when Stern started putting porn stars on his show, "there was a huge amount of people who listened…and bought and rented movies."[37] A favorite among adolescent boys, Stern is known for pushing the envelope in pop culture and has even had porn producer and performer Max Hardcore on his show, a man that even some in the industry feel goes too far. A misogynist and bully, Stern often taunts the women from the porn industry by asking them personal and demeaning questions about their private lives, gets them to do demonstrations of oral sex with dildos on camera, and in some cases, asks them to describe their childhood sexual abuse as a way to titillate his audience. As feminist activist and author Jackson Katz writes: "Stern seeks out and destroys a variety of human targets, but his specialty— and a good part of the reason for his popularity with men—is his sexual bullying of women. He constantly belittles, ridicules, and provokes women—often young, surgically enhanced, and desperate to please men —to degrade themselves sexually for their moment of fame."[38] Howard Stern personifies the porn culture we live in, and for this he is well rewarded; in 2006 he was the second-highest paid celebrity in the world, with an income of $302 million.

As pornographic imagery increasingly filters down into mainstream pop culture, the porn industry has grown in volume and power. Porn should not be understood as an avant-garde "art form" allowing for the creativity and playfulness of independent directors, performers, and producers. It needs to be understood as a business whose product evolves with a specifically capitalist logic. Moreover, this is a business with considerable political clout, with the capacity to lobby politicians, engage in expensive legal battles, and use public relations to influence public debate. As with the tobacco industry, this is not a simple matter of consumer choice; rather, the business is increasingly able to deploy a sophisticated and well-resourced marketing machine, not just to push its wares but also to cast the industry's image in a positive light. As a major industry, the porn business does not just construct and sell a product; it constructs a world in which the product *can* be sold: the technologies, the business models, the enthusiastic consumers, the compliant performers, the tolerant laws, even the ideologies that proclaim porn to be the apogee of empowerment and liberation. One major sign of how mainstream porn has become is its interconnections with large non-porn corporations that form the DNA of our economy. The next chapter takes an in-depth look at just how porn functions today as big business.

THREE

From the Backstreet to Wall Street

The Big Business of Porn

Mainstream corporations are still discreet about the
profits that adult entertainment brings them; they prefer to
keep it on the down-low. But those profits are very real.
                        —Alex Henderson, "Making Bank," *XBIZ*

The size of the porn industry today is staggering. Though reliable numbers are hard to find, the global industry has been estimated to be worth around $96 billion in 2006, with the U.S. market worth approximately $13 billion. Each year, over 13,000 films are released, and despite their modest budgets, pornography revenues rival those of all the major Hollywood studios combined. There are 420 million Internet porn pages, 4.2 million porn Web sites, and 68 million search engine requests for porn daily.[1] While videos and DVDs drove the rapid growth of the pornography market in the two decades from the mid-1970s to the mid-1990s, it is the rapid growth of the Internet, especially broadband access, that has galvanized continued market expansion in recent years. Andrew Edmond, president and CEO of Flying Crocodile, a $20-million pornography Internet business, stated that "a lot of people [outside adult entertainment], get distracted from the business model by [the sex]. It is just as sophisticated and multilayered as any other market place. We operate just like any Fortune 500 company."[2]

The scale of the pornography business has important implications. In a profound sense, the entertainment industries do not just influence us; they are our culture, constituting our identities, our conceptions of the world, and our norms of acceptable behavior. But the scale of the porn business has more far-reaching ramifications. Porn is a key driver of new technological innovations, shapes technological developments, and has pioneered new business models, which have then diffused into the wider economy.[3] In turn, evolving technologies and business techniques have shaped the content and format of pornography. Porn is embedded in an increasingly complex and extensive value chain, linking not just producers and distributors but also bankers, software, hotel chains, cell phone and Internet companies. Like other businesses, porn is subject to the discipline of capital markets and competition, with trends toward market segmentation and industry concentration.

A key factor driving the growth of the porn market has been the development of technologies allowing users to buy and consume porn in private, without embarrassing trips to seedy stores or video rental shops. These technologies also enable pornography to be viewed anywhere, anytime; even the cell phone market for porn reached $775 million in Europe in 2007, and $27 million in the States. According to the Britain-based Juniper Research Company, the global market is expected to reach $3.5 billion in 2010.[4] Porn does not just benefit from these technologies, however—it has helped create the technologies that expand its own market. As Blaise Cronin and Elisabeth Davenport put it, "Certainly, it is universally acknowledged by information technology experts that the adult entertainment industry has been at the leading edge in terms of building high-performance Web sites with state-of-the-art features and functionality."[5]

Porn has proven to be a reliable, highly profitable market segment that has accelerated the development of media technologies, from VCRs and DVDs to file-sharing networks, video-on-demand for cable, streamed video over the Internet for PCs, and most recently, video for cell phones.[6] Video uses vast quantities of data, and the demand for porn has driven the development of core cross-platform technologies for data compression, search, and transmission. File-sharing networks such as Kazaa, Gnutella, and Limewire are better known for music, but are widely used for porn video files as well. According to historian Jonathan Coopersmith, a common pattern across these various technologies is for pornography to blaze the trail, then gradually decline as a proportion of total business as the media mature and develop more general commercial use.[7] The percentage of pornography on the Internet declined from about 20 percent to 5 percent between 1997 and 2002, according to Amanda Spink and Bernard J. Jansen.[8]

The porn business has also been a pioneer of new business models such as Internet subscription and advertising techniques that help to make commercial video profitable, opening the way for commercial viability of video-sharing Web sites such as YouTube and television series downloads to cell phones and iPods. The porn industry has been able to exploit the unregulated, freewheeling nature of business on the Web, which makes it easy for small companies to enter new markets with very little capital and pursue international strategies, while the jurisdictional ambiguity of Internet geography facilitates the avoidance of taxation and regulation. The porn industry has also developed marketing devices that have later diffused to other Internet sectors, such as free "supersites" that build traffic and cross-link to numerous providers. It has also led the development of Web-based subscription business models, antifraud security, and micro-payment systems for pay-per-view customers.[9]

That porn is first and foremost a business means that the content itself is shaped by the contours of marketing, technology, and competition in the industry. The low cost of entry and the intense competition to find and hold users have led to a proliferation of porn sites and extensive experimentation with formats, subgenres, and delivery systems. The rate of evolution of the industry is far faster than in the old days of print, when competition between *Playboy* and *Penthouse* gently pushed the envelope of what was considered acceptable. Where users once relied on a local porn store with limited selection, they can now avidly check hundreds of sites in minutes. It is perhaps not surprising that Web-based competition for eyes and wallets is fueling a rapid increase in porn depicting extreme situations, violence, and pseudo-child pornography. In a similar way, classic games such as Monopoly and Scrabble remained unchanged for decades. Now that gaming has moved largely to computers and the Web, the intense competition drives a market for thousands of new games every year, ever more interactive, violent, and sexually explicit.

The growing similarity between the porn and the video game industry is more than coincidental.[10] New technologies and business models are driving a convergence in entertainment platforms, so that young adults increasingly use their computers for watching television and videos and for playing games. The general public is not far behind. In early 2009, new TV sets with beefed-up computing power started coming on the market advertised as "Internet ready," ready to plug into your home Internet connection. But there is also convergence in form and content, so that the line between games and porn is becoming blurred. Porn producers are experimenting with interactive interfaces so that users can click or speak to direct performers to engage in specific acts. Sites specializing in "simulated" child porn have borrowed from the game industry the use of increasingly realistic animated graphic representations of the human form, which can be programmed to behave in any way imaginable. At the same time, the "rewards" for winning in games such as *Grand Theft Auto* include the chance to rape or kill a simulated woman. And just as games give physical feedback to players via vibrating controllers, the porn industry is beginning to experiment with "virtual sex." "Real Touch" was launched at the 2008 AVN trade show, a "machine that, when connected to your computer via USB, simulates the mouth, vagina, or anus of a real human, matching the on-screen action from supplied pornography." The porn will, of course, be proprietary and premium priced.[11]

Just like the gaming industry, the porn industry engages in the normal business activities that other industries pursue. Porn businesses raise capital, hire managers and accountants, undergo mergers and acquisitions, organize trade shows, and enter into co-marketing arrangements with other companies. Private Media Group was the first diversified adult entertainment company to gain a listing on the NASDAQ exchange (though it should be noted that porn businesses have struggled to raise capital through public share offerings). There is now an investment firm that deals specifically with the porn industry. Called Adult-Vest, the company boasts that it brings together "accredited investors, hedge funds, venture capital funds, private equity funds, investment banks, and broker dealers with growing adult entertainment companies and gentlemen's clubs who are looking to sell their business, raise capital, or go public. Investors can utilize their AdultVest.com membership to research a wide variety of private placements, reverse mergers, IPO's, public offerings, buyouts, joint ventures, and business opportunities."[12]

While these activities are in themselves unremarkably normal business operations, they signal that porn is becoming a mainstream, normal business—a legitimate business, one that is being taken more seriously by Wall Street and the media. These other businesses become allies and collaborators, with a vested interest in the growth and continued viability of the porn business. As Stephen Yagielowicz stated in an article for *XBIZ:* "The corporatization of porn isn't something that will happen or is happening, it is something that has happened—and if you're unaware of that fact then there truly is no longer a seat at the table for you. It's Las Vegas all over again: the independent owners, renegade mobsters and visionary entrepreneurs pushed aside by mega-corporations that saw a better way of doing things and brought the discipline needed to attain a whole new level of success to the remaining players."[13]

The economic connections between porn and mainstream industries were the focus of a 2007 article by Alex Henderson on Xbiz.com, a business Web site for the porn industry. Henderson begins by noting that although executives from mainstream companies don't want to talk about their connections to porn, they are indeed "profiting nicely, consistently and discreetly from adult entertainment." Some of the examples he gives illustrate the multiple ways that porn has increasingly become interconnected with companies that are household names. In the cable television business, for example, porn is distributed by Time Warner Cable, Cox Communications, and Comcast—the latter being the largest cable TV providers in the United States (Comcast also owns E! Entertainment, a cable station that often carries porn-friendly documentaries, such as one on Jenna Jameson, as well as the show *The Girls Next Door*). Although it is difficult to come by any precise numbers, Kagen Research "estimated that in 2005, cable operators earned about $282 million from adult video-on-demand and approximately $199 million from adult pay-per-view sales, though other researchers have said that the numbers are much higher."[14] Pornography is also distributed via satellite TV, with one of the biggest companies, DirecTV, offering Playboy's Spice Network and LFP Broadcasting's Hustler TV.

DirecTV has an interesting history, as it was sold by General Motors in 2003 to Rupert Murdoch's News Corp. Murdoch owns the Fox Television Network, Twentieth Century Fox, the *New York Post*, the LA Dodgers, and *TV Guide*, to name just a few. Murdoch at that time also owned the second-largest satellite provider, EchoStar Communications Corporation, which, according to the *New York Times*, made more money selling hard-core pornography films through its satellite subsidiary than all of Playboy's holdings combined.[15] An example of synergy here is that Murdoch also owns HarperCollins, the company that published Jenna Jameson's best-selling book *How to Make Love Like a Porn Star.* In 2006, the Liberty Media group took control of DirecTV, and it also has part ownership in Sirius Radio, which carries the Howard Stern Show, a show that serves as an advertisement for the porn industry by regularly inviting porn stars.

Another major distributor of porn is iN DEMAND, which, as one of the nation's largest pay-per-view distributors, is owned in part by Comcast and Time Warner. Time Warner also owns HBO, which regularly features pro-porn documentaries such as *Pornucopia*. The WB network, owned by Time Warner, ran a reality show starring Ron Jeremy, a well-known has-been porn actor. Jeremy is the first porn actor to be the star of a network show. Time Warner's other ventures include CNN, Castle Rock, AOL, *Sports Illustrated*, and part ownership of Amazon, a major distributor of porn in its own right.

Porn has been a major source of revenue for hotels, with chains such as Holiday Inn, Marriott, Hilton, Sheraton, Radisson, and Hyatt offering a variety of pornographic movies. Henderson puts the annual revenues from hotel porn at more than $500 million. While there have been some groups, especially right-wing ones, that have lobbied the hotel industry to stop selling porn, the debate really became more public in the 2008 presidential primaries when Mitt Romney, a high-ranking Mormon who had been on the board of Marriott Hotels from 1992 to 2001, was heavily criticized for not pushing the hotel chain to stop selling porn. Pressure was brought to bear on Marriott by the Mormon Church, but the owners refused to stop selling porn. Romney tried to distance himself from the hotel chain during his bid to become the Republican candidate, but after he lost, he quietly rejoined the Marriott board. Henderson points out that hotel porn not only makes money for the hotels but also for the companies that supply it, which include mega-giants such as LodgeNet and On-Command.[16]

Microsoft also makes money from the porn industry as the industry spends what Henderson calls "a fortune" on various financial, accounting, and graphic design software. Search engines such as Google, Yahoo!, Microsoft's Internet Explorer, Apple's Safari, and Mozilla Firefox are used to search for porn, and credit card companies are increasingly making money from porn transactions as the industry moves away from brick-and-mortar stores that still take cash to Web sites that require credit card payment. Henderson points out some of the more hidden mainstream industry partners of porn: real estate and banking. For the former, the porn industry "brings high profit to realtors in the San Fernando Valley, and in many different parts of the U.S., Europe and Asia, real estate people prosper when they sell or rent commercial property to adult webmasters or sex toy manufacturers."[17] Banks also make money from the porn industry as the revenue it generates is invested in stocks, bonds, mutual funds, and so on. Indeed, everyone in the supply chain from production to consumption is complicit in building and strengthening the porn industry.

The porn industry is carefully nurturing a more respectable and mainstream image as it seeks to build not only partner organizations but legitimacy. A May 13, 1999, press release from Private Media Group reads, "We are committed to meeting our goals to increase shareholder value, on a quarter-by-quarter basis, taking us forward as a complete lifestyle global company, providing our services to the mainstream adult communities of the world."[18] In early 2009, adult entertainment studio Pink Visual launched PVExposed.com, a promotional site designed to give media outlets and financial analysts a source for the latest news and announcements from the company. "We created PVExposed as a way to showcase all our products in a safe for work environment where we could build traffic from our various, disparate campaigns like 'Erection '08' and 'Plant Your Wood,'" said Kim Kysar, brand and product manager for Pink Visual.[19]

Just as the gambling industry, from racetracks to casinos, has sought to reposition itself by adopting the label "gaming" industry and emphasizing its contributions to government revenues, so the porn industry is seeking to position itself as part of the entertainment and "lifestyle" sector.[20] There are now a number of PR companies whose job is to promote porn in the mainstream entertainment industry. Brian Gross, the president of BSG Public Relations, which counts *Adult Video News*, *Penthouse Films*, and Joanna Angel (a gonzo porn producer and performer) among its clients, is quoted as saying that in the porn industry there is a consistent demand for mainstream attention, but "the adult industry can't advertise the same way other industries can, they can't market their products like other industries."[21] The solution is to garner publicity in mainstream media by placing stories, people, and products that advertise the porn industry. In the case of pornographer Joanna Angel, Gross has repackaged her as a mainstream spokeswoman for punk and Goth sex and tattoo culture. In addition, thanks to Gross, she not only appears frequently in tattoo magazines, she also writes columns for *Spin* magazine and has been featured in the *New York Times*.[22] In 2008, Indiana University invited Angel to speak on campus—she showed clips from her movies and handed out sex toys.

The industry has also been successful at product placement wherein actors playing leading roles are seen consuming pornography, or where porn is just folded into part of the story line. In the 2004 independent movie *Sideways*, the main character, a mild-mannered man played by Paul Giamatti, is seen reading Hustler's *Barely Legal* magazine, which features women who look younger than eighteen. No comment is made in the film about the magazine; it is just simply part of the scenery. A more blatant example appeared in season 3 of Showtime's *Weeds*, where one of the lead characters, Andy Botwin, played by Justin Kirk, gets a job on a porn set. The well-known porn performer Lexington Steele, appearing mostly naked, is in the background of a number of scenes, simulating penetration. Again, much of the dialogue had little to do with pornography; it was just a mere backdrop to the story. In the movie *I Am Legend*, starring Will Smith, two of Joanna Angel's movies are displayed in one scene that takes place at Tower Records.[23] Porn performers are now increasingly showing up in pop culture to such a degree that the *Los Angeles Times* ran a story called "Porn Stars Are the New Crossover Artists." The article mentioned Sasha Grey and ex-porn performers Traci Lords and Katie Morgan appearing in *Zack and Miri Make a Porno*. The article continues: "As pornography has evolved from a shadowy racket to a multibillion-dollar global industry based in San Fernando Valley office blocks, top porn stars become just one more celebrity life form among many: dishing behind-the-scenes gossip on talk radio, dashing off autographs for besotted trade-show fans and generally marketing themselves as aggressively as any NBA MVP or 'American Idol' champ."[24] Indeed, the article itself is one more example of how porn is now a newsworthy story.

Zack and Miri Make a Porno was big news in the porn industry. Interviewed by *XBIZ*, director Kevin Smith expressed his fondness for porn. Asked what sort of an impact porn had had on him professionally and personally, Smith replied:

> You gotta remember I've been involved with porn, in one way or another, since I was eleven years old. Whether it be trying to steal some skin mags from the magazine store in town, to trying to track down stag films in neighbors' houses, friends' houses—maybe their parents had 'em, because my parents never kept that kind of thing, so I had to look for it elsewhere. Before the days of internet, where it is easily accessible, it was tough to get your hands on grown up stuff. Part of the reason I took the job at RST Video back when I did in 1989, was because it was a mom and pop shop, and they actually had a porn room, as opposed to Blockbuster Video. So, I'm like, "Finally, I'll be able to take home porn flicks without having to rent them on my parents account. This is gonna rock." And that led me to making *Clerks*. So, without porn, I'm not talking to you today.[25]

Another film that makes porn the focus of a comedy is Adam Sandler's forthcoming *Born to Be a Star*. The film is about a teen who goes to Hollywood to follow in the footsteps of his porn star parents. *XBIZ News* made this a top story since it is well aware that movies with a porn theme help to mainstream porn.[26] After reading the *XBIZ* story, Dawn Hill, the editor of the Web site for the sex toy company Liberator Bedroom Adventure Gear, contacted the production house to offer its products as props in the film. According to a follow-up article in *XBIZ*, the prop master liked the products and now actresses in the movie will be wearing Liberator Lingerie and Liberator Latex costumes.[27] This is not the first time that Liberator goods have been in mainstream movies. In the movie *Meet the Fockers*, Barbra Streisand was carrying around one of their products. According to Acme Andersson, a writer for *XBIZ*, "Liberator's products had such a big role in Joel and Ethan Coen's *Burn After Reading* that they should be SAG-eligible. Expect to see more of the products in *Jack Goes Boating*, which Philip Seymour Hoffman is directing and producing."[28] Liberator's vice president, Joshua Maurice, told Andersson that the company has developed contacts with those people who are responsible for placing products in movies.

Mainstream positioning also requires that an industry present a more socially responsible face and pursue modes of self-regulation that try to stop the more blatant abuses, while fending off more unwelcome governmental regulation.[29] In 1991, the industry launched the Free Speech Coalition to engage in lobbying, public relations, and litigation. Its mission is to serve as an organization that "helps limit the legal risks of being an adult business, increases the profitability of its members, promotes the acceptance of the industry in America's business community, and supports greater public tolerance for freedom of sexual speech." Its current 2007–9 strategic plan calls for an Internal and External Communications Plan that identifies "audiences (industry, members, media, legislators, etc)," and develops "methods and materials to reach those audiences." It also promulgates a Code of Ethics and Best Practices.[30]

Another organization founded to provide the industry with a socially responsible image is the Association of Sites Advocating Child Protection. Formed in 1996, the association sells itself as a "non-profit organization dedicated to eliminating child pornography from the Internet. ASACP battles child pornography through its CP reporting hotline, and by organizing the efforts of the online adult industry to combat the heinous crime of child sexual abuse. ASACP also works to help parents prevent children from viewing age-inappropriate material online."[31] Meanwhile, in 2002 the Free Speech Coalition lobbied successfully to change the law on child pornography to allow the industry to use women who, while eighteen years of age, actually look much younger. In an example of utter hypocrisy, Hustler is one of the members of the Association of Sites Advocating Child Protection, the same Hustler that runs *Barely Legal* and advertises itself as "the world's #1 teen magazine with the largest collection of teen sweethearts found anywhere."[32]

Similar to other businesses, the pornographers go to great lengths to study and understand the psychology of consumer behavior. Although there is still very little actual research conducted on porn consumers, Jack Morrison has written articles for *AVN* that draw from a range of areas in an attempt to build a knowledge base about consumer behavior. In one notable article, Morrison discussed the work of Dr. Al Cooper, a Stanford University psychologist, who focused on cyber-sex addiction. The most exciting finding, according to *AVN*, is that 20 percent of porn surfers are addicts, and in a true capitalist approach, the article has a heading called "Exploiting the Data." Here Morrison writes, "I have three specific recommendations for adult Webmasters, each of which has the potential to add millions of dollars of extra revenue to the online adult industry. Some of these recommendations may seem to be controversial, but these techniques are used in mainstream business every day." Morrison suggests the following:

> In order to secure the ongoing revenue from such consumers, adult Webmasters should make it substantially easier to indulge that behavior. The most effective way to do this is probably to include links to additional pay sites/paid content inside your own pay site. This is done on a few sites which have "pay-per-view" elements, but in most cases, links to additional sites are exterior, either as an exit to the tour or in the exit out (at which point the consumer has probably had an orgasm and is thus less likely to buy another paid membership). The goal should be to keep the consumer within the Website and sell additional memberships for additional materials.[33]

In another article, Morrison interviewed a dozen top porn webmasters about their best marketing practices. He came up with a list of twenty-nine, including creating a spokesperson for the site, starting a Yahoo! discussion group about the site, creating more free sites, and starting a newsletter for consumers. Getting into even more detail, he adds a basic rule: "Top Webmasters spend around 50 percent of their time on getting traffic to their sites, 20 percent of their time on content development (graphics, site appearance, updating members areas, building free sites, etc.), and 30 percent on general business issues (looking at statistics, communicating with other Webmasters, following up on contacts from trade shows, maintaining relationships.)"[34] As porn continues to grow, the research on consumer behavior will most likely become more sophisticated and, no doubt, more exploitive.

Clearly, pornography has become big business, stepping more boldly into national and international markets and wielding direct political and legislative influence. The power of the industry continues to be magnified by the trend toward increasing ownership concentration and the emergence of larger, well-capitalized firms with brand names and extensive operations. Moreover, the industry's links to mainstream finance, media, and communications chains provide it with powerful allies. As the porn industry's clout increases, so too will the pornographization of our society.

FOUR

Grooming for Gonzo

Becoming a Man in a Porn Culture

The awkward truth, according to one study, is that 90 percent of 8-to-16-year-olds have viewed pornography online. Considering the standard climax to even the most vanilla hard-core scene today, that means there is an entire generation of young people who think sex ends with a money shot to the face.

—*Details*

One of the arguments I hear regularly is that it is perfectly natural for boys and men to like porn. Males are more visual, so the argument goes, and they need more sex than women, so porn is simply a way to satisfy a biological urge. What proponents of this argument miss is that it is anti-male to believe that there is something essential in men that leads them to desire porn, gonzo or otherwise. What feminists argue is that men are socialized by the culture into a specific type of masculinity that makes porn both normal and pleasurable. If we take seriously the notion that we are all cultural beings, then we need to think about the ways that boys become men and how this process creates a consumer base for porn that is degrading to women. What became clear when feminists started to explore male socialization is that although the type of masculinity a boy adopts will depend on multiple factors such as religion, race, and class, the dominant masculinity today is, as Robert Jensen argues, one in which "men are assumed to be naturally competitive, and aggressive."[1]

But as Jensen and a whole host of researchers show, there is nothing natural about boys being shoved, coerced, seduced, and manipulated into conformity the second they enter a world brimming with gender expectations and assumptions about how real men have to be strong, powerful, and unemotional. From parents, schools, peer groups, sports and, of course, media, boys are taught that any deviation from the norm will result in swift punishments, the worst of which is being called "a girl." Few insults carry as much weight and few insults do as much damage to both boys and girls, since the boy is being told that the worst thing he can be is a female.

This has profound effects on the emotional lives of boys as they are, as psychiatrist James Gilligan argues, "taught that to want love or care from others is to be passive, dependent, unaggressive, and unambitious or, in short, unmanly; and that they will be subjected to shaming, ridicule, and disrespect, if they appear unmanly in the eyes of others."[2] To be "unmanly" is, of course, within our gender binary system, to be feminine, and here lies the essence of gender socialization for males: they need, at all times, to distance themselves as much as possible from anything constructed by the culture as feminine. The feminine hence becomes feared—and that which we fear, we also learn to despise.

This is damaging to boys on many levels, not least because they are children who need the love and emotional connection of caregivers, most of whom today are still women, in order to develop a healthy emotional life. But to survive in this world of masculinity and all the bullying and jockeying for power that comes with it, a boy needs to learn how to disconnect from his own emotions and those of others. Public displays of fear, empathy, and sadness—indeed, anything that suggests vulnerability—are dangerous for many boys as the alpha males of the pack are only too happy to provide a lesson on what happens to boys who fail to show sufficient manliness. This leads to many boys becoming emotionally stunted as they reach adulthood because they have learned to wear the mask of masculinity that hides their deeply felt emotions. This mask may feel like a poor fit to a young boy, but after wearing it for many years, the mask begins to mold to his skin, and after a while, it becomes almost like a second skin.[3]

Helping to reinforce masculinity are the massive media and toy industries, which seem to be cemented in gender apartheid. In 2008, on a trip to Toys "R" Us with my nieces and nephews, aged between eight and thirteen, I couldn't believe how much the store had changed from when I used to go with my own son a decade earlier. While there was some gender division among the toys in the 1990s, today the store has an almost tangible gender barrier down the middle. One half was full of toy guns, knives, swords, wrestling figures, and violent computer games, and the other half magically turned pink with princess dresses, dolls, makeup, and hairdryers. My two nephews walked out with the latest wrestling figures, and my two nieces each had a pink Barbie hairdryer and a pink makeup bag, all bought by their loving feminist aunt. I did try to steer them to the few gender-neutral items, such as jigsaws and board games, but was stopped short by the look of disgust across all four faces.

When we arrived home, my nephews eagerly unwrapped their toys as they watched *Casino Royale*, with Daniel Craig playing alpha male James Bond. With his ruggedly handsome face, rock-hard body, smooth delivery of lethal violence against his opponents, and bevy of beautiful women falling over him, Craig must have seemed like a very appealing role model for my nephews, reared on pop culture. I watched their faces as Craig, now on the receiving end of the violence, was being tortured—by having his testicles whacked with a carpet beater, no less. Rather than showing pain, he responded with sarcastic quips and sneering put-downs. I wondered what my nephews were taking away from this scene and how it fit with all the other gender lessons they had learned.

Studies show that today's children, especially boys, live in a media culture that is awash in violence. The Henry J. Kaiser Foundation lists the following statistics on its media violence fact sheet:

- Nearly two out of three TV programs contained some violence, averaging about six violent acts per hour.
- Fewer than 5 percent of these programs featured an anti-violence theme or pro-social message emphasizing alternatives to or consequences of violence.
- Violence was found to be more prevalent in children's programming (69 percent) than in other types of programming (57 per-

cent). In a typical hour of programming, children's shows featured more than twice as many violent incidents (fourteen) than other types of programming (six).

- The average child who watches two hours of cartoons a day may see nearly ten thousand violent incidents each year, of which the researchers estimate that at least five hundred pose a high risk for learning and imitating aggression and becoming desensitized to violence.[4]

Alongside television's steady diet of violence is an enormously profitable video game industry, which generated worldwide over $26.5 billion in 2007. While many of these games depict images of hypersexualized violence, one of the worst, and most profitable, is *Grand Theft Auto*. When *GTA IV* hit the market in April 2008, on its first day of release it sold a record 2.5 million units in North America. Sociologist Matt Ezzell describes some of the scenes from a video montage of *GTA IV* called *The Ladies of Liberty City: Very Bad Things.* These scenes focus specifically on the sexual interactions between Niko, the protagonist of the game, and women, most of whom are prostitutes and strippers.

The Ladies of Liberty City opened with graphic images of women stripping, pole-dancing, and giving the protagonist a lap-dance. The next scene showed Niko shooting a woman in the middle of the street. It went on to show Niko picking up prostitutes.... He approaches one woman who says, "I'll suck your cock real nice." "Get in," he replies, before driving her to a baseball field. Once parked, he says, "You get what you pay for, right?" The woman sits on his lap. As they bounce up and down, the woman squeals, "Fuck the shit out if it! Yeah, you nasty fucker!" They finish, and Niko says, "Life is strange, don't you think?" The woman gets out of the car and walks away. As she does, Niko pulls out a gun and shoots her several times. You can hear her scream as Niko says, "Stay down or I will finish you off!" She does not get up.[5]

These sorts of messages targeted at boys help shape the ways they develop their masculine identity. As boys turn into men, these messages are in turn absorbed into their sexual identities, and the more media they are exposed to, the more they become desensitized to the visual depiction of violence, no matter how brutal or sexualized that violence is.[6] In this emotional economy, porn is appealing; it offers men a no-strings-attached, intense, disconnected sexual experience, where men always get to have as much sex as they want in ways that shore up their masculinity. The sex acts are always successful, ending in supposed orgasm for both, and he is protected from rejection or ridicule since in porn, women never say no to men's sexual demands, nor do they question their penis size or technique. In this world, men dispense with romantic dinners, vanilla sex, and postcoital affection and get down to the business of fucking. In porn, sex is the vehicle by which men are rendered all powerful and women all powerless; and for a short time a man gets to see what life would look like if only women unquestionably consented to men's sexual demands.

For some men, especially those who are overconformists to masculinity, gonzo is going to be instantly appealing because they can easily identify with the male performer's show of extreme masculinity and violence. However, it would be a mistake to assume that all men instantly and easily take to gonzo porn since that would assume that all men are similarly socialized into a more violent masculinity. Men who adopt a less "manly" type of masculinity may well be turned off by watching a woman being called a cunt as she is roughly penetrated by any number of men, so pornographers, being the savvy businessmen they are, develop techniques to groom reluctant gonzo viewers. While these techniques vary, what they all have in common is the way they render away the humanity of women in porn.

HOW PORN SOCIALIZES THE USERS: THE BITCH LOVES IT

The first and most important way pornographers get men to buy into gonzo sex is by depicting and describing women as fuck objects who are deserving of sexual use and abuse. It is especially important for the pornographers to shred the humanity of the women in the images, as many porn users have sustained and intimate relationships with women in the real world. Even though we live in a culture that devalues women, men still manage to develop loving connections with mothers, sisters, daughters, friends, lovers, and wives. To erode any empathy that many men may have for the women in porn—an emotion that would most likely end up derailing the porn experience as they might feel sorry for her—the porn needs to construct porn women in ways that clearly demarcate them from the women men know and love.

The most obvious technique that the pornographers employ here is to verbally segregate this group of women by calling them cunts, whores, sluts, cumdumpsters, beavers, and so on. In gonzo, a woman is never referred to as a woman; instead, she is reduced to a sexual object. But reducing women to just sex objects is not enough for gonzo, and they are further referred to as dirty, nasty, and filthy. No wonder we never see any kissing or touching in porn. Who would want to kiss or caress dirty, nasty, filthy cunts/whores/sluts?

In porn, sex is framed as not just consensual but as something that the woman seeks out because she loves to be sexually used. This also is a method for lessening any guilt the user may feel as he can reassure himself that she is not being hurt, or if she is, it is what she wants. Take for example the description of "Gauge" on the site Ass Plundering. "Gauge gives a new meaning to the word whore. Any less than 2 guys at once means she won't be satisfied. Her tight holes need to be ravaged by big cocks at the same time for her to have fun."[7] The images surrounding this text show Gauge being orally, vaginally, and anally penetrated by three men at the same time. One of the images shows a red, raw, and swollen anus while others show her face contorted as she is supposedly having an orgasm. The images and the written text together, as well as the movie, which presents her begging for more, collude to seduce the viewer into believing that no matter how cruelly her body is being treated, she belongs to a special breed of women that enjoy sexual mistreatment.

Similarly, on the British Bukkake site, the text reads, "If you like horny bitches that like to drench themselves in hot jizz, this is the site for you. These girls know how to do it up right and you're guaranteed to get off when you see their dripping faces full of cum."[8] These women (or rather, "horny bitches") are not, according to the text, being coerced by anybody to participate in acts that most girlfriends or wives would absolutely refuse to do. Rather, we are told that the "horny bitches" are different from the women the user knows because they actually seek out and enjoy being debased.

The process of dehumanizing a group as a way to legitimize and justify cruelty against its individual members is not something that porn producers invented. It has been a tried and trusted method adopted by many oppressors; the Nazi propaganda machine effectively turned Jews into "kikes," racists defined African Americans as "niggers" rather than humans, and homophobes have an almost limitless list of terms for gays and lesbians that strip them of humanity. Once the humanness of these individuals is collectively rendered invisible by their membership in a socially denigrated group, then it is that much easier to commit acts of violence against them.

In porn, the women's lack of human qualities often results in men's inability to see just how violent the sex act is. No matter how cruel the sex, the one question I can always count on hearing from a man after my presentation is, "Women enjoy what they are doing, so why is porn a problem?" Of course, these men have no empirical evidence to support this, just their observations of the porn that they masturbate to. When I ask them if they would like to see their wives, girlfriends, or sisters in this position—in an attempt to humanize the porn performers—they are quick to respond that their loved ones are different from the women in porn; their women would never "choose" such a job. The image these men seem to have of women in porn is of a woman accidentally stumbling onto a porn set one day, and realizing that this is what she has been looking for all her life. That these women are acting, and may have come to porn not so much through choice but due to a lack of alternatives is rarely considered because this premise threatens to puncture the fantasy world created by both pornographer and user.

The degree to which users will fool themselves into believing that porn performers have found their one true vocation is evident all over porn discussion sites, where men swap stories about how most porn performers love what they do. On Adult DVD Talk, Nookie Monster contributes to the discussion on the "Porn chicks who Love it" thread by singing the praise of Cynthia in the movie *Exotica 6* because, by the end of a three-way scene, "she is quivering all over and her legs twitching. Halfway into the scene she goes crazy as she gets the living hell fucked out of her. Its one of the best scenes I have ever seen in porn.... She starts out joking with the guys, almost taunting them before they even fuck, and by the end of the scene that have broken her pride and made her like a women [sic] possessed quivering and screaming for more cock and to be fucked harder."[9] If we take a close look at what is happening to this woman, with lots of men treating her body in ways that even this porn user describes as getting "the living hell fucked out of her," then no wonder she is quivering and twitching, though it could well be due to exhaustion and pain, not sexual arousal. Needless to say, no one participating in the thread mentions this possibility.

The men[10] who post to these porn discussion boards also buy into the myth that doing porn is not something a woman does for money, but that it's a calling, and it is their love of sex—not the need to earn a living—that drove these women to the industry. Some of the men on the porn sites do acknowledge that these women get paid for what they do, but they assume that the money is seen as a kind of icing on the cake, since they would choose to do this even if no money was involved. Take, for example, a recent discussion on the Sir Rodney porn review site. The reviewer (Sir Rodney) is discussing the site West Coast Gang Bangs, which he finds "especially exciting because it's real, featuring real amateurs (mostly swingers) fulfilling a fantasy. Honestly, we get extra hard just writing about it." Well, it turns out that some of the users aren't getting hard enough as they recognize some of the women from other porn movies and feel angry that they have been deceived. But Anonymous chimes in with a post to salvage the "real amateurs" fantasy by offering the helpful insight that even though they are porn stars, it doesn't mean that they "cant [sic] swing on the side!"[11]

The more ardent fans who post on Adult DVD Talk attend porn promotion shows (such as the Adult Entertainment Expo) and talk about how these women are so hot for sex that they just spontaneously started making out with each other or talked dirty to the customers. Malte Decker, for example, evidently had firsthand experience of just how much Ava Devine is "hungry for cok [sic]" since during a signing and interview he was at "she grabbed most of the man's [*sic*] dicks...and she was rubbing my dick throughout the whole interview and started sucking it after the last question."[12] Irrespective of whether this story is true or not, the point of the post is to reinforce just how much porn stars supposedly love their job.

Pornstarlover is particularly perturbed about a movie featuring one of his favorite porn stars, Delilah Strong, where she "fucks two black guys and has them cum into 'shot' glasses. She ends up swallowing 5 loads but after the first 3 she looks pretty uncomfortable. In fact, she looks like wanting to throw up at the last cumshot. In the end she is all sunshine again and it may have been just acting."[13] The way this fan, and indeed many others, talk themselves into believing what they want to believe is to construct an argument that Delilah was acting when she looked "uncomfortable," and not acting when she was "all sunshine." It is hardly worth pointing out here that it could well be the other way around and the real acting was managing to look happy after drinking five different ejaculates.

If porn performers truly don't like what is happening to them, then the fantasy that users have erected about women and porn begins to crumble, and they are left with the stark reality that maybe these women are not "fuck dolls," but are instead human beings with real emotions and feelings. If this is the case, then users would have to admit to becoming aroused to images of women being sexually mistreated. For those men who are not sexually sadistic or cruel, this could well be psychologically intolerable, so they have to work very hard at maintaining the fantasy that porn women are indeed unlike most women they meet in the real world.

Ultimately, however, the ability to keep porn women separate from the women they date and hook up with is eroded as the more men watch porn, the more the stories become part of their social construction of reality. Men may think that the porn images are locked in that part of the brain marked fantasy, never to leak into the real world, but I hear over and over again from female students how their boyfriends are increasingly demanding porn sex from them. Whether it be ejaculating on their partner's face or pounding anal sex, these men want to play out porn in the real world. And from male students I increasingly hear how they thought that they could separate the two worlds, only to find out that industrially produced porn images do indeed seep into their intimate lives.

BORING PORN

Once the user has been socialized into gonzo porn, there is an abundance of images for him to choose from. At first these images may well be exciting, but the more seasoned user will soon find that porn, because of its formulaic nature, becomes predictable. There are X number of minutes given over to oral sex, often leading to the woman gagging, then anal, then double penetration, and then ejaculation. And while the next film may have a few more minutes on one particular act, or may have anal before oral, the story unfolds in much the same way as it did in the previous films, and the images begin to look the same. Missing from porn is anything that looks or feels remotely like intimacy and connection, the two ingredients that make sex interesting and exciting in the real world. Drained of these, porn becomes monotonous and predictable to the point that users need to eventually seek out more extreme acts as a way to keep them interested and stimulated. This is why, Robert Jensen argues, pornographers "offer men sexual gymnastics and circus acts that are saturated with cruelty toward women; they sexualize the degradation of women."[14]

Realizing that heightening the level of degradation is what keeps men interested in and aroused by porn helps us to understand why today's porn looks the way it does. The acts that porn amplifies are designed to deliver the maximum amount of degradation. Probably the most degrading of acts in contemporary porn is ass-to-mouth (ATM), where a woman is expected to put a penis in her mouth that has just been in her anus (or in another woman's anus). What heightened sexual enjoyment is to be had for the man from going from an anus to a mouth outside of the actual degradation of the woman? That some fans enjoy watching this debasement is evident on the Adult DVD talk; in a thread called "Dirty A2M & Messy Anal-Bloopers & Unexpected Leak," fans post their favorite scenes and discuss them in detail, with some listing hundreds of scenes where women were clearly shown having to suck a penis covered in visible fecal matter. Mediasmart 2, one of the most energetic of posters on this thread, describes a scene from *Assault that Ass #1* in vivid detail:

> There is intense anal pounding followed by the guy pulling out, sticking the dick in poor Paris's face to cum, and as he cums the dick rubs on her chin and lips and lo and behold it smears brown-ness all over her. There's no ambiguity whatsoever to this scene, it is crap, and lots of it. To cap it all, having seen the dirtiness on his cock, the guy then mutters "suck" in a low guttural voice, and Paris, perhaps not even realizing yet that her chin is entirely brown, sucks away. Its the closest thing to a moment of Zen you can ever get in porn, your eyes are just glued to the screen just waiting for her to figure out what is going on.

Similarly, Balou shares his favorite scene: "At 1:54:17 Rocco pulls his cock out of the ass of a dark haired hungarian amateur slut and makes ATM to a blond girl. He doesn't hit her mouth at once, so his cock is first at her nose. When he slides into her mouth, you see a very little dark piece of shit remaining on her nose.... Gentlemen, this thread must never die, I love dirty anal so much."[15] The pleasure for many of these fans seems to be in watching the real looks of disbelief, disgust, and distaste flash on the women's faces when they realize just what they are going to have to put in their mouths. It is a pleasure gained from watching somebody totally dehumanized and humiliated.

The desire to see women utterly degraded and powerless explains in part why anal sex has become so popular in porn. In the real world this act is becoming more common,[16] but I doubt that many women are seeking out the type of anal sex that the pornographers depict. What generally makes anal sex so appealing in porn is the potential pain and harm that robotic and mechanistic thrusting can cause women. One porn executive explains why users like anal: "Essentially it comes from [every man] who's unhappily married, and he looked at his wife who just nagged at him about this or that or whatnot, and he says, 'I'd like to fuck you in the ass.' He's angry at her, right? And he can't, so he would rather watch some girl taking it up the ass and fantasize at that point he's doing whatever girl happened to be mean to him that particular day."[17] Similarly, one producer at the Expo told me that he was specializing in anal-themed movies because "men like to see just how far the women will go with the cocks up her ass. I like to see them pushed to the edge, so I make films I like to watch."

A quick glance at the Adult DVD Talk forum suggests that fans are indeed on the lookout for scenes where the woman is suffering real pain. A popular thread—called Painful Anal—has numerous posts where fans list their favorite scenes and discuss at great length their enjoyment at watching the woman cry, scream, or simply become too overwhelmed to do anything. Nunsploitation, for example, especially likes a scene from *Dirty Anal Kelly in Rome* where the male performer Rocco is very rough with "Kelly." At one point, "he takes her arms, holds them behind her back and just plows her ass mercilessly showing no concerns for her yelps and howls. Her face goes from angry and defiant to overwhelmed." For Nunsploitation, this is an "awesome anal scene." Another post, this time by AC Cream, illustrates how users are quick to point out that they normally don't get off on violence, but these scenes are especially appealing:

> The most real painful scene I've ever seen is Gang-Bang Auditions #3 from Diabolic. The scene with Aspen Brock. When it gets to where Lexington is in her pu$$y & Mr. Marcus is in her a$$. The guys start asking her questions like "You like that dick in your a$$?," but she is in such pain her answers are hard to understand. She tried to say something like "I loooove iiiit," but then the tears started flowing. I think 1 of the other guys in the scene said "aaaah look, she's crying." ... In this scene combined with the humor & the rareness of a porn chick not handling dick gave me major Bone-age I recall.[18]

For those men who really like to see pain and suffering, nobody is better to watch than performer Max Hardcore. I have seen many Max Hardcore movies, and it is hard to believe that he is anything but a sexual sadist. In a 2005 interview, he outlined the type of acts he "pioneered": "Positions like pile driver, where I would gape the girls [sic] asses wide open, and provide a clear view for the camera, was unknown before I came along. I also created the technique of cumming in a girl's ass, having her squeeze it out into a glass, and then chuck the load down." He continued by boasting that over time he "developed many other unique maneuvers, most notably, vigorous throat fucking, creating gallons of throat slime over a girl's upside down face, and even causing them to puke. A little later, I started pissing down their throats several times during a scene, often causing them to vomit uncontrollably while still reaming their throats."[19] The story of Max Hardcore is really the story of contemporary porn. Once considered an outlier by the industry for his extreme porn, he is now increasingly being brought back into the fold. A sign of his newfound status was an October 2007 appearance on *The Howard Stern Show*. As porn becomes more extreme and cruel, men like Hardcore move from the margins to the center of the porn world. Although he was found guilty on ten counts of federal obscenity charges in June 2008 and was sentenced to forty-six months in prison, Hardcore remains a major figure in the porn world, not least because he was one of the founding fathers of gonzo. Veteran of well over a hundred movies, possessed of a large fan base and a well-traveled Web site, Hardcore will likely find that his stay in prison has little impact on his popularity.

At the 2008 EXPO, I walked over to Hardcore's booth, which was surrounded by male autograph seekers. It was easy to spot him in his signature cowboy hat, but as I approached, hoping for an interview, I froze. There was the real Max Hardcore doing what he does best, raging at a woman. Red in the face, sweating profusely, walking up and down like a caged animal, and speaking through gritted teeth, Hardcore let a female porn performer have the full force of his fury. The woman, who, I later found out, was his "girlfriend" Layla, sat perfectly still, not moving a muscle. At one point, Max Hardcore shook with rage and Layla began to cry. The scene was frightening, and she clearly was intimidated as she went to the bathroom to get away from him. I followed her to see if she was okay, only to watch a Max Hardcore security guard take her by the arm and firmly walk her around the convention hall, controlling her every move.

The scene reminded me of *Hardcore*, a British documentary that follows "Felicity" from London to Los Angeles as she attempts to break into porn.[20] Felicity is shown being cajoled and manipulated by her pimp-agent to perform anal sex. Felicity steadfastly refuses, and we watch her pimp become increasingly angry, telling her that to make real money in porn you have to be willing to do anal. In the end, the pimp sets up a meeting between her and Hardcore, obviously in an attempt to get Hardcore to do the grooming necessary to persuade Felicity to agree. While she is clearly frightened about meeting him and has heard he is abusive to women, Felicity nonetheless agrees to go to Hardcore's house. What follows is a dreadful scene where Hardcore walks into the room and within a few seconds is anally raping her. Felicity tries to defuse the situation by joking with him, and all the while he is thrusting his penis into her anus. She tells Hardcore repeatedly that she is scared of him, and he tells her to relax, that he is not really scary at all.

The next scene shows her agreeing to make a film with Hardcore, and while we don't see what he does to her, we hear him gagging her with his penis. Felicity then runs up the stairs, crying hysterically. Hardcore runs after her and soothes the crying Felicity, stroking her hair and telling her that she is special and unique. As she begins to calm down, he suddenly changes his tone and becomes abusive, calling her "a fucking loser" and "fucking pathetic." His rage builds to the point that he is red in the face as he accuses her of shirking her responsibility as a single mother. Thoroughly intimidated, Felicity agrees to continue filming, at which point the documentary crew members step in and talk her into leaving. But by then it is too late, as Felicity has been thoroughly brutalized.

The methods that Hardcore used to groom Felicity are the very ones he adopts in his best-selling series Cherry Poppers. The series features Max Hardcore bullying, coercing, and seducing women dressed as schoolgirls into agreeing to perform oral, anal, and vaginal sex. The techniques Hardcore uses in his movies to debase women are still among

the most extreme in gonzo, and many porn fans who post to Adult DVD
say he is too violent for their tastes. Another Porn Addict, for example,
shares his current distaste for Hardcore movies:

> A couple of days ago I took delivery of a couple of Max Hardcore
> discs...which I viewed soon after in anticipation. Until this point I
> hadn't seen any of Max's releases for a long time. Previous to this
> I had seen maybe 8 or 9 of Max's films (all seen around 1997).... All
> I can say is this. His films are not the same as they used to be. One
> of the titles that I bought—*Max Faktor 11*—is so extreme in parts
> that I've actually forced myself to destroy it so I don't watch it again.
> Yes there were parts here and there which I enjoyed seeing, and I
> loved Max previously for what I perceived to be his anal porn excel-
> lence/dolly-girl themed movies. But this was something else. I've
> heard some say that the girls in his movies are acting, but certainly
> with girl number 3 in this flick I'm sure that this can't have been the
> case. In real tears in parts it was obviously too much for her and I
> hate to think of the mental mark it has probably left on her. Nobody
> deserves that Max. Also, girls giving head is one thing. But ram-
> ming your cock into their throats so that they have to suffer such
> obvious physical discomfort and unease? Hey Max, that's really not
> right dude.

VirginSurgeon attempts to explain to Another Porn Addict how some
women actually enjoy the treatment handed out by Hardcore.

> You have to understand a'lot [*sic*] of these porn performers enjoy sex,
> enjoy being dominated to the point of tears.
>   Something tells me you didin't [*sic*] have this problem until after
> you "popped your load" why else would you destroy the tape, you
> liked it, and that scares you.
>   This is a problem with your guilt, not Max Hardcore!!

Another Porn Addict responds by stressing that he did not feel guilty
but rather disgusted, even though he makes clear that he did enjoy parts
of the movie. To which VirginSurgeon responds:

Fair enough, you drew your line in the sand and don't wish to cross.

You have to understand that many of the videos you watched and enjoyed may have had a women [*sic*] who disliked or didn't want to be doing what she was doing, but she was a good enough actress not to show it. Therefore, is it okay to facilitate your orgasms just as long as your [*sic*] not intuned [*sic*] to the feelings of the performer, hence if you act well but don't like the sex, it's okay—you're not being disrespected, however if you're a bad actress, and don't like the sex, I'll boycott the manufacturer?[21]

Notice here that the debate eventually shifts away from actual violence in the real world toward how good at acting the women are. VirginSurgeon has his own line in the sand: as long as the woman is acting like she enjoys it, it's fine because then the viewer can feel less guilty; that is, as long as he is not "intuned" with her real emotions.

The question here is how did VirginSurgeon, and, to a lesser degree, Another Porn Addict, end up so completely disconnected from women's pain that they can watch Hardcore gag a woman until she vomits, drench her in urine and then make her drink it, and then have a civilized debate about the pleasures involved in masturbating to such scenes? One key factor leading to this level of disconnection is that porn trains men to become desensitized to women's pain. As one fan, Anon, explains to Another Porn Addict: "A few years ago I joined Maxhardcore.com to see what all the fuss was about and, while I found a lot of the girls really hot in their teeny outfits, Max's attitude and actions in a lot of the clips left me feeling shellshock, sickened and dirty. Probably how you felt watching that batch of DVDs. But. Just as porn moves on, so did my tastes, and gradually I realised I was enjoying Max's extreme scenes more and more—whether thats [*sic*] corruption or desensitisation I dont [*sic*] know. All I do know is that I've gone from being a one time Max hater to a Max Hardcore fan."[22] Anon's analysis is borne out by studies that show that the more porn men watch, the more desensitized they become. The words he uses to describe his feelings when he first watched Hardcore's movies—"shellshock, sickened and dirty"—

speak to a powerful negative reaction. Yet he then says his tastes moved on and he began to enjoy the scenes. It would appear that Anon became desensitized to the women's pain since it is impossible to enjoy Hardcore's images if you have any empathy for the women. They look so distressed and in such pain that it feels like you are watching actual torture.

FROM FUCK DOLLS TO REAL DOLLS:
HOW FANTASY MESHES WITH REALITY

The loathing and contempt toward women evident in Max Hardcore's videos might be more overt than in most gonzo porn, but it is only a more extreme version of what is played out on women's bodies throughout the industry. No surprise, then, that the message boards are filled with users who, like pornographers, refer to women as whores, cunts, and sluts. I was thus surprised when one day I came upon a message board that refers to women as "honey," "sweetie," "darling," "beauty," and "my love." How is it that these particular women escape the hate, I wondered.

After some research, I realized that what made these "women" special is that they never complain, never say no, and have three orifices always available for penetration, irrespective of time or place. They don't grimace when a man ejaculates in their mouth, and their anuses and vaginas have no limits. They have absolutely no needs outside of pleasing men, they ask for nothing, they don't require dinner or conversation before sex. For their total acquiescence, these women are rewarded with outpourings of love. In fact these women are so loved that men are even willing to marry them as "a nice way to show your devotion to your lady." Perhaps unsurprisingly, these perfect "women" are not human beings at all but life-sized sex dolls.[23]

I interviewed one of the representatives of the company RealDoll at the Expo in Las Vegas, and he told me, with a straight face, that these dolls are "great for men who want to learn how to be with a woman." Not only do these dolls make men "feel more confident around women, they also help men to develop relationships." Advertising itself as the "home of the world's finest love doll," RealDoll has been in business since 1996. One of their products will set the buyer back about $6,500, and he will have to wait an average of eighteen weeks to get his doll delivered. The Web site boasts:

> Our dolls feature completely articulated skeletons which allow for anatomically correct positioning, an exclusive blend of the best silicone rubbers for an ultra flesh-like feel, and each doll is custom made to your specifications.
>
> We offer an extensive list of options, including 10 female body types and 16 interchangable [*sic*] female faces. RealDolls are completely customizable, all the way down to the make up and fingernail colors. If you've ever dreamed of creating your ideal partner, then you have come to the right place.[24]

On the site the prospective buyer can also purchase accessories, which include RealDoll clothing, pubic hair patches ("trimmed or natural"), extra wigs, extra tongues, extra eyes, and a labia repair kit.

RealDoll was given a boost in 2007 with the release of the popular movie *Lars and the Real Girl*. Lars, played by Ryan Gosling, is depicted as a sweet, childlike loner who has difficulty making friends with real people. He orders a RealDoll and takes her around town, introducing her as his girlfriend. During the interview at the Expo, the RealDoll representative told me that the company had served as consultants for the film and that the week it was released, their RealDoll Web site got so many hits, it crashed.

When reading men's postings on the Doll Forum,[25] it often feels like they have indeed found their "ideal partner." They talk at length about the personalities of their dolls and share what feels like personal details of an intimate sexual relationship. Dollylama's post on his four dolls' "style and personality" provides insight into just how real these men take their dolls to be. He starts with his description of Natasha, who is a "a sweet sensual vixen who likes to cuddle and watch movies and . . . loves to loung [*sic*] around in her black teddy and an old blue silk shirt of mine." He then compares her to his other dolls, Brandy, Tiffany, and Amber (posting printed as written):

Brandy is a southern trailer girl who loves to watch porn and go down while I play with her nice boobies. Brandy is a little sex maniac with a strong oral fixation she is not big on conversation but she usually has her mouth full.

Tiffany is very quiet and demure. she loves her french maid out-fit and white fishnet body stocking. recently she borrowed brandys boots and refuses to give them back. now Tiffany prefers to lounge on the sofa and watch action fliks or sit back and stare at Brandy while she goes to town. Recently she has been sneaking in to my room to get a little more naughty. (I knew it was a matter of time before she would let out her wild side). It is usually the quiet ones that get the most freaky.

Now the girls are all jealous of the newest arrival Amber Lynne...Amber arrived last night. She quickly found an auburn and blond culrly wigg, black gartered stockings and a white tank top (what is it with girls stealing my shirts?)

Amber kicked Natasha to the foot of the bed and made herselfe at home. Amber has turned into a bohemian artist that like to hogg the bed. I think she is wanting to take over the place as leading laddy. time will tell....

So this is how my girls have developed thier own unique person-alitys. each one is very different from the rest. am curious as to how other dolls have made themselves known[26]

Other men discuss their own particular personality preferences of their ladies, lest you think that Dollylama is the only man to anthropomor-phize his dolls.

Owners swap messages about how to dress, clean, make up, and have sex with the dolls, as well as to commiserate when dolls are sent off to be repaired or cleaned. One man waiting for his doll is told that all of the forum members have been through it, and waiting doesn't get any easier with time but "its [sic] worth every second."[27] The forum is full of pornlike pictures that men take of their dolls. As one owner posts a picture, the others weigh in with words of admiration ("she's so hot") and expressions of envy ("you lucky bastard"), and never with negative or unpleasant-sounding postings about the somewhat strange behavior exhibited by an adult male dressing up a doll that he routinely sticks his penis into.

For many of the men on this message board there is a sense that the porn world and the real world have meshed into one, and they have ceased to know the difference between fantasy and reality. It is tempting to see these men as a breed apart from regular porn users, who supposedly do know the difference between the two. But, as we shall see, the fantasy versus reality debate is itself dogged by the fantastical thinking that men can masturbate to porn images and walk away from them, untouched by the misogyny that makes pornography interesting and unpredictable.

FIVE

Leaky Images

How Porn Seeps into Men's Lives

> Porn cannot show rape-fantasy because it might
> confuse people who will mistake the fantasy for reality.
> —Duefuss, Adult DVD Talk

I vividly remember one of the most difficult lectures I ever gave, at a small private Catholic school in the Midwest. It started off on a bad note when the (mostly male) audience members began whistling and stamping their feet as the first slide, of a *Playboy* cover, appeared on the screen. While speaking, I could hear the male students groaning and shuffling to express their dissent. I finished my lecture and invited questions. A sea of mostly male hands immediately came up from the center of the auditorium, often a sign that the students are angry and have waited till this very moment to let it rip. The first comment set the tone for the next hour, with the accusation that I was a feminist (true) who hated men (not true) and was too quick to blame them for using porn. The blame, they said, lay with the women in porn since they were the ones making megabucks doing something that they liked. I was heavily criticized by the male students for exaggerating the effects of porn; they said that they had used porn and had never raped a woman. No rape, no effect. The hostility in the room was palpable and this led, as usual, to near silence on the part of the female students.

A few days later I gave a talk at a large northeastern state university, and the response was markedly different. I presented my slide show to a crowd of well over five hundred students, who appeared highly engaged in both the lecture and the Q&A discussion. At one point, when a female student was voicing her distress about men's use of porn, another one shouted that she wanted to know what men get out of using porn, aside from an orgasm. I suggested that maybe one of the hundreds of men in the room might want to answer that. There was a hush and then a lone hand went up. A twenty-something student got up and set the tone for the next ninety minutes, saying, "I am really anxious about speaking, but I have to tell you what has happened to me." What followed was a heartrending story of his compulsive porn use and his own despair over what felt like an inability to stop using. One of his most poignant comments was how much he looked forward to school vacations since his lack of Internet access at home meant he could get a break from the porn. He sat down, and rather than maintaining an embarrassed silence, men started getting up to tell their own stories about the negative ways that porn had affected them. Although not all compulsive users, these men talked about their feelings of inadequacy relating to sex after using porn. Whether it was their inability to bring their girlfriends to a screaming orgasm, their need to conjure up porn images in order to reach their own orgasm with their girlfriends, their "too small" penis, or their tendency to ejaculate "too quickly," they were using porn sex as their yardstick—and they all failed to measure up. The discussion ended only when the security guards needed to lock the building for the night.

What made these two presentations unusual was not so much the depth of emotion shown by any individual audience member as the degree to which anger or sadness dominated the collective discussion. I usually get audiences who are more mixed in their responses, so the atmosphere vacillates between the two extremes. Thankfully, some spaces in between are less emotionally charged.

Over the years I have come to understand how and why my presentation stirs up extreme emotions in men. What I do in my presentations is take the very images that users have viewed privately and with pleasure, and I project them onto a screen in a public forum. In the decidedly nonsexual arena of a college auditorium, men are asked to think critically about what the images say about women, men, and sexuality. Stripped of an erection, men are invited to examine their porn use in a reflective manner while thinking seriously about how images seep into their lives.

The men in the small Catholic college dismissed this opportunity to explore their sexuality and it was apparent that, knowingly or not, they adhered to the porn world's story: pornography is fun and harmless fantasy. My questioning the real-world implications of such fantasy elicited neither interest nor curiosity but a kind of consuming rage that closed down the possibility of reflection, analysis, and reason. The rage was directed at two places, both female—either the women in the industry or me—and it certainly conveyed to all women in the room what happens to those of us who don't follow the porn party line. Conversely, the men who were concerned about their use seized the opportunity to explore how porn had affected them; the result was a serious and painful reflection of their porn use that left me, and many people in the audience, deeply moved.

I suspect that the reason many men reject the opportunity to ask reflective questions is that they don't want to end up in pain, despairing about how porn affects their sexuality, relationships, and interactions with women. Moving out of the porn world's tightly controlled version of reality and into a space where one has to delve inside for an emotional stocktaking of porn's impact on the body and mind is not easy. For most of their lives, the culture told men that pornography is fun and harmless and all about fantasy.

Many of the men seeking out a one-on-one discussion after presentations tell me that they became increasingly agitated while listening as they began realizing just how their porn use had spilled over into their sex lives, whether with wives, girlfriends, or hookup partners. What they had thought were idiosyncratic problems suddenly looked somewhat different when porn was added into the equation. That pornography has clearly had an effect on men's lives is not a surprise to those of us who study media images.

Academics who study the effects of media tend to focus on the ways that images construct reality for the viewer. Media scholars accept that images have some effect in the real world. By telling stories, images help to shape how we think about ourselves as gendered beings, as well as about the world that surrounds us. What is of interest is not necessarily the overt message of one particular image but the cumulative effect of the subtextual themes found in the system of images, which together create a particular way of looking at the world. For example, one fashion advertisement may not be that influential in itself, but add up the hundreds of fashion ads that we encounter daily, and you begin to hear a particular story about women's bodies, femininity, and consumerism. Human beings develop their identity and sense of reality out of the stories the culture tells, and while pornography is not the only producer of stories about sex, relationships, and sexuality, it is possibly the most powerful.

Asking how porn affects its users is to open up the proverbial can of worms. Some argue that porn has no effect in the real world, while others, especially anti-porn feminists, view pornography as material that encourages and justifies the oppression of women. Probably the biggest single argument marshaled against porn having an effect on users is the "Porn is fantasy" claim, which argues that fantasy is in the head and stays in the head, never to leak into the real world of relationships, sex, love, and intimacy. This argument holds that men are not simply dupes who look at porn in a literal sense, taking the images at face value, but rather sophisticated consumers who enjoy porn for the playful fantasy it is, enjoying its excessive transgressions, silly plotlines, caricatured bodies, and over-the-top sexual shenanigans that always end in screaming orgasms for her and copious amounts of semen for him. Afterward, the argument continues, guys go back to the real world, unaffected and unchanged. To argue otherwise, some porn advocates maintain, is to fall into the trap of confusing fantasy with reality.

Indeed, pornography, like most media images, creates a world that, on some level, we know is not true. But it is an enormous leap to say that because porn is not an accurate version of how things are in the world, it then has no real-world effects. Many women, for example, know that the image of the model in the ads is an airbrushed, technologically enhanced version of the real thing, but that doesn't stop us from buying products in the hope that we can imitate an image of an unreal woman. No matter how fantastical the images of women are, they do, to varying degrees, affect the lives of most women.[1] One powerful example of this effect is the growth of the plastic surgery industry. According to the American Society of Aesthetic and Plastic Surgery, in the last ten years there has been a 465 percent increase in the total number of cosmetic procedures:

over 12 million procedures occur annually (for liposuction, face-lifts, the "bionic package"—that is, the tummy tuck, the breast job, the facial rejuvenation). We now spend just under $12.5 billion a year on plastic surgery, and that figure is rapidly increasing.

The main pushers of the "Porn is fantasy" argument are the pornographers and the users, not surprisingly, given that both often have a massive financial and/or emotional investment in it. What is surprising is how many people, even those who don't like porn, buy this argument, insisting that the carefully constructed images that are formulaically scripted and produced by the multibillion-dollar porn industry belong in the realm of sexual fantasy, not reality. Psychologist Michael Bader, for example, in an article on the effects of pornography, claims: "Pornography is the visual enactment of a sexual fantasy. That's fantasy—to be distinguished from reality. That's fantasy—to be distinguished from an intention, wish, or even attitude. A fantasy occurs in the imagination. The imagination is creative, capable of all sorts of tricks and distortions." According to this position, porn is just fantasy and fantasy occurs in the imagination, which, Bader argues correctly, is creative in its capacity to play with ideas, images, and themes. To provide an example of some of these "tricks" and "distortions" at work, Bader lets the reader into a fantasy he had recently in which he daydreamed that his brother died: "In the daydream, lots of people came to console me in my grief. Now, in reality I love my brother and don't have a shred of resentment toward him. What I did have at the time was a need for a certain kind of love and attention. The meaning of my daydream was *not* 'you wish your brother was dead.' The real meaning of my daydream was, 'You're so guilty about wanting attention that you think the only way you can get it is if you suffer a terrible tragedy.' The meaning of a fantasy is often the opposite of its plot; whatever the meaning, it's subjective and can't easily be inferred from its story line."[2] Using his daydream as his data, Bader informs his readers that it is similarly impossible to know just how men think about women when they are masturbating to porn, since they, like Bader, are using their imagination in creative ways.

I can't comment on what Bader's fantasy about his brother may or may not have meant. What is clear, though, is that this daydream is something Bader made up in his own head, from his own experiences, feelings, and desires. He presumably was not thinking of how best to conjure up this fantasy so that he could then pay people to enact it so he could sell it, in image form, to lots of people who would buy it and use it for their own purposes, sexual or otherwise. What seems remarkable to me is that Bader is comparing his own personal fantasy to those images produced by an enormous industry whose goal, in the real world, is to maximize profits by selling to men a product that facilitates masturbation. In other words, these are not "fantasies" constructed in the head of each individual porn user, based on his own creative imagination, past histories, longings, and experiences, but highly formulaic, factory-line images created by a savvy group of capitalists. Whatever Bader's daydream means, it is his and he owns it from the first moment of inception. Because of this, it cannot be compared to what goes on in the heads of men when they masturbate to images that are not of their own making. Ironically, what the "Porn is fantasy" camp misses is that porn actually works to limit our imagination and capacity to be sexually creative by delivering images that are mind-numbingly repetitive in content and dulling in their monotony.

There are literally hundreds of people I could quote who say the same thing as Bader, but I chose him because he is not a run-of-the-mill porn apologist. In fact, in the beginning of his article, he decries porn for being dehumanizing to women, and he is not a pornographer, he is a psychologist. Also, his article appeared on Alternet, a progressive Web site that regularly publishes articles on how the mainstream media, with their right-wing tilt, distort the way people think about politics, culture, and power. Progressives have, for good reason, singled out the media as a major form of (mis)education in the age of monopoly capitalism in which a few companies dominate the market and use their economic and political power to deliver messages that sell a particular worldview that legitimizes massive economic and social inequality. But many of these same progressives argue against the view that porn has an effect on men in the real world, preferring instead to call anti-porn feminists unsophisticated thinkers who don't appreciate how images can be playful and open to numerous interpretations. So now we are in a somewhat strange place where people who argue that mainstream corporate media have the power to shape, mold, influence, manipulate, and seduce viewers simultaneously deny that porn has an effect on their consumers.

Consider how many of us in media studies accept that Fox News, Rush Limbaugh, and Glenn Beck, to name a few, do indeed construct a fantasy world totally at odds with reality. We wouldn't dismiss the effects of right-wing media by saying that their fantastical messages won't leak into the real world of local, national, and global politics. When we see the right-wing media construct a world where people of color are labeled as thugs and welfare cheats, where the poor are derided for their supposed unwillingness to work, where immigrants are accused of taking jobs from whites, and where Arabs are singled out as terrorists, we don't argue that people will view this as fantasy. We don't minimize the power of these right-wing images to shape ideas in the real world by erecting a mythical barrier between fantasy and reality. We understand that such a barrage of imagery is going to affect society in ways that are hard for progressives to tolerate.

Why, then, do many of these same progressives refuse to engage in a thoughtful analysis of how porn affects the culture? For some, measuring porn's real-world effects boils down to one extreme and ultimately misleading question: "Does it lead to rape?" What is overlooked here is the more subtle question of how porn shapes the culture and the men who use it. No anti-porn feminist I know has suggested that there is one image, or even a few, that could lead a nonrapist to rape; the argument, rather, is that taken together, pornographic images create a world that is at best inhospitable to women, and at worst dangerous to their physical and emotional well-being. In an unfair and inaccurate article that is emblematic of how anti-porn feminist work is misrepresented, Daniel Bernardi claims that Andrea Dworkin and Catharine MacKinnon believed that "watching pornography leads men to rape women."[3] Neither Dworkin nor MacKinnon, pioneers in developing a radical feminist critique of pornography, saw porn in such simplistic terms. Rather, both argued that porn has a complicated and multilayered effect on male sexuality, and that rape, rather than simply being caused by porn, is a cultural practice that has been woven into the fabric of a male-dominated society. Pornography, they argued, is one important agent of such a society since it so perfectly encodes woman-hating ideology, but to see it as simplistically and unquestionably leading to rape is to ignore how porn operates within the wider context of a society that is brimming with sexist imagery and ideology.

If, then, we replace the "Does porn cause rape?" question with more nuanced questions that ask how porn messages shape our reality and our culture, we avoid falling into the images-lead-to-rape discussion. What this reformulation does is highlight the ways that the stories in pornography, by virtue of their consistency and coherence, create a worldview that the user integrates into his reservoir of beliefs that form his ways of understanding, seeing, and interpreting what goes on around him.

By placing porn use within a cultural context, we can begin to see how powerful it really is. As boys grow up to be men, they are inundated with messages from the media, messages that both objectify women's bodies and depict women as sex objects who exist for male pleasure. These images are part and parcel of the visual landscape and hence are unavoidable. They come at boys and men from video games, movies, television, ads, and men's magazines, and they supply them with a narrative about women, men, and sexuality. What porn does is to take these cultural messages about women and present them in a succinct way that leaves little room for multiple interpretations. While there are some media images that can be read in a number of ways (called polysemic in media studies) by different people, gonzo porn, particularly—with its overt contempt for women and incessant story line of how women like to be humiliated and debased—delivers a clear message to men, who have already developed a somewhat pornographic gaze by virtue of being brought up in a society filled with sexist pop culture images.

To say that the way users look at a porn image is, in large part, defined by the culture that they grew up in is to say that the context within which images are consumed shapes the way that meaning is produced. One way to understand this is to compare sexist images to racist ones. This is not to say that sexism and racism are the same, just that images that legitimize different types of oppression can work in similar ways. One particularly racist image was that of Stepin Fetchit, an image developed by Lincoln Theodore Monroe Andrew Perry that was popular with (white) moviegoers in the 1930s. With his slow mannerisms and his constant refrain of "Yes, massa," Perry constructed an image of black men as ingratiating half-wits. African Americans protested these images as they viewed them as having very real effects on the way whites thought about blacks. I doubt that African Americans would have been persuaded by the argument that these images were just playful fantasies of white people and that white viewers were sophisticated enough to know that these media images were mere comedic entertainment, and hence they could separate blacks in the media—half-wits—from real blacks—their neighbors and coworkers.

Now, no media theorist would argue that such images alone would make a nonracist white take out a lifetime membership with the KKK; nor would they have an immediate or powerful effect in a society where blacks and whites were already treated as full and equal citizens. However, put these images in a society with a long history of racism, where the dominant ideology is that blacks are lazy, shiftless, violence-prone freeloaders, and you begin to see how the Stepin Fetchit images didn't change the views of the average white person so much as they delivered to the white population ideas that were floating around in the culture in a form that was compelling, easy to understand—and even easier to get away with. After all, it was supposedly just entertainment.

It is no accident that black civil rights movements have consistently opposed the racist messages—from *Birth of a Nation* to Don Imus— that the media spew on a regular basis. Every group that has fought for liberation understands intuitively what media theorists took decades to realize, namely, that media images play a major role in the systematic dehumanization of an oppressed group. These images never stand alone but are implicated in the broader system of messages that legitimize the ongoing oppression of a group, and their power is often derived not from shifting attitudes and behavior but from strengthening and normalizing the ideology that condones oppression.

If we take these arguments and apply them to pornography, we see that some of porn's effects might be more subtle than causing an immediate change in attitudes and behaviors. By the time they first encounter porn, most men have internalized the sexist ideology of our culture, and porn, rather than being an aberration, actually cements and consolidates their ideas about sexuality.[4] And it does this in a way that gives them intense sexual pleasure. This framing of sexist ideology as sexy and hot gives porn a pass to deliver messages about women that in any other form would be seen as completely unacceptable.

Imagine what would happen if suddenly we saw a slew of dramas and sitcoms on television where, say, blacks or Jews were repeatedly referred to in a racist or anti-Semitic way, where they got their hair pulled, faces slapped, and choked by white men pushing foreign objects into their mouths. My guess is that there would be an outcry and the images would not be defended on the grounds that they were just fantasy but rather would be seen for what they are: depictions of cruel acts that one group is perpetrating against another group. By wrapping the violence in a sexual cloak, porn renders it invisible, and those of us who protest the violence are consequently defined as anti-sex, not anti-violence.

To see just how invisible sexual violence is in pornography, we can go back to Daniel Bernardi's article. Bernardi is quick to pull apart anti-porn feminists for arguing that porn has any real-world effects, accusing Andrea Dworkin and Catharine MacKinnon of being unsophisticated scholars who "neglect to think about the weakness of their methodology," but he then critiques racist images in porn as "colorized hate" that could have a very real effect on the lives of people of color.[5] The obvious question here is that if racist porn images can have a detrimental effect on people of color in general, then why can't images of women—black, white, Asian, Latina—being choked and ejaculated on while being called cunts have a negative effect on women of all colors?

The answer to this is that porn does indeed help to shape the world-views of men who masturbate to it. I know this first and foremost from the hundreds, if not thousands, of men I have spoken with over the years about their porn use. While there are a slew of psychological studies that support this claim,[6] what I find more useful are the many conversations that I've had with males after my lectures. These are not self-selected men since the lecture is often mandated by teachers, coaches, or fraternities. It is in these discussions that the complexity of porn use is best captured because the men are speaking organically about their lives in ways that make sense to them rather than responding to a researcher's predesigned set of questions. Obviously these men are not representative of every man who uses porn, especially as they are aged mainly between eighteen and twenty-four and working toward a college degree, but patterns have emerged over twenty years that speak to the multiple ways that porn affects the real lives of men. The stories I have heard sound very similar to the ones discussed by Pamela Paul—who interviewed a cross section of men—in her book *Pornified*, suggesting that the men who speak to me are not that different from the general population of men who use pornography.[7]

What I hear most is that these men feel like sexual losers. They thought college would present easy opportunities for sex, assume that other guys are "getting it," and conclude that something must be amiss with them or the women they are trying to hook up with. They worry they're not good-looking enough, smooth enough, or masculine enough to score, and since the porn view of the world suggests that women are constantly available, these men are bewildered by rejection. They often express deep shame about their inability to hook up, and this shame morphs into anger at their female peers who, unlike porn women, have the word "no" in their vocabulary.

Given the increasing prevalence of hooking up in the culture, especially on college campuses, these men's perceptions that other guys seem to have no problem finding sex is not completely inaccurate. Where they seem to lose touch with reality is in the degree to which they assume this is the norm. In the porn world of never-ending sex, every interaction with a woman—be it a student, a doctor, a maid, a teacher, or just a stranger—ends up sexualized. Add to this the stories that men regale each other with about their latest conquest, stories that often sound like the porn movie they just watched, and you have a constructed world of constant male access to every woman a man meets. When the real world doesn't play out like this, then disappointment and anger make sense.

Hooking up, however, brings its own set of disappointments since the mind-blowing porn sex they were anticipating looks nothing like the sex they are actually having. Because porn has been the only form of sex education for many of these young and impressionable men, they envisioned having the type of sex that they have been masturbating to: exciting, deep-thrusting penetration of the hookup's orifices that goes on and on, ending in her having a screaming orgasm. The erection needed for this sex is more difficult to sustain than they anticipated as their penis, unlike the Viagra-pumped porn penis, has limits. They are disappointed with what they see as their too-quick ejaculations, their inability to perform over and over again, and their unsophisticated techniques. Adam grew up watching his father's porn and feels that "porn taught me all I know about sex. My parents never mentioned the word sex at home, and sex ed in school was a fucking joke. I had this image of how great sex would be, both of us going at it for hours. So it was kind of a shock the way the real thing turned out...she didn't [have an orgasm] and I came really quickly."

With these feelings of inadequacy also come feelings of anger toward the hookup, as she is not as willing as Pornland women to have porn-like sex. Pornland women don't seem to mind extreme acts, so why is the one lying next to him in bed kicking up such a fuss? The sex she wants is more vanilla, but as a connoisseur of porn sex, he finds this boring. One student told me, "I love porn and I try out the sex on my girlfriend but she isn't interested. I dumped the last girl I was with because she wanted to keep the sex straight. That's not for me. If women don't want to try different things, then I am not interested." He continued to say that he really wants to give his latest sex partner a "facial" (pornspeak for ejaculating on the face), but she refuses.

What troubles many of these men most is that they need to pull up the porn images in their head in order to have an orgasm with their partner. They replay porn scenes in their mind or think about having sex with their favorite porn star when they are with their partners. Dan was concerned about his sexual performance with women: "I can't get the pictures of anal sex out of my head when having sex, and I am not really focusing on the girl but on the last anal scene I watched." I asked him if he thought porn had in any way affected his sexuality, to which he answered, "I don't know. I started looking at porn before I had sex, so porn is pretty much how I learned about sex. It can be a kind of problem to think about porn as much as I do, especially when with my girlfriend. It means I am not really present with her, my head is somewhere else."

Some think a way to spice up the sex is by getting their partners to watch porn and act out the scenes; others suggest threesomes, bondage, or S&M. Then there are those who tell me that all they can think about is the porn they plan to watch as soon as the sex is over. Some men have told me that they even cut the sex short so that the woman will leave and he can then turn to porn. Tim told me that one of his "tricks" is to "get her off quickly and tell her that she has to go because my roommate is due back…that way I get to have sex and watch a porno." For these men, it is gonzo movies and not features that are the porn of choice. Jeremy, for example, said, "I watch only certain movies with girls because they like the more tame ones, but when it's just me alone, then I go straight to the real ones." Here he clearly sees gonzo porn as more "real" than features.

One pattern I have seen emerge is the way many of these men don't mind the porn images intruding into their sex lives as long as the sex partner is a hookup. They start to mind when they have met someone they want to forge a relationship with and they are unable to get rid of the images. Try as they may, scenes from their favorite movies come hurtling back as they become aroused. They find themselves comparing their girlfriend to their favorite porn performers, with the girlfriend coming off the loser. Andy put it succinctly: "When we have sex, I try not to think of some scenes from porn that I like, and then I feel guilty because I can't help myself when I do think about that. I feel like a shit because she doesn't even know I watch porn." Tony, voicing a similar sentiment, said, "I hope she never knows what's going through my mind when we have sex. She'd hate me."

Breasts play a big role here as men have become accustomed to getting aroused to large, silicone-enhanced ones, and their girlfriends' seem small and uninviting by comparison. Pubic hair has become a big turnoff, especially today when many young women in the real world are removing it, so a woman who has "ungroomed" hair is less desirable. Josh told me how over the years the type of woman's body he likes has come to resemble porn performers in that he likes them "shaved, oiled, and well-toned." I asked him how he would feel if his girlfriend didn't match up, to which he replied, "I would think that she didn't take care of herself…that she needed to make herself look good, not just for me, but for herself also." Also disappointing is that these women do not behave like the women in porn—they are not begging for rough sex, nor do they respond orgasmically to every touch.

Many of these men don't want to think of their girlfriends in the same way they think of porn women, but they find it increasingly difficult to separate the two. Robert explained that he had used porn for years but when he started going out with his girlfriend he decided to "stop using porn altogether. I got rid of my movies and cancelled my memberships for the Web sites. I thought it would be that easy, but it's not, I still think of porn a lot and it feels like I am sort of cheating on my girlfriend." There are times when men come to speak to me with their girlfriends in tow, and she is more often than not baffled by his desire to introduce porn into their sex life. She feels that the relationship needs more time to develop; he thinks it needs more porn. After one lecture a boyfriend and girlfriend came to speak to me about his porn use. She was very upset that he wanted to bring porn into the relationship. His comment to me and her was "We don't have to watch it a lot, just enough to give us some ideas." His girlfriend didn't respond so I asked her how she felt about this, to which she replied, "I feel cheap. I know he watches porn and I don't mind it too much, but I don't want it to come into our relationship. I don't like it when he wants me to do certain things he saw in porn. I can tell what these are just by the way he acts." The intimacy, igniting of senses, and connections developed when skin meets skin are all either absent or overridden by the industrial product that these men have come to depend on for sexual pleasure. Trained by the porn culture to see sex as disconnected from intimacy, users develop an orientation to sex that is instrumental rather than emotional. No wonder one man described pornography as teaching him "how to masturbate *into* a woman."[8]

What is new over the last five years or so is college-age men telling me about their addiction to pornography. I used to be somewhat skeptical of the addiction model, thinking that it was a way for men to avoid taking responsibility for their porn use. However, I am not the only one to hear this, as therapists are increasingly seeing men who are addicted in the clinical sense. The Portman Clinic in London, a well-known treatment center for a range of addictions and behaviors, has reported that its "casebook has shifted significantly in recent years, for one principal reason: Internet pornography." According to the director of the clinic, Stanley Ruszczynski, "The number of patients who are either addicted or otherwise adversely affected by it [pornography] is 'phenomenal.' Referral letters mention it regularly, and if they don't the patient will often mention it during his assessment."[9] Similarly, sex therapists Wendy Maltz and Larry Maltz discuss in their book on the harms of porn how therapists are increasingly seeing porn addicts become a major part of their practice. They found both in their practice and from interviewing other therapists that "what used to be a small problem for relatively few people had grown to a societal issue that was spilling over and causing problems in the lives of countless everyday people."[10]

The men I speak to at colleges who are addicted do indeed end up in serious trouble; they neglect their schoolwork, spend huge amounts of money they don't have, become isolated from others, and often suffer depression. They know that something is wrong, feel out of control, and don't know how to stop. While men may share their favorite porn stories, they don't tend to talk to each other about their addictive use, which further adds to their feelings of isolation. Ted described his addiction in this way: "I never thought I would become so dependent on porn for sex. I can't get away from it, even though I know that this is no longer just a phase in my life. It feels more permanent and I don't know how to stop it." Eric came to me in tears, saying he was scared and felt "like such a loser" for watching so much porn. I asked him how much he used and he responded, "Before class, after class, and recently I have been staying in my dorm room all night watching. I am worried about how much I have been watching lately, and how much time I spend on porn sites." Another student told me, "I try to stay away from porn but I just keep going back on the computer. I tell myself that this will be the last time, and then the next day it starts all over again." This seems to be such a problem on some campuses that the counseling center is now offering support groups for such men. Whenever I hear these stories, I feel both sad for the men and outraged at the porn industry for hijacking the men's sexuality to the point that they feel so out of control.

Some of the worst stories I hear are from men who have become so desensitized that they have started using harder porn and end up masturbating to images that had previously disgusted them. Many of these men are deeply ashamed and frightened as they don't know where all this will end. Phil told me, "Sometimes I can't believe the porn I like. I feel like a freak," and Anthony sees it as a "slippery slope I never thought

I would slide down. I never thought of myself as a guy who would like the really hard-core porn, but that's what's happened to me." Some speak of moving toward more violent images while others have become increasingly interested in bondage and even child porn. Because accessing child porn is illegal, many of the students said that they had not actively gone searching for it but had accidentally come across it while surfing porn sites. This had piqued their interest, although most of the men I spoke to are very disturbed by their sexual interest in these pictures.

Students are not the only group becoming bored by and desensitized to porn images of adult women. In interviews I did with seven incarcerated sex offenders, aged from their late thirties to early sixties, all said that the quality and quantity of their porn use changed drastically after the introduction of the Internet. Prior to the Internet, they would regularly use pornography (of adult women) but after the introduction of the Internet, they began to use it compulsively, some of them even losing their jobs because of it. For this group of men, the regular gonzo pornography became boring, and they moved into more violent, fetishistic pornography, often that which looked like overt torture. When this also started to become boring, most of the men moved into child pornography. Some accidentally came across child porn while surfing porn sites, and others sought it out to masturbate to something other than the usual porn. The average length of time between downloading the first child porn and sexually assaulting a child was one year. Most men told me that before becoming addicted to Internet porn, they had not been sexually interested in children.[11]

One of the men, Jim, who was in prison for raping a woman, talked at length about his love of violent pornography. He said he needed to see a woman in pain in order to get aroused. This was true also for his actual rapes in the real world; he said that he needed to see his victim terrified in order to complete the rape. Jim had started using his father's *Playboy* from an early age but soon graduated to violent porn, looking for that which focused on torture and rape. I want to be clear that I am not suggesting that most men are like Jim—however, I'll never forget that Jim, in a tone that suggested no remorse, admitted candidly to me that using porn before a rape "got me in the mood."

The connection between porn and rape is without a doubt the most debated and most controversial question of porn's effects. Some argue that porn causes men to rape, while others counter that sexually aggressive men seek out more violent pornography and would rape with or without the visual stimuli. Studies, however, suggest that there is a link between porn consumption and violence against women. Neil Malamuth, one of the most well-known psychologists studying the effects of porn, and colleagues reviewed a broad range of studies and concluded that "experimental research shows that exposure to non-violent or violent pornography results in increases in both attitudes supporting sexual aggression and in actual aggression."[12] Moreover, in their own study, Malamuth and his fellow researchers found: "When we considered men who were previously determined to be at high risk for sexual aggression...we found that those who are additionally very frequent users of pornography[13] were much more likely to have engaged in sexual aggression than their counterparts who consume pornography less frequently."[14] What needs to be pointed out here is that the pornography the men in this study consumed was in magazine form and tended to be soft-core (*Playboy*, *Penthouse*, *Chic*), with *Hustler* being the most hard-core. Today, *Hustler* magazine is tame compared to the violence in mainstream gonzo porn. It would seem that contemporary porn, with its body-punishing sex, would have an even greater effect as it shows women actually enjoying being brutalized.

The studies provide some indication of effects, but what I find most compelling are the stories I hear from women who were raped by men who used porn. These women don't need scientific data to tell them that some men who consume pornography will rape. In some of these women's experiences, pornography was actually present at the time of the rape, as the men made them study it to see how to play out the sex activity they wanted. This scenario is most common in child rape, where pornography is used as both a grooming tool and an instructional manual. After all, what better way to explain to a child how to perform sex than showing her pictures of it? And afterward, in many cases, the perpetrator took pictures of the child naked to both terrorize her into silence with the threat of showing them to family or friends or to add to his stash. Over the course of my lecturing, I have had at least twenty women come up to me after the presentation, with looks of utter dread on their faces, to tell me that they were sure that they were going to see pictures of their own childhood rape appear on the screen. The depth of trauma suffered is apparent in this anxiety, as I don't show child porn in my lectures, and in reality, it is highly improbable that I would have found one specific picture among the millions floating around. But laws of probability don't mean anything to a traumatized individual, who is certain that her rapist is omnipotent and that pictures of her will absolutely, without doubt, surface.

And then there are the women who have been raped as adults by boyfriends, husbands, teachers, priests, doctors, colleagues, and strangers, who either made them act like the women in porn or told them about their porn use as they raped them. I have heard from wives who were forced to put a centerfold over their face as their husbands raped them; girlfriends who, during the assault, had to moan just like the woman in the movie; women who thought they could trust a male friend only to be drugged and raped while the camera was recording; and students who went to fraternity parties and were gang-raped by the brothers as a porn movie was playing in the background. Traveling the country, I have heard just about every possible way that porn is used against women, children, and some men. I have listened to stories of lives devastated by men who use porn, and for these survivors, porn is not a fantasy but a nightmarish reality.

How porn is implicated in rape is complex and multilayered. Clearly, not all men who use porn rape, but what porn does is create what some feminists call a "rape culture" by normalizing, legitimizing, and condoning violence against women. In image after image, violent and abusive sex is presented as hot and deeply satisfying for all parties. These messages in porn chip away at the social norms that define violence against women as deviant and unacceptable, norms that are already constantly under assault in a male-dominated society. In most mass-produced images a woman has no bodily integrity, boundaries, or borders that need to be respected. Combined, these images tell us that violation of these boundaries is what she seeks out and enjoys. This is one among many rape myths that porn disseminates to users. Embedded in porn are numerous other myths, all of which seek to present sexual assault as a consensual act rather than an act of violence. One way to illustrate this is to select examples from porn that reinforce the myths:[15]

RAPE MYTH: Women don't know their own minds; men know better what women really want and need sexually.

PORN EXAMPLE: "Lystra is homesick and wants to move back to Korea. Professor Lawrence…knows what's best for his best students—like his cock inside her moist, little hole."[16]

RAPE MYTH: A woman might not want it at first, but once she gets a taste of hot sex, she can't get enough.

PORN EXAMPLE: "Katie was a bit reluctant at first but after two hard cocks stretched her tight ass wide open she screamed with joy."[17]

RAPE MYTH: Women are by nature sexually manipulative.

PORN EXAMPLE: "Jaclyn Case is pretty smart about how she tricks boys into coming over and giving IT to her. She's also pretty specific about how she wants her pussy serviced."[18]

RAPE MYTH: Women are sluts who get what they deserve.

PORN EXAMPLE: "Gia is a nasty little whore that can't seem to get enough cock. We make sure this slut gets what she deserves and more!"[19]

RAPE MYTH: All women are whores at heart and want to be fucked by any available man.

PORN EXAMPLE: "Vanessa might seem like a sweet girl, but deep inside, she's a whore wanting big white dick."[20]

Not every man who uses porn will swallow these rape myths whole. To argue such a point does not account for the variations that exist among users and would reduce the effects debate to one effect—rape. But what anti-porn feminists are saying is that such myths promote a culture that will affect men in myriad ways: some will rape but many more will beg, nag, and cajole their partners into sex or certain sex acts, and more still will lose interest in sex with other human beings. Some will use women and disregard them when done, some will be critical of their partner's looks and performance, and many will see women as one-dimensional sex objects who are less deserving of respect and dignity than men, both in and out of the bedroom. Whatever the effect, men cannot walk away from these images unchanged.

One way to think about effects is to turn the question around; rather than asking how porn affects users, we could ask, Under what conditions would the images in porn not have an effect? In other words, what do men need to be exposed to in order to counter the stories in porn? In media studies we ask similar questions when discussing how to immunize people to the constant flow of consumerist ideology that is paired with capitalism. Often the answer lies in providing people with a counter-ideology that both reveals the fabricated nature of consumer ideology and offers an alternative vision of the world. A counter-ideology to porn would similarly need to disrupt and interrupt its messages, and it would have to be as powerful and as pleasurable as porn, telling men that porn's image of women is a lie, fabricated to sell a particular version of sex. This alternative ideology would also need to present a different vision of heterosexual sex, one built on gender equality and justice. Few men are exposed to such a feminist ideology; rather, most men (and women) are fed the dominant sexist ideology on a daily basis to such a degree that gender inequality seems a natural and biologically deter-mined reality. Porn not only milks this ideology for all its worth, it also wraps it up and hands it back to men in a highly sexualized form. In the absence of a counter-ideology, this pleasurable sexist ideology becomes the dominant way of thinking and making sense of the world. While porn is by no means the only socializing agent, thanks to its intense im-agery and effect on the body, it is a powerful persuader that erodes men's ability to see women as equal and as deserving of the same human rights that they themselves take for granted.

SIX

Visible or Invisible

Growing Up Female in a Porn Culture

> Women are much more understanding and aware of their true purpose in life than ever before. That purpose, of course, is to be receptacles of love; in other words, fuck dolls.
>
> —Max Hardcore, pornographer

> Fashion also is taking more aesthetic cues from porn, including the growing popularity of genital piercing and shaving, which was popularized by adult film actors.
>
> —Reed Johnson

At a lecture I was giving at a large West Coast university in the spring of 2008, the female students talked extensively about how much they preferred to have a completely waxed pubic area as it made them feel "clean," "hot," and "well groomed." As they excitedly insisted that they themselves chose to have a Brazilian wax, one student let slip that her boyfriend had complained when she decided to give up on waxing. Then there was silence. I asked the student to say more about her boyfriend's preferences and how she felt about his criticism. After she spoke, other students joined in, only now the conversation took a very different turn. The excitement in the room gave way to a subdued discussion of how some boyfriends had even refused to have sex with nonwaxed girlfriends, saying they "looked gross." One student told the group that her boyfriend bought her a waxing kit for Valentine's Day, while yet another sent out an e-mail to his friends joking about his girlfriend's "hairy beaver." No, she did not break up with him; she got waxed instead.

Two weeks after the waxing discussion, I was at an East Coast Ivy League school, where some female students became increasingly angry during my presentation. They accused me of denying them the free choice to embrace our hypersexualized porn culture, an idea that was especially repugnant because, as rising members of the next generation's elite, they saw no limits or constraints on them as women. Then one student made a joke about the "trick" that many of them employ as a way to avoid hookup sex. What is this trick? These women purposely don't shave or wax as they are getting ready to go out that night so they will feel too embarrassed to participate in hookup sex. As she spoke, I watched as others nodded their heads in agreement. When I asked why they couldn't just say no to sex, they informed me that once you have a few drinks in you and are at a party or a bar, it is too hard to say no. I was speechless—these women, who had just been arguing that I had denied them agency in my discussion of porn culture, saw no contradiction in telling me that they couldn't say no to sex. The next day I flew to Utah to give a lecture in a small college which, although not a religious college, had a good percentage of Mormons and Catholics. I told them about the lecture the previous night and asked them if they knew what the trick was. It turns out that trick is everywhere.

I tell this story because it neatly captures on many levels how the porn culture is affecting young women's lives. The reality is that women don't need to look at porn to be profoundly affected by it because images, representations, and messages of porn are now delivered to women via pop culture. Women today are still not major consumers of hardcore porn; they are, however, whether they know or it or not, internalizing porn ideology, an ideology that often masquerades as advice on how to be hot, rebellious, and cool in order to attract (and hopefully keep) a man. An excellent example is genital waxing, which first became popular in porn and then filtered down into women's media such as *Cosmopolitan*, a magazine that regularly features stories and tips on what "grooming" methods women should adopt to attract a man. *Sex and the City*, that hugely successful show with an almost cult following, also used waxing as a story line. For instance, in the movie, Miranda is chastised by Samantha for "letting herself go" by having pubic hair.

What my conversations with college students reveal is how conformity to porn culture is defined by young women as a free choice. I hear this mantra everywhere, yet when one digs deeper, it is clear that the idea of choice is more complicated than originally thought. To talk about women's free choice is to enter into the tricky terrain of how much free will we really have as human beings. While we all have some power to act as the author of our own lives, we are not free-floating individuals who come into the world with a ready-made set of identities; rather, to paraphrase Karl Marx, we are social beings who construct our identities within a particular set of social, economic, and political conditions, which are often not of our own making. This is especially true of our gender identity, as gender is a social invention and hence our notion of what is "normal" feminine behavior is shaped by external forces.

To illustrate this point, we can look at women's "choices" in the post–Second World War era. At first glance, it looked like women were eagerly giving up their wartime jobs to go home and look after their husbands and kids; it appeared that women as a group suddenly and collectively chose to return to being housewives and mothers. It was only after that period, thanks to feminist historians and writers, that we found out that what drove them home was a complex set of circumstances that included women being fired or demoted to make room for men, the inability of married women to find employment, the growth of suburbia, and the lack of child care. What, then, appeared as free will were actually economic and social forces that cohered to limit women's life choices. Not least of these were the media images and sitcoms such as *Ozzie and Harriet* and *Leave It to Beaver,* which depicted the housewife as the idealized woman: feminine, nurturing, and blissful in her role as cleaner, caretaker, nanny, chauffeur, and nurse. This was the dominant image of femininity that was celebrated and perpetuated by the media. The only problem was that the image was a lie. As Betty Friedan revealed in *The Feminine Mystique,* many real women were miserable, lonely, and overburdened with the daily duties of holding the family together.[1] But media images do not have to tell the truth to be believed or internalized as many women of that era compared themselves to Harriet Nelson or June Cleaver—and found themselves deficient.

Today's women are not being forced back to the home, but that does not mean that they are not similarly affected by cultural constructions of idealized femininity. In her book on women and pop culture, Ariel Levy asks why women are still conforming to mainstream images of women since, she argues, "Women today have staggeringly different opportunities and expectations than our mothers did."[2] This is true, especially for white middle-class women, but we are still cultural beings who develop our identities out of the dominant images that surround us. The Stepford Wife image, which drove previous generations of women crazy with its insistence on sparkling floors and perfectly orchestrated meals, has all but disappeared, and in its place we now have the Stepford Slut: a hypersexualized, young, thin, toned, hairless, and, in many cases, surgically enhanced woman with a come-hither look on her face. Harriet Nelson and June Cleaver have morphed into Britney, Rihanna, Beyoncé, Paris, Lindsay, and so on. They represent images of contemporary idealized femininity—in a word, hot—that are held up for women, especially young women, to emulate. Women today are still held captive by images that ultimately tell lies about women. The biggest lie is that conforming to this hypersexualized image will give women real power in the world, since in a porn culture, our power rests, we are told, not in our ability to shape the institutions that determine our life chances but in having a hot body that men desire and women envy.

In today's image-based culture, there is no escaping the image and no respite from its power when it is relentless in its visibility. If you think that I am exaggerating, then flip through a magazine at the supermarket checkout, channel surf, take a drive to look at billboards, or watch TV ads. Many of these images are of celebrities—women who have fast become the role models of today. With their wealth, designer clothes, expensive homes, and flashy lifestyles, these women do seem enviable to girls and young women since they appear to embody a type of power that demands attention and visibility.

For us noncelebrities who can't afford a personal stylist, the magazines dissect the "look," giving us tips on how to craft the image at a fraction of the price. They instruct us on what clothes to buy, what shoes to wear, how to do our hair and makeup, and what behavior to adopt to look as hot as our favorite celebrity. The low-slung jeans, the short skirt that rides up our legs as we sit down, the thong, the tattoo on the lower back, the pierced belly button, the low-cut top that shows cleavage, the high heels that contort our calves, and the pouting glossed lips all conspire to make us look like a bargain-basement version of the real thing. To get anywhere close to achieving the "look," we, of course, need to spend money—lots of it—as today femininity comes in the form of consumer products that reshape the body and face. The magazines that instruct us in the latest "must-have" fashions have no shortage of ads that depict, in excruciating detail, what it means to be feminine in today's porn culture.

While the fashion industry has always pushed clothes that sexualize women's bodies, the difference today is that the "look" is, in part, inspired by the sex industry. We are now expected to wear this attire everywhere: in school, on the street, and at work. Teachers, including elementary school teachers, often complain that their female students look more like they are going to a party than coming to school. It is as if we females now have to carry the marker of sex on us all the time, less we forget (or men forget) what our real role is in this society.

Among hypersexualized celebrities, Paris Hilton ranks high. The story of how she was catapulted to the A-list is one all about porn culture. Once a minor-league celebrity known mainly for her vast bank account, in 2004, her then-boyfriend, Rick Salomon—thirteen years her senior—released a videotape of them having sex, called *1 Night in Paris*, and she instantly became a household name. Thanks to that tape, Hilton is now talked about all over the porn discussion boards as "a filthy slut" who got what she deserved. The fact that Salomon was the one who orchestrated the whole thing (she sued him over the release) does not prevent her from being mocked and derided by porn users and pop culture commentators alike. Over the years, Hilton has been labeled a kind of super "slut"—a term used to demarcate the supposed good girls from the bad. Her antics have garnered a devoted following among girls and young women, as well as massive visibility as one of the most photographed women in the world. Hilton gets away with being anointed as a "slut" because she is fabulously rich; the wealth acts as a kind of upmarket cleansing cream that instantly rubs off the dirt. For most girls and women, however, especially those from the working class, the dirt sticks like mud.

Take, for example, Britney Spears. At seventeen Spears released her debut single, called "...Baby One More Time," which became an instant international success. In the accompanying video, Spears is dressed in a school uniform with a knotted shirt that reveals a bare midriff, socks, and braided hair as she writhes around asking her ex-boyfriend to "hit me, baby, one more time." Spears later went on to employ Gregory Dark to direct her videos; Dark is a longtime porn director whose films include *The Devil in Miss Jones*, *New Wave Hookers*, and *Let Me Tell Ya 'Bout Black Chicks*. Her meltdowns in public, together with the famous image of her sans underwear, have contributed to a kind of public humiliation: we collectively flog her for her trashy ways, yet we put her on a pedestal for embodying a kind of uncouth hot sexiness. Unlike Hilton, Spears was not born into great wealth, so the attacks on her mothering, appearance, and partying tend to carry a subtext of classism in which Spears is described as a trailer-trash slut who, despite her millions, can't escape her roots.

Another celebrity who was similarly loved and hated for her so-called slutty behavior was Anna Nicole Smith, a woman whose life was filled with sexual exploitation yet one who was elevated in pop culture to the status of a kind of iconic slut who was willing and happy to sleep, strip, and marry her way to the top. Even in death this woman was trashed, consistently referred to as an "ex–porn star" rather than a woman dogged by poverty and abuse who suffered the terrible tragedy of losing a child. A few months after the overdose death of Smith's son, *Hustler* magazine ran a cartoon under the title "Anna Nicole Smith's Son's Autopsy." Two doctors, both wearing white coats splashed with blood, stand in front of a shrouded dead body. One says to the other, "We'll have to invent a cover story. All the tests conclude he died of embarrassment." What is startling about this cartoon is not only the contempt it shows for both Smith's son's death and Smith's pain at burying her son, but the way in which the cartoonist understood the degree to which the porn industry turned Smith into the laughingstock of America and how this must have affected her son.

People not immersed in pop culture tend to assume that what we see today is just more of the same stuff that previous generations grew up on. After all, every generation has had its hot and sultry stars who led expensive and wild lives compared to the rest of us. But what is different about today is not only the hypersexualization of mass-produced images but also the degree to which such images have overwhelmed and crowded out any alternative images of being female. Today's tidal wave of soft-core porn images has normalized the porn star look in everyday culture to such a degree that anything less looks dowdy, prim, and downright boring. Today, a girl or young woman looking for an alternative to the Britney, Paris, Lindsay look will soon come to the grim realization that the only alternative to looking fuckable is to be invisible.

One show that popularized porn culture was *Sex and the City*, a show that supposedly celebrated female independence from men. At first glance this series was a bit different from others in its representation of female friendships and the power of women to form bonds that sustain them in their everyday lives. It also seemed to provide a space for women to talk about their own sexual desires, desires that were depicted as edgy, rebellious, and fun. However, these women claimed a sexuality that was ultimately traditional rather than resistant. Getting a man and keeping him were central to the narrative, and week after week we heard about the trials and tribulations of four white, privileged heterosexual women who seemed to find men who take their sexual cues from porn.

Porn-type sex is a fixture on the show, which regularly featured plotlines about men who like to watch porn as they have sex, men who are aroused by female urination, men who want group sex, men who can get aroused only by masturbating to porn, men who are into S&M, men who want anal sex, and men who are willing to have only hookup sex and not a relationship. In one episode, called "Models and Mortals," Carrie (Sarah Jessica Parker) finds out that a male friend of hers is secretly taping his girlfriends as they have sex. Rather than being appalled at this invasion of privacy, Carrie is immediately interested and sits down with him to watch the tapes. Later in the show, Samantha (Kim Cattrall) shows some interest in the man, and when she finds out that he tapes his girlfriends, she becomes even more determined to have hookup sex with him. Another one of the story lines of the show was Charlotte's (Kristin Davis) first husband's inability to sustain an erection during sex. One night Charlotte hears noises coming from the bathroom and, thinking that her husband is crying, she walks in, only to see him masturbating to porn. Shocked at first, Charlotte later glues pictures of herself in the magazines.

These examples show how the *Sex and the City* women capitulated to the pornography that invades their sex lives. In their desire to get a man and keep him, they were willing to do anything, even if they felt uncomfortable. In the episode about urination, for example, Carrie is clearly uncomfortable with the idea, but eventually offers to either pour warm liquid on her partner or urinate with the door open so he can hear her. The idea that these women are independent is undermined by their dependency on men and male approval. At the end of the final season, Carrie is living with an emotionally unavailable artist in Paris and is saved by the equally emotionally unavailable Mr. Big. In the movie released in the summer of 2008, Mr. Big leaves her standing at the altar, but in typical *Sex and the City* style, Carrie eventually forgives him and marries him.

What critics have noted about the show and the movie is the role that consuming products plays in the lives of the women. Media scholar Angela McRobbie notes that the "show functions as a televisual magazine and shop window for the successful launching of shoes, accessories and fashion lines well beyond the means of average female viewers."[3] The *Sex and the City* women are described as being independent not because they refuse to submit to men's power but because they can afford to buy their own high-end goods. Through the endless buying of goods, the women constructed their femininity, styling and restyling themselves depending on their latest purchase. Their bodies and their clothes spoke to a conventional—albeit upmarket—femininity that was constructed out of the culture's mainstream images. Nowhere did we see a resistance to the fabricated image; rather, their very sexuality was dependent on the products they consumed. These women looked hot because they were perfectly turned out in designer gear. In one episode, in which Carrie has a first date with Mr. Big, she vows not to have sex with him, but the dress she buys for the occasion says otherwise, and the two do have sex—the dress becoming the marker of her sexuality. The problem with this is that women's so-called independence became seamlessly meshed with their ability to consume rather than being about a feminist worldview that insists on equality in heterosexual relationships.

Nowhere is this pseudo-independence more celebrated than in *Cosmopolitan*, a magazine that claims to have "served as an agent for social change, encouraging women everywhere to go after what they want (whether it be in the boardroom or the bedroom)." It is hard to see how *Cosmopolitan* helped women advance in corporate America, given that most of the Cosmo girl's time is taken up with perfecting her body and her sexual technique. But this doesn't stop the magazine from boasting that "we here at *Cosmo* are happy to have played such a significant role in women's history. And we look forward to many more years of empowering chicks everywhere."[4] In porn culture empowering women translates into "chicks" having lots of sex, and no magazine does more than *Cosmopolitan* to teach women how to perform porn sex in a way that is all about male pleasure.

With headlines every month promising "Hot New Sex Tricks," "21 Naughty Sex Tips," "Little Mouth Moves That Make Sex Hotter," "67 New Blow-His-Mind Moves," "8 Sex Positions You Haven't Thought Of," and so on, women seem to experience no authentic sexual pleasure; rather, what she wants and enjoys is what he wants and enjoys. While there might be an odd article here and there on what to wear to climb the corporate ladder, the magazine as a whole is all about "him" and "his" needs, wants, desires, tastes, and, most importantly, orgasm. In *Cosmopolitan*, as in much of pop culture, her pleasure is derived not from being a desiring subject but from being a desired object.

Women's magazines that focus on "him" are not new, as earlier generations were also inundated with stories about "him," but then the idea was to stimulate his taste buds rather than his penis. *Cosmopolitan* is the contemporary equivalent of *Ladies' Home Journal* in that it pretends to be about women, but it is in fact all about getting him, pleasing him, and (hopefully) keeping him. For previous generations of women, the secret to a happy relationship lay in being a good cook, cleaner, and mother— for the young women of today, the secret is, well, just being a good lay. If the reader is going to *Cosmopolitan* for tips on how to build a relationship or ways of developing intimacy, she will be disappointed, as conversation only matters in the world of *Cosmo* if it is about talking dirty.

With its manipulative "We are all girls together" tone coupled with the wise older mentor approach that promises to teach young women all they need to know to keep "him coming back for more," *Cosmopolitan*, like most women's magazines, masquerades as a friend and teacher to young women trying to navigate the tricky terrain of developing a sexual identity in a porn culture. *Cosmopolitan*'s power is its promise to be a guide and friend, and it promotes itself as one of the few magazines that really understand what the reader is going through. A promotional ad for *Cosmopolitan* geared toward advertisers boasts that it is "its readers' best friend, cheerleader and shrink."[5]

In *Cosmopolitan*, hypersexualization is normalized by virtue of both the quantity of articles on sex and the degree to which they are explicit. For example, one article instructs the reader, in a somewhat clinical manner, on how to bring a man to orgasm: "While gripping the base of the penis steadily in one hand, place the head between your lips, circling your tongue around the crown. When you sense your guy is incredibly revved up, give his frenulum a few fast tongue licks." For the uninitiated, the magazine explains that the frenulum is "the tiny ridge of flesh on the underside of his manhood, where the head meets the shaft."[6]

Cosmopolitan is quick to suggest using porn as a way to spice up sex. In one article, entitled "7 Bad Girl Bedroom Moves You Must Master," the reader is told to take "the plunge into porn" as it "will add fiery fervor into your real-life bump and grinds." The article quotes a reader who, after watching porn with her boyfriend, evidently ended up "having sex so hot that the porn looked tame in comparison." The article suggests that if the reader feels embarrassed, she should "drive to a store in another neighborhood, shop online, or go to a place that stocks X-rated."[7]

In the world that *Cosmopolitan* constructs for the reader, a world of blow jobs, multiple sexual positions, anonymous porn sex, and screaming orgasms (usually his), saying no to his erection is unthinkable. The options on offer in *Cosmopolitan* always concern the type of sex to have and how often. What is not on offer is the option to refuse his demands since he has (an unspoken and unarticulated) right of access to the female body. Indeed, readers are warned that not having sex on demand might end the "relationship." Psychologist Gail Thoen, for example, informs *Cosmopolitan*'s readers that "constant cuddling with no follow-through (i.e., sex) can be frustrating to guys" and what's more, "he is not going to like it if you leave him high and dry all the time."[8] The reader is pulled into a highly sexual world where technique is the key, and intimacy, love, and connection appear only rarely as issues worthy of discussion. The message transmitted loud and clear is that if you want a man, then not only must you have sex with him, you must learn ways to do it better and hotter than his previous girlfriends.

That the magazine teaches women how to have porn sex is clear in an article that ostensibly helps women deal with the etiquette of how to behave in the morning after the first sexual encounter. Women are told: "Don't Stay Too Long." The article warns women that "just because he had sex with you doesn't mean he's ready to be attached at the hip for the day." Actually, the entire day seems like a long shot—"Bo" informs readers that "I was dating this girl who wanted to hang out the next morning, but after only a couple of hours with her, I realized I wasn't ready to be that close." What advice does *Cosmopolitan* have for women in this situation? "Skip out after coffee but before breakfast."[9]

Media targeted to women create a social reality that is so over-whelmingly consistent it is almost a closed system of messages. In this way, it is the sheer ubiquity of the hypersexualized images that gives them power since they normalize and publicize a coherent story about women, femininity, and sexuality. Because these messages are every-where, they take on an aura of such familiarity that we believe them to be our very own personal and individual ways of thinking. They have the power to seep into the core part of our identities to such a degree that we think that we are freely choosing to look and act a certain way be-cause it makes us feel confident, desirable, and happy. But as scholar Rosalind Gill points out, if the look was "the outcome of everyone's in-dividual, idiosyncratic preferences, surely there would be greater diver-sity, rather than a growing homogeneity organized round a slim, toned, hairless body."[10]

This highly disciplined body has now become the key site where gender is enacted and displayed on a daily basis. To be feminine requires not only the accoutrements of hypersexuality—high heels, tight clothes, and so on—but also a body that adheres to an extremely strict set of standards. We need to look like we spend hours in the gym exhausting ourselves as we work out, but whatever the shape of the body, it is never good enough. Women have so internalized the male gaze that they have now become their own worst critics. When they go shopping for clothes or look in a mirror, they dissect themselves piece by piece. Whatever the problem, and there is always a problem—the breasts are too small, the thighs not toned enough, the butt too flat or too round, the stomach too large—the result is a deep sense of self-disgust and loathing. The body becomes our enemy, threatening to erupt into fatness at any time, so we need to be hypervigilant. What we end up with is what Gill calls a "self-policing narcissistic gaze," a gaze that is so internalized that we no longer need external forces to control the way we think or act.[11]

We cannot talk about the contemporary feminine body without mention of the complicated relationship that most women and girls have to food: we want it, enjoy it, and yet feel guilty for eating it. The need to eat is taken as a sign of weakness, as not measuring up to being a real woman since celebrity women manage to survive on minimal amounts of food. Whenever I am in places where women congregate— the hairdresser, gym, clothes shops—I hear long and involved conversations about dieting. Women recite lengthy lists about what they have eaten, what they intend to eat, and what they need to stop eating. A kind of shame hangs over the conversations as everyone assumes that they are too fat and hence weak willed.

In her excellent book on body image and food, feminist philosopher Susan Bordo looks at the ways the culture helps shape women's ideas about what constitutes the perfect body.[12] The bodies of the women we see in magazines and on television are actually very unusual in their measurements and proportions, with long necks, broad shoulders, and high waists. Yet because these are more or less the only images we see, we take them to be the norm rather than the exception and assume that the problem lies with us and not the fashion and media industries that insist on using a very specific body type. This is what the media do: they take the abnormal body and make it normal by virtue of its visibility, while making the normal bodies of real women look abnormal by virtue of their invisibility. The result is a massive image disorder on the part of society. Since we all develop notions of ourselves from cultural messages and images, it would seem that a truly disordered female is one who actually likes her body.

Bordo's discussion of the way culture shapes notions of the body asks us to rethink the idea that women with eating disorders are somehow deviants. Women who starve themselves are actually overconforming to the societal message about what constitutes female perfection. They have taken in the messages and come to what looks like a very reasonable conclusion: thin women are prized in this culture, I want to be prized, and therefore I need to be thin, which means that I can't eat. How can it be any different in a world where anorexic-looking women such as Kate Moss, Victoria Beckham, Mary Kate Olsen, and Lindsay Lohan are praised by the celebrity magazines for their "look"? I do not mean to be glib here about the devastating effects of starving one's body. I have seen many students with a long list of health problems due to long-term starvation. But somewhere in this discussion, we need to see the society as pathological rather than the adolescent girl in the hospital ward who is being diagnosed with multiple disorders.

Many of the young women I have spoken to who have been hospitalized for eating disorders talk about all the new tricks they learned from fellow patients for losing weight even faster. Not many talk about their hospitalizations in terms of recovery. While many of these young women end up hospitalized for complex reasons, the cultural obsession with female thinness has to figure in somewhere for most of them. Yet these recovery programs do not have classes on media literacy and cultural constructions of gender or rap sessions on resisting sexist imagery. Instead the focus is squarely on the individual female and her assumed psychological problems, which somehow dropped from the sky. One story that demonstrates the cultural components of this so-called individual disorder is writer Abra Chernik's experience of having a day out from the hospital, where she is being treated for anorexia.[13] Close to death, Chernik goes to the mall and takes a "fat test" at a sporting goods store. She learns she is this week's winner, with the lowest percentage of body fat, and everyone in the store breaks into applause. Chernik then returns to the hospital, where she is meant to recover with intense therapy that explores her personal problems. Meanwhile, the culture is left intact.

Understanding culture as a socializing agent requires exploring how and why some girls and young women conform and others resist. For all the visual onslaught, not every young woman looks or acts like she take her cues from *Cosmopolitan* or *Maxim*. One reason for this is that conforming to a dominant image is not an all-or-nothing act but rather a series of acts that place women and girls at different points on the continuum of conformity to nonconformity. Where any individual sits at any given time on this continuum depends on her past and present experiences as well as family relationships, media consumption, peer group affiliations and sexual, racial, and class identity. We are not, after all, blank slates onto which images are projected.

Given the complex ways that we form our sexual and gender identities, it is almost impossible to predict, with precision, how any one individual will act at any one time. This does not mean, though, that we can't make predictions on a macro level. What we can say is that the more one way of being female is elevated above and beyond others, the more a substantial proportion of the population will gravitate toward that which is most socially accepted, condoned, and rewarded. The more the hypersexualized image crowds out other images of women and girls, the fewer options females have of resisting what cultural critic Neil Postman called "the seduction of the eloquence of the image."[14]

Conforming to the image is seductive as it not only offers women an identity that is in keeping with the majority but also confers a whole host of pleasures, since looking hot does garner the kind of male attention that can sometimes feel empowering. Indeed, getting people to consent to any system, even if it's inherently oppressive, is made easier if conformity brings with it psychological, social, and/or material gains. Many women know what it's like to be sexually wanted by a man: the way he holds you in his gaze, the way he finds everything you say worthy of attention, the way you suddenly become the most compelling person in the world. This is the kind of attention we don't normally get from men when we are giving a presentation, having a political conversation, or telling them to do the dishes. No, this is an attention men shower on women they want sexually, and it feels like real power, but it is ephemeral because it is being given to women by men who increasingly, thanks to the porn culture, see women as interchangeable hookup partners. To feel that sense of power, women need to keep sexing themselves up so they can become visible to the next man who is going to, for a short time, hold her in his lustful gaze.

Those girls and young women who resist the wages of sexual objectification have to form an identity that is in opposition to mainstream culture. What I find is that these young women and girls tend to have someone in their life—be it a mother, an older woman mentor, or a coach—who provides some form of immunization to the cultural messages. But often this immunization is short-lived. Every summer I co-teach an institute in media literacy, and many of the participants are parents or teachers. Year after year we hear the same story: they are working hard to provide their daughters or students with ways to resist the culture, and in their early years the girls seem to be internalizing the counter-ideology. However, at some point, usually around puberty but increasingly earlier, the girls begin to adopt more conventional feminine behavior as their peer group becomes the most salient socializing force.[15] This makes sense because adolescence is the developmental stage that is all about fitting in. Indeed, in a strange way, one becomes visible in adolescence by looking like everyone else, and to look and act differently is to be rendered invisible.

What many of these young women and girls need to be able to continue resisting the dominant culture is clearly a peer group of like-minded people as well as an ideology that reveals the fabricated, exploitative, and consumerist nature of contemporary femininity. Alternative ideologies such as feminism that critique dominant conceptions of femininity are either caricatured or ignored in mainstream media. Absent such a worldview and a community of like-minded people, many young women speak about feeling isolated and alone in their refusal to conform to the porn culture. The stories are the same: they have a lot of difficulty in negotiating the outsider status that they have been forced to take on. They not only refuse to sex themselves up, they also refuse to have hookup sex, which means that they have a difficult time finding men who are interested in them.

HOOKUP SEX AS PORN SEX

One of the most noticeable shifts in girls' and young women's behavior over the last decade or so is their increasing participation in what is called hookup sex—those encounters that can be anything from a grope to full sexual intercourse but have the common feature that there is no expectation of a relationship, intimacy, or connection.[16] Sex is what you expect, and sex is what you get. In a large-scale survey of 7,000 students, sociologist Michael Kimmel found that by their senior year, "students had averaged nearly seven hookups during their collegiate careers. About one-fourth (24 percent) say that they have never hooked up, while slightly more than that (28 percent) have hooked up ten times or more."[17]

Given its lack of commitment and intimate connection, hookup sex is a lot like porn sex, and it is being played out in the real world. If porn and women's media are to be believed, then these women are having as good a time as the men. But studies are finding that women do hope for more than just sex from a hookup encounter, as many express a desire for the hookup to evolve into a relationship. Sociologist Kathleen Bogle, for example, found in her study of college-age students that many of the women "were interested in turning hookup partners into boyfriends," while the men interviewed "preferred to hookup with no strings attached."[18]

Now, it would be a mistake to glorify sex for women in the pre-hookup days, as feminists such as Shere Hite have documented just how unfulfilling sex was with men who were clueless about women's bodies and sexual desires. But if previous generations of men didn't understand women's bodies, then what must this generation of men be like who have grown up on porn? As my colleague Robert Jensen always says, "If men are going to porn to learn about women's sexuality, then they will certainly be disappointed." In porn a man just has to have an erection for a woman to be suddenly overtaken by orgasmic responses. Porn sex assumes that women are turned on by what turns men on, so if he enjoys pounding anal sex, then she does too. Little surprise that studies show that men in hookups experience orgasm more often than women, or that they report more sexual satisfaction from the encounters.[19]

But not having orgasms is not the only thing women in hookup sex have to worry about. Studies have found that women who partici- pate in hookups have lower self-esteem and higher levels of depres- sion, and they experience regret over the hookups.[20] Grello and her colleagues, for example, found that the more depressed females had more sex partners, and the more partners they had, the more they re- gretted the hookup. The authors suggest that one possible explanation for this is that "depressed females may be seeking external validation from sex. They may be maintaining a vicious depressive cycle by un- consciously engaging in sex in doomed relationships. Possibly, these females' negative feelings of self-worth or isolation may increase their desire to be wanted by or intimate with another. Thus, if they sensed a potential romance would result from the encounter, they may have en- gaged in sexual behavior with a casual sex partner in an attempt to feel better, at least temporarily."[21]

Probably one of the most interesting findings of this study is that males who engaged in hookup sex reported the least depressive symp- toms of any group. They also reported feeling more pleasure and less guilt than the females who participated in hookups. One reason for this could be the way that masculinity is socially constructed, since the more sex partners a man has, the more he is conforming to the idealized image of manhood.

With hookup sex comes, for women and girls, an increased possibil- ity of being labeled a slut—a term that is used to control and stigmatize female sexual desire and behavior. There is, after all, no male equiva- lent of a slut since men who are thought to be highly sexually active are called a stud or a player—labels most men would happily take on. What it means to be a "slut" shifts over time, as previous generations of women carried the label just for having sex before marriage. But for all of women's so-called sexual empowerment today, the effects of being labeled a slut are as devastating now as they were in the past. A study by academics Wendy Walter-Bailey and Jesse Goodman shows that these girls and young women "often resort to self-destructive behaviors such as drug and alcohol abuse, eating disorders, self-mutilation, academic withdrawal, or risky sexual conduct."[22]

Walter-Bailey and Goodman found that the girls most likely to be labeled as sluts are those who "act too casual and/or flaunt their sexuality" as well as those who "flirt too heavily, blossom too early, or dress too scantily."[23] But here's the problem in a hypersexualized society: conforming to the mainstream norms means girls and young women have to engage in the very behaviors that get them labeled a slut. This is what feminist philosopher Marilyn Frye calls the classic double bind of the oppressed, in that they are faced with "situations in which options are reduced to a very few and all of them expose one to penalty, censure or deprivation."[24]

All of this is further complicated by the fact that in hookup culture, the norms are never clearly defined, so young women are always vulnerable to being labeled a slut.[25] The line between being a good girl and being a bad one is fuzzy, and any girl or woman can inadvertently step over that line at any time, since it is other people who decide if a girl is a slut. Once that line is crossed, it is almost impossible to get rid of the label.

Some of the students I interviewed who had been defined as sluts got the label because ex-boyfriends started to spread rumors, while others were labeled by girlfriends who felt threatened by their boyfriends' interest in the "slut." Whatever the reason one gets labeled a slut, we are putting our girls and young women in an impossible situation because they have to act and dress like a "slut" while avoiding being labeled as one.

Other studies have found that women experience "unwanted sex" (in other words, rape) more frequently in hookups than in dating or long-term relationships. One study in which 178 college students were interviewed found that of the experiences students called "unwanted intercourse," 78 percent occurred during a hookup, as opposed to 8.3 percent on a date and 13.9 percent in an ongoing relationship.[26] This makes perfect sense when we think about the lack of clear borders set up during a hookup. In an ongoing relationship, couples can discuss and negotiate sexual boundaries as the relationship develops, but in a hookup, there will typically be little discussion regarding who is thinking of doing what and how far each one wants to go sexually. Talking or drawing boundaries is not what a hookup is about.

Men brought up in a porn culture will have a distorted view of sex, since in porn everyone is having hookup anal, vaginal, and oral sex all the time. Kimmel found that men across the country think that on any given weekend, 80 percent of male college students are having sex. According to Kimmel, the actual percentage is 5–10 percent.[27] The man may likely expect his hookup to conform somewhat to what he sees as the norm; why should he be getting less than everyone else? She, on the other hand, might decide that her comfort zone is some touching, maybe oral sex, but not full sexual intercourse. Throw in some alcohol for good measure, and you have a perfect setup for hookup rape. I can't begin to count how many students have told me a story that sounds like the above, but rarely do they say they were raped. They will see the experience as a hookup gone too far, or view themselves as an idiot for not stopping the man, but they do not regard what happened as actual rape. One reason for this is that these women feel culpable as they agreed in the first place to the hookup. In other cases they will ask him to stop, and if he doesn't, then they do what he wants, because they do not want to wake up the next day as a rape victim. They would much rather blame themselves because then at least they don't have to take on an identity that marks them as powerless.

Why, then, are girls and women agreeing to have sex under emotionally shallow and at times physically dangerous circumstances? Bogle says it is because there is no clear alternative on college campuses,[28] and while I agree with this, I think there is something else going on: in this hypersexualized culture, we are socializing girls into seeing themselves as legitimate sex objects who are deserving of sexual use (and abuse). The person who best explained this to me was not an expert in women's studies but an incarcerated child rapist. During an interview in a Connecticut prison, John told me how he carefully and strategically groomed his ten-year-old stepdaughter into "consenting" to have sex with him, and then causally mentioned that his job was made easy because "the culture did a lot of the grooming for me."

As John has been through many years of therapy in prison, he had the lingo down pat, and in his eagerness to show off his knowledge to me, he used the word "groom" many times. This is a term psychologists use to describe the way perpetrators socialize, seduce, and manipulate their victims into accepting and often "agreeing" to sexual abuse. John explained how, in his "conscious desire to desensitize her," he used the questions she would ask (What is a blow job? What does a penis taste like?) as an entrée to introducing her first to adult porn and then to child porn. John was very clear that the sexualized pop culture images his stepdaughter had been exposed to from an early age, as well as the sexualized conversations that such images generated in her peer group, had developed a precocious sexual curiosity that "made grooming her easy."

While not all men are a "John," the insight he had on how the culture facilitates sexual abuse is worth taking seriously as he picked up on a trend in the society that no doubt other men, incarcerated perpetrators and nonincarcerated ones, are exploiting. By inundating girls and women with the message that their most worthy attribute is their sexual hotness and crowding out other messages, pop culture is grooming them just like an individual perpetrator would. It is slowly chipping away at their self-esteem, stripping them of a sense of themselves as whole human beings, and providing them with an identity that emphasizes sex and de-emphasizes every other human attribute.

The American Psychological Association's study on the sexualization of girls found that there was ample evidence to conclude that sexualizing girls "has negative effects in a variety of domains, including cognitive functioning, physical and mental health, sexuality, and attitudes and beliefs."[29] Some of these effects include more risky sexual behavior, higher rates of eating disorders, depression, and low self-esteem as well as reduced academic performance. These are the same symptoms found in girls and women who have been sexually assaulted; in terms of effect, then, we appear to be turning out a generation of girls who have been "assaulted" by the very culture they live in. And there is no avoiding the culture. The very act of socialization involves internalizing the cultural norms and attitudes. If the culture is now one big collective perpetrator, then we can assume that an ever-increasing number of girls and women are going to develop emotional, cognitive, and sexual problems as they are socialized into seeing themselves as mere sex objects, and not much else.

Where is female sexual agency in all of this? When feminists in the 1960s and '70s fought for sexual liberation, they fought for the right to want, desire, and enjoy sex—but on their own terms. They argued that their sexuality had been defined by men, and they wanted it back. What they got was not what they expected: a hypersexuality that is generic, formulaic, and plasticized. It is a sexuality that has its roots in porn and is now so mainstream that it is fast becoming normalized. One of the men interviewed by Bogle said he saw hookup culture as a "guy's paradise."[30] Yes, Pornland is indeed paradise for these men, as it is sex with no strings attached. And for women it is business as usual: men defining our sexuality in ways that serve them, not us. Only now this sexuality is sold to us as empowering. A new twist on an old theme.

SEVEN

Racy Sex, Sexy Racism

Porn from the Dark Side

> The consumer never had it so good.... Definitely those niches
> are being fulfilled, interracial, all black, ethnic.
> —James A, owner of West Coast Productions

> Just throw it all in a blender and see what comes out.
> —Video Team owner Christian Mann
> on interracial and ethnic porn

In April 2007, radio show legend Don Imus finally overstepped the
mark with his vile description of the Rutgers University women's bas-
ketball team as "nappy-headed hos." Following a concerted campaign
by the African American community, CBS fired him amid a public outcry and a mass exodus of corporate sponsors from his show. But what
barely merited a comment, let alone outcry from the media, was a press
release issued three weeks later from the porn company *Kick Ass Pictures*
announcing its intention to donate $1 from every sale of its new movie,
titled *Nappy Headed Hos*, to the Don Imus retirement fund. And this
movie is just one among countless that have "hos" in the title, a shorthand way the porn industry commonly refers to black women.

Over the years, thanks in large part to the civil rights movement,
blatant examples of racism that were once commonplace in mainstream
media have become less acceptable. The old "Stepin Fetchit"–type movies that depicted black men as imbeciles or *The Birth of a Nation*–type
movies that showed black men as violent rapists of white women would
not be tolerated today. This does not mean that racist depictions are a
thing of the past, just that the media industry has to operate with some

restraint since we have, as a society, made some surface attempt at rein-
ing in the most vulgar and crass demonstrations of racism. Not so for the
porn industry, which gets away with a level of racism that is breathtaking
in its contempt and loathing for people of color.

Consider the August 2007 release of *Long Dong Black Kong*, which
caused quite a stir in the porn industry with charges of racism for using
the word Kong to describe the black male performer. Invoking the "only
a joke" defense, Peter Reynolds, vice president of Adam and Eve, the
movie's distributor, recommended that "we should all not take ourselves
so seriously," as the "name is totally innocent."[1] Given the overtly racist titles of recent porn movies that feature black men—*Hot Black Thug,
Black Poles in White Holes, Huge Black Cock on White Pussy*, and *Monster
Black Penises*—the *Long Dong Black Kong* title does, at first glance, seem
fairly tame by comparison. However, by referring to black men as mon-
sters, this movie came too close for comfort for many porn producers. It exposed what the porn industry would prefer to keep below the
surface—that black men are routinely depicted as monstrous in their
uncontrolled desire for white women.

The *Long Dong Black Kong* movie belongs to a genre called "interracial" by the industry. According to an article in *Adult Video News*, this is
one of the fastest growing and most bootlegged subgenres in gonzo pornography today.[2] While the term interracial suggests a grab bag of color,
with performers of different races having sex with each other, in reality,
interracial porn features mainly black men with white (often blonde)
women, with titles such as *Black on Blondes, White Pussy-Black Cocks*, and
White Sluts on Black Snakes. If porn users want to see other racial or ethnic mixes, they have to go to categories marked "Black" (which refers to
porn with black women performers), "Asian," "Latin," or "Ethnic," all
of which are burgeoning genres in porn.

The racial politics of the porn industry today mirror those of pop
culture in that the majority of people involved in the production end
of the business is white. This white control has led Jake Stead, a well-
known black performer, to accuse the industry of "rampant racism" in its
failure to provide black producers with the start-up capital, networks, or
access to distribution channels that many white producers enjoy.[3] Jesse
Spencer, aka Mr. Marcus, performer and owner of the production com-

pany MSEX, similarly faults the industry for its overrepresentation of white producers and performers and calls for a greater black presence. In an interview for *XBIZ*, he offers a solution to racism in porn: "I think it has to be up to the black performers to create product for our people and our market, because no one is going to do it for us."[4] Who exactly is included in the "us" category is unclear because it's hard to imagine how black women, or any women of color, would benefit from Mr. Marcus's proposal.

Black women do not fare well in the porn industry because the "plum" jobs for porn performers—the contract employment with the two major porn-feature studios, Vivid and Wicked—are reserved mainly for white women. These studios, with their chic image, sophisticated marketing practices, and guarantee of regular work, afford their contract women an income and level of visibility that makes them the envy of the industry. (Jenna Jameson, of course, is held up as the quintessential example of just how far a contract porn star can go.) With surgically enhanced bodies, perfectly coiffed hair, and glamorous makeup, these women act as PR agents for the porn industry, showing up regularly on Howard Stern, E! Entertainment, or in the pages of *Maxim*. As the porn industry increasingly wiggles its way into pop culture, it is no surprise that it uses mainly white women as the "acceptable" face of porn; their all-American-girl looks seamlessly mesh with the blonde, blue-eyed images that grace screens, celebrity magazines, and billboards across North America.

In porn, women of color are generally relegated to gonzo, a genre that has little glamour, security, or chic status. Here women have few fan club Web sites, do not make it to pop culture, and have to endure body-punishing sex. But while the sex acts are typical gonzo, the way the written text frames the sex is unique as it racializes the bodies and sexual behavior of the performer. In all-white porn, no one ever refers to the man's penis as "a white cock" or the woman's vagina as "white pussy," but introduce a person of color, and suddenly all players have a racialized sexuality, where the race of the performer(s) is described in ways that make women a little "sluttier" and the men more hypermasculinized.

It is this harnessing of gender to race that makes women of color a particularly useful group to exploit in gonzo porn, since gonzo porn works only to the degree that the women in it are debased and dehumanized. As a woman of color, the porn performer embodies two subordinate categories, such as Asian fuckbucket, black ho, or Latina slut. All past and present racist stereotypes are dredged up and thrown in her face while she is being orally, anally, and vaginally penetrated by any number of men. When men (irrespective of race) ejaculate on her face and body, they often make reference to her skin color, and her debased status as a woman is seamlessly melded with, and reinforced by, her supposed debased status as a person of color. In the process, her race and gender become inseparable and her body carries the status of dual subordination.

RACIALIZING THE SLUT: WOMEN OF COLOR IN PORN

It is no surprise that Asian women are the most popular women of color in porn, given the long-standing stereotypes of them as sexually servile geishas, lotus blossoms, and China dolls. Depicted as perfect sex objects with well-honed sexual skills, Asian women come to porn with a baggage of stereotypes that makes them the idealized women of the porn world. In most sites and movies specializing in Asian women ("Asian" being used in porn as a shorthand for a whole range of ethnicities), we see a mind-numbing replaying of the image of Asian women as sexually exotic, enticing, and submissive in both the text and pictures. Using words such as naive, obedient, petite, cute, and innocent, the Web sites are full of images of Asian women, who, we are told, will do anything to please a man, since this is what they are bred for. It seems from these sites, however, that Asian women are interested in pleasing only white men because Asian men are almost completely absent as sex partners.

The introductory text on Hustler's Web site Asian Fever sums up the way Asian women are caricatured in porn: "Asian Fever features scorching scenes of the sexual excesses these submissive Far East nymphos are famous for. No one knows how to please a man like an Asian slut can, and these exotic beauties prove it."[5] Notice here how Asian women are defined as being super slutty thanks to their assumed sexual excesses, submissiveness, skill, and beauty. Their supposed submissiveness is eroticized as they are presented as completely powerless to resist any sexual demands men may have. Their powerlessness is further enhanced by the ways these women are "childified"—they are presented as naive, innocent, and lacking any adult agency. The more childish the woman seems, the greater the ability of the male to exploit and manipulate.

The bodies of these women are similarly described as immature, and of course, given that this is porn, it is always their vaginas that are constructed as the most childlike. Words like "tiny," "little," and "tight" are used as a way to develop an image of a vagina that seems more like a child's than a woman's. Many of these sites promise the viewer the pleasure of seeing a "tight Asian cunt filled with a huge cock," thereby sexualizing female discomfort. In keeping with the gonzo script, these women are depicted as loving rough sex and are happy to take the abuse handed out to them.

For "authenticity," the Web sites often write the English text in chopstick font, play Asian-sounding music in the background, and have the women speaking in broken English. While all of these sites are deeply racist in the way they caricature Asian cultures, one of the worst offenders is a site called Me Fuck You Long Time (a spoof of a line borrowed from *Full Metal Jacket*), which offers the viewer movies of "Asian Sluts Getting Fucked by American Cocks." Referring to the women as "fuckbuckets," this site has multiple images of women being gagged by so-called American cocks. On the right-hand side of the site is an American flag, a tank, and the Statue of Liberty, and on the left is an Asian woman holding a Chinese flag. Just below her is a streaming video of an Asian woman having ejaculate squirted on her face.[6] The not-so-subtle message here is that no matter what really happened in past wars, today the Americans are the real winners as they get to fuck Asian women any way they want. To the winner goes utter and complete access to the losing side's women, and what better way to represent this than to have a continuous video of the losing side's woman being degraded in the best way porn knows: a face covered in ejaculate.

Sometimes the industries of trafficking and sex tourism, which supply Western men with cut-rate women and girls, are referenced for an extra thrill. The text promoting the film *Asian Street Hookers* advertises "real Asian freaks from southeast Asia," and to make really sure that the user knows that they are talking about trafficking in women, they boast:

"The Oriental Express flies to Thailand and the Philippines—and once again imports the sexiest dolls around."[7] Indeed, if the pleasure in porn is watching a woman rendered powerless, then trafficked women are about as powerless as you can get. They are in a foreign country with no support systems, their passport is usually confiscated by the pimp, they have no money, often they can't speak the language, and they are at the mercy of the sex traffickers who would just as soon kill them as let them leave. In this subordinated state, a woman has to submit to any sexual use and abuse brought to bear on her body. In Pornland sex, this state of utter oppression is about as hot as you can get.

Whereas Asian women are seen as biologically disposed to being subservient, black women are presented as the very opposite. The idea that black women lack the traditional feminine quality of subservience is not something that porn invented; it has been around for some years and has at times found its way into governmental reports, most notably the Moynihan Report (1965), which blamed black poverty on black women's emasculation of black men.[8] As ridiculous as this is, black women in particular, and the black community in general, have paid a heavy price for the pathologizing of black women as unrestrained "bitches" steamrollering over black men. Now, in porn, these women get their comeuppance.

As they are in the rest of society, black women are unequally treated in the industry, often earning less than their white female counterparts for the same acts and scenes; very few black women actually become well known and are thus denied the added wealth that comes with having a name in the industry. In his book on the black porn industry, Lawrence Ross quotes the well-known black porn actor Lexington Steele as saying: "In a boy/girl scene, one girl one guy, no anal sex, the market dictates a minimum of $800 to $900 per scene for the girl.... Now a white girl will start at $800 and go up from there, but a black girl will have to start at $500, and then hit a ceiling of about $800. So the black girl hits a ceiling at the white girl's minimum."[9]

With film names like *Juicy Black Butt, Horny Black Pussy, Bad Black Babes,* and *Black Pussy Stuffed,* the race of the woman is clearly transmitted to the potential user. Wading through numerous sites featuring black women, what appears as a common theme is the framing of these women as aggressive and mouthy. They are constantly referred to as having an "attitude," and the job of porn sex is to train them—domesticate them, if you will—into a subordinate state. They are presented as having a particularly excessive and uncontrollable type of sexuality that takes a real man, be he black or white, to handle.

A whole subgenre of black porn is depicted as taking place in the ghetto, a location that is described as sexually lawless, debauched, and brimming with hos, pimps, and gang-bangers. The black women who populate the porn world become not just sluts and whores, but ghetto sluts and hos, which makes them even more dehumanized than their white counterparts. On some of these sites the women are depicted as unkempt, poorly dressed, and lacking in style. The story here is that they need a pimp to turn them into presentable prostitutes, and not to worry, there is no shortage of pimps, usually black, eager to take on the job.

On Pimp My Black Teen—a spoof of the popular *Pimp My Ride* MTV series—the headline on the site reads: "We find ordinary black teens from the ghetto and pimp them out extreme-makeover style." This site, like many other pimp sites, has pictures of so-called before and after makeovers, in which a teenage black woman is shown in sweat pants and jeans for the "before"—and sexy, revealing underwear for the "after." One caption reads, "We caught up with Reneeka looking like a tattered hood rat. Once we styled her fine brown ass, her wet pussy took a long black cock just fine."[10] Above the text are pictures of "Reneeka" giving oral sex to a black male, her face smeared with ejaculate.

But while "ghetto" black women may try to clean themselves up to look more sexy and hot, there is no escaping their roots, as exemplified in the case of Saxxx: "Saxxx tried to clean herself up, but there was no fooling us, she was still a low down dirty ghetto ho! So I rammed her head into the couch as I worked her snatch like a jack hammer, then proceeded to fire a messy load all over her face."[11] Indeed, it is their so-called ghetto style that seems to make these women more appealing, as one fan, comparing white and black women performers, told Ross that white women "are all fake and shit, fake tits and fake ass on the camera, you know what I am saying? But the black chicks are the real deal. Like you could actually get with them."[12]

One image of black women that is common in both mainstream pop culture, especially hip-hop, and porn, is the reduction of them to a "big black booty." Some sites put booty in their title—like Big Booty Cuties, Black Booty Cam—while others make clear that the black women's buttocks are the focus of attention—Sweet Chocolate Butt, Black Ass Fucks, Phat Ass Ebony, and Black Ass Fucking. And virtually every black porn site talks about the "booty" in their promo text, promising lots of "big black round asses." African American writers such as Patricia Hill Collins have explored how this fetishization of black women's buttocks is rooted in the belief that black women are especially promiscuous and that their "booty" is the only part worthy of notice, thus reducing black women to sexual objects devoid of humanity, individuality, and dignity.[13] Instead of a whole person, the black woman becomes an appendage to a big black booty, one that she is willing to shake at any man, no matter what his race.

It is impossible to know with any certainty who buys these movies with black women, but articles in *Adult Video News* and on the XBIZ Web site suggest that when both male and female porn performers are black, then it is mainly geared toward a black audience. Lawrence Ross, in his interviews with the fans of this genre, found the majority to be black, and their reason for buying these movies was that for them, "black porn is the manifestation of a fetish. Black skin is looked at as being a sort of hypersexuality, an explosive combination that is more exciting and hotter than general-market or white sex."[14] If Ross is correct, then the dominant white-produced stereotypes of blacks as having what Cornel West mockingly refers to as "dirty, disgusting, and funky sex"[15] would seem to have gained some traction with black men.

Also, black men have been socialized over the years by the increasingly pornographic images in mainstream hip-hop. Highly sexualized images of black women are a staple of these videos, and while, as some black critics argue, these images reinstate black women as sexually desirable in a society where the beauty standard is racist,[16] they do so in ways that objectify their bodies and teach boys and young men that they are not equal partners but rather fuck objects who deserve to be treated just like the women in porn videos. Hip-hop helped develop the black porn genre, and Mireille Miller-Young argues that "white pornographers were acutely interested in how black men consumed images of black women—how they fetishized them in popular culture—so that they could expand their market beyond the standard white male consumers who generally purchased adult tapes featuring black sexuality."[17] Hip-hop was the main source of information for porn producers eager to open up the black male market; it would seem, given the growth in the number of black porn movies released, that it successfully provided a blueprint for porn imagery.[18]

There are now a growing number of sites that depict sex between white men and black women, and if the porn boards are any reflections, the majority of these viewers appear to be white. It seems that when either the male or female porn performer is white, then the audience is mainly white men. This makes sense given how racial conflict is constructed, articulated, and exploited as a way to enhance the sexual debasement of women. On the site White Dicks in Black Chicks—where the banner reads, "White Guys Violate Ebony Babes"—the sex is regular gonzo, but the text constructs a scenario of acute economic deprivation and subsequent sexual exploitation:

> What a fuckin' hot day it was when we found Carmen. She was walking out of the grocery store with her shirt up and her big fat tits hanging out. We had to say something to her. A fine black woman like this. But when we tried to approach her she wasn't having it. This woman may be the most racist black woman we've ever met. She couldn't stand the white man. Calling them perverts, ingrates, honkeys, even threatening to get her gang members to kick the shit out of them. But we had an angle. See Carmen has two kids and they need milk but Carmen is a little low on cash right now so we made her a proposition. One thousand bucks to fuck a white man. Our final offer. She accepted alright and when we got back to the house she also got a mouthful of white cum to wash down that milk.[19]

On the site is a large picture of "Carmen" on all fours with a penis entering her anus. The message here is that her gender, race, and class locations have visually and viscerally brought her to knees.

This site is nothing compared to the actual sexual violence that black women in Ghetto Gaggers suffer at the hands of white men. Promoting itself as a site that delivers "Ghetto Fabulous Face Fucked Beyatches," the home page has many pictures of black women with lots of semen dripping off their faces. Surrounding these images are smaller ones of the women being anally, orally, and vaginally penetrated. Unlike much of gonzo, there is no attempt to even pretend that these women like the sex, as they are shown close to tears, grimacing, and, in many cases, thoroughly disgusted by the semen that is all over their eyes, mouth, and nose. Although the entire site is very disturbing, one of the worst images is of "Vixen," who looks utterly exhausted. The text accompanying the images reads: "Vixen is a sassy ghetto fabulous beyatch with more atti- tude than Harlem has crack. She needed a learnin' by some white cocks to remove the sass from her chicken head bobbin' back and forth ghetto ass. We did just that. Two cocks in her holes, we ran train on her ass, slapped the taste out of her mouth and dumped two loads all over that sexy beyatch. Ghetto Gaggers, we destroy ghetto hoes, and it be showin' like a mutha fukka!"[20]

It's apparent that these pornographers see sex as a punishment for Vixen's failure to act like a subservient female. The violence of this site is not lost on fans, who, on the porn discussion board Adult DVD Talk, share their favorite scenes. Hotboy 1999 tells his virtual friends that "i love the hardcore face fucking, the women drooling, the gagging, and the puke scenes" and asks for suggestions for more gagging and puke scenes. Panas answers, "If you like the roughest it could be the Jes- sica scene, where she is extremely uncomfortable and at a point she stops the scene crying. If you like vomit go for Baby Doll, a scene where she starts vomiting from the very start."[21] Indeed, on the free teaser, any- one can watch "Baby Doll" vomit over and over again as she is gagged. The role of such violence is to feminize her into being a real woman, and who better to deliver this message in a racist society than white men.

Asian women and black women are not the only women to be ra- cially exploited by the porn industry; there is also a market for other ethnic groups, especially Latina women, and lately for Arab women. Irrespective of the ethnic group, the framing of the narrative is exactly the same—the women's race makes them that bit sluttier than "regular," white porn women. For men of color, the story is often more complicated.

RACIALIZING THE STUD:
MEN OF COLOR IN PORN

While there are literally thousands of images of Asian women on these porn sites, there are very few Asian men as sex partners. This mirrors pop culture, where apart from a few sagely old men dispensing wisdom in broken English or a kung fu–type fighter, Asian men are virtually absent in media, especially as intimate partners of Asian women, or any women, for that matter. The lack of Asian male characters as lovers, husbands, boyfriends, or even porn performers is, according to Darrell Hamamoto, an Asian American professor at the University of California, Davis, and a porn producer, due to the widely held stereotype of Asian men as asexual nerds.[22] But if we move over to gay porn, we see plenty of Asian men who are portrayed as anything but asexual. Some of these sites have Asian-on-Asian male sex, but when an Asian male is paired with a white man, he is identified in much the same way as Asian women—cute, petite, innocent. The word that often is used to describe Asian men in porn is "twinks," a term used in gay slang to mean a young, attractive, slightly built gay male. The stereotypes that make Asian men attractive as feminized gay men are the very ones that make them unappealing in straight porn, since to be a feminized man would undo the strict gender demarcation present in straight porn.

It seems that the hyperfeminization of Asian women in pop culture and porn leaks down to Asian men, whereby the group as a whole becomes feminized as the sexual object of white masculinity. This "demasculinization" of Asian men in Western culture was the topic of discussion on Adult DVD Talk when a user asked why there were no Asian male porn stars. Mixed in with the predictable racist assumptions—"Asian men tend to have smaller genital size"—there was a range of posts that illustrated ways in which white men view Asian men as lacking masculinity. One user wrote that "even if a white woman might like an asian male, she might not want to sleep with him because of the way people view the masculinity (or lack thereof)," to which another responded:

> But: porn isn't so much about "real life." Like any kind of show business, it emphasizes "image" and exaggerates. Since it is about sex, there is a tendency to exaggerate masculinity vs. feminity [sic]. And like it or not, there is a tendency to *perceive* individuals of certain races and/or "types" as more masculine (or feminine as the case may be) than others. I would say that in the eyes of many, black guys top the list in terms of masculinity (as defined in terms of size, muscularity, physical power, dick size, aggressiveness, and self-confidence), while the common *perception* of Asian guys...would put them lower on that list. White guys would fall, on average, somewhere in between.[23]

What is remarkable about this post is the way the writer (Eduardo911) so neatly sums up how race is gendered to the degree that one group represents masculinity (blacks), one group femininity (Asians), and one group (whites) floats somewhere in the middle of the continuum. When this racial landscape is disrupted, porn users become somewhat uneasy, as in the case of the porn site Asian Man, which advertises itself as being about the "sexual adventures of an Asian man and beautiful girls from all over the world." The readers' reviews on the Sir Rodney site (a porn-review site) are very mixed, with many reviewers unsure as to how Asian the site owner and performer, Rick, really is. Some insist he is Asian, while others, such as Anonymous, argue that "Asian-man is a ripped off [sic]. This asshole who owns the site is not even Asian or Chinese."[24]

For those who believe that Rick is indeed Asian, there is a lot of support for having an Asian man as the lead male performer, or, as Anonymous puts it, "the site's unique feature is that it features an asian in the male role."[25] But for all the hype about this site featuring an Asian man, the male porn performer goes to great lengths to conceal his racial identity. In every still image on the site he hides his face, sometimes to the point of chopping off the top of a picture, or even blacking out his head. In the movies, his face is buried in the body of the woman he is penetrating or the camera is held at an angle that conceals his face. Although it is the norm in heterosexual porn to minimize the images of the male performer, perhaps for fear that the sight will make the viewer uncomfortable while watching (and possibly enjoying) another male become aroused, this site takes it to an extreme. It would seem that Rick, or whoever the owner is, feels unsure about how well an Asian man would be received by consumers, so he makes him everyman by blocking out distinguishing racial characteristics.

One other site that promotes Asian men as heterosexual porn performers is Phuck Fu Masters, owned by Asian American porn producer Jack Lee. The story told on the site is that two amateurs from Hong Kong come to America for instruction from a porn master in how to become the first-ever Asian male porn stars, and the viewers get to see them honing their skills on, mainly, white women. The text on the site both pokes fun at and reinforces traditional stereotypes of Chinese people, with constant references to Chinese food delivery, kung fu, and chi. Interestingly, the site also emphasizes just how new to porn sex these men are. Rarely in porn is reference made to the inexperience of the male performers since their masculinity is tied to their sexual prowess, but here on a site with Asian men, the theme is that the male performers need to be taught by a master. And who, in Pornland sex, is the master best suited to teach Asian men how to have sex? A black man, of course, in the form of Santino Lee, veteran porn performer and producer. So on this site, run by an Asian man, there is still a replaying of the hypermasculine black male and the feminized Asian dichotomy by making the former the "master" of the latter.

Jack Lee has been quoted as saying that he started this Web site because "there's a demand from many Asian men to see guys like themselves portrayed as sex symbols," and that for him and his Asian viewers, it "is an Asian Pride thing."[26] These are almost the exact same sentiments expressed by professor and pornographer Darrell Hamamoto, although Hamamoto uses somewhat more scholarly language to justify his entry into the porn world. Creator of *Skin on Skin*, a porn movie using only Asian American performers, Hamamoto sees his porn movie as "a proudly erect statement on Asian American male sexuality." How he gets to this somewhat twisted position is through a very reasonable assessment of how Asian American sexuality has been "warped by White supremacist thought/behavior, the history of anti-Asian exterminationism, colonialism, removal and relocation, deportation, and anti-miscegenation laws."[27] There is no doubt that such overtly racist practices would have a major impact on every facet of life, including sexuality, and Hamamoto's outrage is well justified, given the racism that Asian Americans continue to experience in this country.

But Hamamoto is really only outraged on behalf of Asian American men and demonstrates utter contempt for Asian American women in his willful failure to adopt any critical analysis of how porn negatively affects the lives of Asian American women. No stranger to sophisticated thinking on how images construct reality, media scholar Hamamoto suddenly sounds like an average porn consumer when he comments, in an interview, that finding Asian American women to appear in porn is easy: "There are tons of Yella womenz who want to appear on camera doing the Wild Thang."[28] Well, certainly, if you surf the Asian porn sites, you will find "tons" of Asian women. But to conclude from this, as Hamamoto does, that Asian American porn is about Asian American women's desire to do the "wild thang," rather than a racist marketing ploy developed by primarily white men to make a profit off long-held racist stereotypes, is simply absurd.

What seems to be blinding Hamamoto to the exploitation of Asian American women in porn is his overwhelming desire to remasculinize the Asian American male. And this is where his project really turns bizarre, for while he critiques the dominant racist image of the emasculated Asian American male, he ultimately uses the dominant sexist image of masculinity—one based on control and dominance of women —as his measure of what a remasculinized Asian man should look like. Within this framework, it makes sense why Hamamoto sees Asian-on-Asian porn as a way to change the image of Asian American men, since Asian men get to play out the ultimate act of masculinity—fucking (over) their own women. This might be, as both Jack Lee and Darrell Hamamato say, a proud statement for Asian American masculinity, but for Asian American women, it is business as usual, with their sexuality still being used in the service of proving the masculinity of the men who are fucking them.

For all the attempts to remasculinize Asian men, it seems that it will take more than a few porn sites to shift the stereotypes of Asian men that have long been part of the collective consciousness of white Americans. As long as Asian men are seen by whites as feminized, it is unlikely that they will ever be of much interest to white male porn users as this muddies the gender demarcation between women and men. If, as argued elsewhere, men go to porn to shore up their masculinity, then they want to see men—real powerful men—fucking women who at the moment of penetration are utterly feminized by their subordinated role. The more masculine the man, the more likely he can subordinate, and the more the user/spectator gets to live out his masculinity vicariously as he watches the scene unfold before him.

If Asian men have occupied the feminized end of the masculinity continuum, then black men have been at the hypermasculinized end. Saddled with ugly stereotyping as violent thugs and rapists, black men are often held up as examples of masculinity run amok, the kind that is uncontained and out of control. In fact, this is the very masculinity that is idealized and glorified in porn, since every male in the porn world is hyperaroused and ready to do what he has to in order to pleasure himself. It would appear that the long-held image of black men as spoilers of white womanhood was in fact tailor-made for porn, so it should be no surprise that the industry has cashed in on these stereotypes in the form of the very successful genre of interracial porn (IP). As one porn retailer puts it: "My customers seem to enjoy black men 'taking advantage' of white women; seducing their white daughters and wives. The more 'wrong' a title is, the more appealing it is. The *Blackzilla* line is one of my best selling series. *Oh No! There's a Negro in My Mom* is also one that sells as soon as it hits the shelves. My customers don't want to see a loving interracial couple; they want to see massive black dicks, satisfying or defiling pretty white girls."[29]

While the movie *Long Dong Black Kong* caused a stir for its racism, it was in fact a perfect title for a porn movie featuring black men and white women, just as the original *King Kong* movie was probably the most dramatic rendering of black masculinity that this country had ever seen when it came out in 1933. Who can forget the image of an out-of-control "black" monster rampaging through the streets of New York, with a defenseless white woman clutched to his chest? No surprise that when the movie was released in Germany in 1934, it was renamed *King Kong and the White Woman.* Although Kong did not have an identifiable penis, we were primed to imagine just what damage he could do to petite Fay Wray as she lay helpless in his arms.

Porn movies that pair black men with white women are very popular with porn consumers. Although there is little empirical research on the consumers of such porn, *AVN* articles suggest that IP is being produced, marketed, and distributed mainly to a white audience. This seems strange given that a relatively short time ago, the thought of a black man just looking at a white woman was enough to work white men up into a lynch-mob frenzy. And now they are buying millions of dollars worth of movies that show, in graphic detail, a black man doing just about everything that can be done to a white woman's body. But it is actually less strange when we realize that in the world of porn, the more a woman—white or of color—is debased, the better the porn experience for the user. And what better way to debase a white woman, in the eyes of white men, than to have her penetrated over and over again by that which has been designated sexually perverse, savage, and debauched? One interracial porn producer says that his most popular movies are those where "the purity of the sacred white women is compromised... even if the white girl is as dirty and diseased-riddled as humanly possible."[30] This explains why interracial porn geared toward white men is almost totally dominated by black male porn performers rather than any other ethnic group.

It is not an easy task in gonzo porn to make any one group look more debauched than the next since everyone in porn is depicted as nothing more than walking genitalia looking for penetration and orgasm. But even in this world, black men are more reduced to their penis than any other group of men, because the action centers around "the big black cock" that can't get enough "white pussy." Described as "huge," "enormous," "monstrous," "gigantic," and "unbelievable" with mind-numbing monotony, the black penis is filmed from every angle to give the porn user a clear image of its size and color. The focal point of these movies is the numerous ways in which the huge black penis can do damage to small white orifices, as constant mention is made of her inability to deal with such a large penis. Or, as one fan put it, the best IP movies are those where "he is giving her more than she can handle." The site White Meat on Black Street, for example, refers to the women as "victims" and promises users "interracial pussy splitting action" because "these horse-hung black dudes are packing so much meat it is a wonder that these tight white pussies don't recoil at the mere sight!"[31]

The movies typically begin with the woman expressing shock at the size of the penis, and in some cases she tells the cameraman that she is not sure she can do the scene. Whether fake or real, as the sex begins you watch the women grimace and move away from the penis, only to be dragged back toward it as it penetrates an orifice. In some of the movies there is more than one man, so she might have penises thrust into her vagina, anus, and mouth at the same time. The usual gonzo sex goes on and on, and the viewer gets to see her gag to the point where tears are streaming down her face. While the penis is thrust into her vagina and the anus, and she is squirming, she says, often through gritted teeth, that she loves "big black cock."

The male porn performers are, like most men in gonzo, depicted as lacking empathy and completely uninterested in the pain or discomfort they are causing the women. While this kind of behavior reduces all men in gonzo to robotic fuckers of women's orifices, for black men it is described as part of their very biological makeup and hence carries the weight of authenticity. And porn users like authenticity. If they suspect they are being fooled, they get upset, as in the case of some fans who are convinced that the penis attached to one of the men in *White Meat on Black Street* is fake. As the users discuss whether the penis is real, one reader writes that "the dick is clearly fake. Watch how he has to hold it on. It doesn't cum realistically either. Stupid niggers trying to fake big dicks."[32] Why the outrage? One possible answer could be that if the penis is fake, then maybe the woman's pain is also fake, and this spoils the thrill of watching the action play out. Also, many of these white men seem somewhat entranced by the black penis, as they seem to be spending a lot of time studying it while masturbating.

In IP movies, the white penis is often held up as inadequate and lacking in potency when compared to black ones. An excellent example of this can be found in one of the most popular series of IP movies, called

Blacks on Blondes, which feature white blonde women with multiple black males. As in most IP, the white performer is "applauded" for being able to take a black penis in her mouth, vagina, and anus. In one particular movie with "Liv Wylder," we see an example of a theme running through IP: the emasculation of the white man by the big black penis. The text on the site reads:

> Bring out the cuckold mask again! Time for another white couple to live out their naughtiest fantasy, and thanks to *Blacks On Blondes* for making it happen! Liv and Hubby have been married for a few years, and she wears her ring proudly. But lately the spark has left the bedroom, if you know what I mean. A few e-mails later, and we've got Hubby in a cage while Boz and Mandingo work Liv over. And when I say they work her over, we mean it. She takes so much black dick it amazed even us. The best part of this whole deal was the end: after Liv has about a gallon of cum all over her face and clothes, and grabs a plastic bowl—for Hubby to beat off in. He does, and his wad was weak, and Liv lets him know that.[33]

The story that the text and images are telling in this movie has deep historical resonance as it is pitting the black male sexuality against white male sexuality, and the loser is without a doubt the latter. The white man's poor performance in the bedroom ("the spark has left the bedroom") as well as his ineffectual semen ("his wad was weak") stand in sharp contrast to the size of the black men's penises, the skill of their sexual performance ("they work her over, we mean it"), and the amount of semen they produce ("a gallon of cum"). To add to the humiliation, the last line lets us know that Liv is only too happy to ridicule her husband in front of the black men. What we have here is a playing out of a stereotype that demarcates the white man as civilized, and therefore somewhat restrained in his bodily functions, versus the uncivilized, animalistic black man who, unencumbered by social norms and dictates of bodily control, really knows how to please a woman. And when push comes to shove, the white woman really prefers the unrestrained sexuality of black men. No wonder one popular series of IP films is called Once You Go Black…You Never Go Back.[34]

This mocking of white masculinity would seem like an odd thing to do in a porn genre that is mainly targeted to white men. Men generally do not like to be ridiculed for having an ineffectual penis, so we need to consider what possible pleasure white men could get from such movies. One possibility could be that the viewer identifies with the black male, and in so doing, he gets to imagine what life would be like if he were, according to the image, an out-of-control savage black man rather than a penis-challenged white man. This would not be the first time in history that white men have identified with black men as a way to enjoy the pleasures of the (assumed) unconstrained body. The blackface minstrel shows that swept through America in the 1830s and 1840s were very popular with white male audiences. Some scholars suggest that the mask of blackness donned by the white performers conferred a freedom on them such that they could "sing, dance, speak, move, and act in ways that were considered inappropriate for white men."[35] When white men watched the minstrels, they saw not white men in blackface but what they thought was authentic black behavior being played out. The reason for this, argues Mel Watkins, is that whites assumed that the minstrel shows depicted something real and essential about blacks, because the shows were "advertised as the real thing. In fact, one group was called 'The Real Nigs'...they were advertised as 'Come to the theatre and get a real look into what plantation life was like.'...It was advertised as a peephole view of what black people were really like."[36]

I would suggest here that IP is not so much a peephole as a peep-show into what whites think is real black sexual behavior. White men get a bird's-eye view of "authentic" black sex at work. The Blacks on Blondes text above perfectly captures, albeit in an extreme form, the image of a white man, sexually caged by his race, peeping at uncaged, uninhibited black men performing sex in a way that really pleases slutty white women. The white man watching this, or indeed any IP movie, gets to shed his whiteness and identify with a group of men who seem to be tailor-made for porn. As the white man unzips, he steps out of the socially constructed cage of whiteness and into a thoroughly debauched world of huge, semen-filled black penises out to rip, tear, pummel, and hammer white women into the utter subordination of becoming a fuckee.

While this debasing of white women might well intensify the sexual thrill for the white user, it has real-world implications for the black community. All forms of oppression, be they gender-, race-, or class-based, require a system of beliefs that justify why one group has power over another. This justification process often comes in the form of negative images of the targeted group as somehow less human than the group in power, and it is this less-than-human status that makes them especially deserving of exploitation, abuse, and degradation. In porn, all people are seen as less than human because everyone is reduced to genitalia. But for whites, this is not presented as a condition of their whiteness, since in our society, whiteness is colorless and hence invisible by virtue of its power status. For people of color, however, it is their very color that constantly makes them visible as a racialized group as they carry the marker of "difference" on their skin. This is why it is impossible in porn for a person of color to have just a vagina or a penis, as their genitalia are always going to be racially visible as "Asian Pussy" or "Black Cock."

The pornographic images that meld the racial with the sexual may make the sex racier, but they also serve to breathe new life into old stereotypes that circulate in mainstream society. While these stereotypes are often a product of the past, they are cemented in the present every time a user masturbates to them. This is a powerful way to deliver racist ideology, as it not only makes visible the supposed sexual debauchery of the targeted group, but also sexualizes the racism in ways that make the actual racism invisible in the mind of most consumers and nonconsumers alike. This is why Don Imus got fired, and why the pornographers get rich.

EIGHT

Children

The Final Taboo

> I believe that most men here will never want to accept the
> possibility that the young teen trend is grotesque because it
> will say so much about them. If you know that something is
> harmful and wrong and you still become aroused then what
> does it mean about who you really are as a man?
>
> —Miss DeRay, porn performer, director,
> photographer, Adult DVD Talk

In the March 2006 special edition of *Vanity Fair*, thirty-year-old Reese Witherspoon is photographed looking wide-eyed and innocent in a girl's party dress. In her left hand she is holding a little girl's doll. Also in the magazine is a photo of then twelve-year-old Dakota Fanning wearing makeup, an off-the shoulder evening gown, and a "bed head" hairdo. Three years later, *Vanity Fair* carries pictures of a scantily clad fifteen-year-old Miley Cyrus with a "fuck me" look on her face. One year after that, in July 2009, *Elle* has a picture of Cyrus in a short black dress and thigh-high black boots. She is spread across a table with her legs apart as she looks seductively into the camera. These four images exemplify a visual landscape that has become so ubiquitous that we hardly glance twice when we see sexualized childified women and sexualized adultified children.

As we become more desensitized to images of hypersexualized young women, the fashion industry has tried to capture our attention by sexualizing young girls. A pioneer of this type of advertising was Calvin Klein, who, in the early 1980s, used the fifteen-year-old Brooke Shields in ads for his jeans with the famous tagline "Do you wanna know what comes between me and my Calvins? Nothing." In the mid-1990s Klein ratcheted up the imagery by using mostly underage teenagers in poses that looked so much like actual child pornography that the Justice Department started to investigate him for possible violation of the law. Klein escaped prosecution, only to come back a few years later with ads for his children's underwear line that featured prepubescent boys and girls wearing only underwear. This time Klein was forced to pull his ads almost overnight due to public outcry.

As pop culture begins to look more and more pornographic, the actual porn industry has had to become more hard-core as a way to distinguish its products from those images found on MTV, in *Cosmopolitan*, and on billboards. The problem for pornographers is that they are quickly running out of new ways to keep users interested. So one of the big questions they have to grapple with today is how to keep maximizing their profits in an already glutted market where consumers are becoming increasingly desensitized to their products. The solutions for them are the same as for all capitalists: find innovative ways to expand both market shares and revenues in existing markets, bring in new customers, and find new market segments and distribution channels. Thus the major task for the porn industry is to keep looking for new niche markets and consumer bases to open up and exploit while staying within the law, or alternatively, working to change the law—an option that the now-mainstream pornography industry increasingly employs.

The main body charged with lobbying lawmakers on behalf of the porn industry is the Free Speech Coalition, an organization that, although founded in 1991, had to wait till 2002 for its first big legal victory, the case of *Ashcroft v. Free Speech Coalition*. Here the Supreme Court ruled in favor of the coalition when it declared the 1996 Child Porn Prevention Act unconstitutional because its definition of child pornography (any visual depiction that appears to be of a minor engaging in sexually explicit conduct) was ruled to be overly broad. The law was narrowed to cover only those images in which an actual person under the age of eighteen (rather than one that simply appears to be) is involved in the making of the porn, thus opening the way for the porn industry to use either computer-generated images of children or real porn performers who, although eighteen or over, are childified to look much younger.

Following the Court's decision, there has been an explosion in the number of sites that childify women, as well as those that use computer-generated imagery. In the former category, the pioneer was Hustler's *Barely Legal* porn magazine, which started in 1974 and is now a popular Web site and video series, with *Barely Legal* 79 released in February of 2008. Hustler is owned by Larry Flynt, a multimillionaire who is known in the porn world for being a risk taker and somewhat of a maverick. It is not surprising that it took the Supreme Court's 2002 decision to open the gates to this new genre, since prior to then, sites such as Barely Legal were vulnerable to prosecution, and few pornographers had either Flynt's money or his will to fight a legal battle. Now that the chance of prosecution has been eliminated, sites with childified women have sprung up all over the Web.[1] Consequently, more users have the opportunity to masturbate to pseudo-child pornography (PCP), images of "girls" being penetrated by any number of men masquerading as fathers, teachers, employers, coaches, and just plain old anonymous child molesters.[2]

Because pornography that uses children (those under eighteen) is still illegal, PCP sites that use adults (those over eighteen) to represent children are never called child pornography by the industry. Instead, almost all of those sites that childify the female porn performer are found in the subgenre called "teen porn" or "teen sex" by the industry. There are any number of ways to access these sites, the most obvious one being Google. Typing "teen porn" into Google yields over 9 million hits, giving the user his choice of thousands of porn sites. A number of these hits are actually for porn portals where "teen porn" is one subcategory of many, and when the user clicks on that category, a list of sites come up that runs for over ninety pages. Moreover, teen porn has its very own portal, which lists hundreds of sub-subgenres such as Pissing Teens, Drunk Teens, Teen Anal Sluts, and Asian Teens.[3]

Even though these sites are also becoming increasingly popular with porn users, with nearly 14 million Internet searches for "teen sex" in 2006, an increase of 61 percent in just two years, and 6 million Internet searches for teen porn, an increase of 45 percent over the same period,[4] there is very little research on either the content or the effects of such sites. One of the main reasons for this could be that those who research the field of child pornography and child sexual abuse prevention have been overwhelmed by the flood of real child pornography that accompanied the growth of the Internet. Since an actual child is used in the making of such imagery, there is an urgent need to track both the producers and consumers of such pornography and to infiltrate the many international child porn rings that swap thousands of child pornography pictures in the relatively safe and anonymous space created by the Internet. To get some idea of the scope of the problem, one Internet ring that was raided in 1998, called the Wonderland Club, operated in over twelve countries, and to join, each prospective member had to have at least 10,000 child pornography images to swap.[5]

Obviously, compared to such a mind-boggling level of actual child abuse, researching PCP images appears less pressing since the women involved are at least eighteen and hence, according to the law, no actual crime is taking place. But if we shift our attention away from production and toward consumption, then we can begin to ask questions regarding the possible effects that PCP and actual child pornography may have in common since both aim to sexually arouse men with images of sexualized "children." If, as researchers argue,[6] real child pornography is used by some men to prepare them for actual assault on a child by both arousing them and desensitizing them to the harm done to children, while at the same time offering a blueprint of how to commit the crime, then is it not possible that PCP sites could play a similar role? The answer to such a question depends to a large degree on just how successful the PCP sites are in constructing a reality for the user that he is in fact masturbating to images of sexualized children, and not of adults, since he presumably goes to these sites with the goal of gazing at females who look or behave somewhat differently from the thousands of females that populate the regular porn sites. So the first step in developing an analysis of effects is actually an investigation into how PCP sites borrow, employ, and mobilize symbols, codes, conventions, and narratives that are found in actual child pornography. It is only after developing such a map of content that we can begin to ask questions about the ways PCP images leak into the real-world attitudes and behaviors of users.

DEVELOPING A MAP OF CONTENT OF PCP SITES

To explore the linkages between PCP sites and actual child pornography, it first makes sense to develop a classification system for the former from the typologies developed to classify the latter. One of the most popular of these, according to Tony Krone, a well-known researcher in the field, is a five-point typology of child pornography.[7] Using this typology not only helps to distill the thousands of PCP sites into a workable number of categories, it also provides a way to understand how users may seamlessly move between the two genres.

The five categories of child pornography described by Krone are

1. images depicting nudity or erotic posing, with no sexual activity;
2. sexual activity between children, or solo masturbation by a child;
3. nonpenetrative sexual activity between adult(s) and child(ren);
4. penetrative sexual activity between adult(s) and child(ren); and
5. sadism or bestiality.

While there are PCP sites that fall into all five categories, the vast majority fit into categories 2, 4, and 5. The acts, narratives, and visual techniques of the PCP sites in 2, 4, and 5 are drawn from the adult genre of pornography, since solo masturbation, penetrative sexual activity, and sadism (not bestiality)[8] are common types of sex acts in mainstream pornography. What follows is a descriptive analysis of those PCP sites that fall into each of the three categories and a discussion of how the sites move from being relatively nonviolent (images of girls masturbating) to images of girls being used sexually in ways that are sadistic and abusive.

Type 2: Sexual activity between children, or solo masturbation by a child

The competition for customers is fierce in the porn industry since the user has a wide range of sites, themes, images, and narratives to choose from. Pornographers know this, so they attempt to pull the user in quickly by giving sites names that are short, to the point, and unambiguous. It is therefore not surprising that many of the sites in this category actually have the word "solo" in the name, along with a word that cues the user into the youthfulness of the females depicted: Solo Teen, Solo Teen Babe, Sexy Girl Solo, Solo Cuties, Solo Gals, Solo Teen Girls. When the user clicks on any one of these sites, the first and most striking feature is the body shape of the female porn performers. In place of the large-breasted, curvaceous bodies that populate regular porn Web sites are small-breasted, slightly built women with adolescent-looking faces that are relatively free of makeup. Many of these performers do look younger than eighteen, but they do not look like children, so pornographers use a range of techniques to make them appear more childlike than they actually are. Primary among these is the use of childhood clothes and props such as stuffed animals, lollipops, pigtails, pastel-colored ribbons, ankle socks, braces on the teeth, and, of course, school uniforms. It is not unusual to see a female porn performer wearing a school uniform, sucking a lollipop, and hugging a teddy bear as she masturbates with a dildo.

Another technique for childifying the woman's body is the removal of all the pubic hair, so the external genitalia look like that of a prepubescent female. What is interesting is that over the years, this technique has lost much of its signifying power as it is now commonplace in porn for women to remove all their pubic hair. One of the results of this is that today, virtually every female porn performer looks like a child, a shift that in itself is cause for concern because porn users who are not looking for pseudo-child images are nonetheless exposed to them when they surf the porn sites.

For all the visual clues of childhood surrounding the women in PCP sites, however, it is the written text accompanying the images that does most of the work in convincing the user that he is masturbating to images of sexual activity involving a minor. The words used to describe the women's bodies (including their vaginas)—"tiny," "small," "petite," "tight," "cute," "teeny"—not only stress their youthfulness but also work to separate them from women on other sites. Most striking is how many of these PCP sites refer to the female as "sweetie," "sweetheart," "little darling," "cutie pie," "honey"—terms of endearment that starkly contrast with the abusive names the women on other sites are commonly called, such as "slut," "whore," "cumdumpster," and "cunt." The use of kinder terms on PCP sites is a method of preserving the notion for the user that these girls are somehow different from the rest of the women who populate the world of porn in that they are not yet used-up whores deserving of verbal abuse. This would explain why so many of these Web sites have the word "innocent" in their name—Innocent Cute, Innocent Dream, Innocent Love, and Petite Innocent.

The reason why girls are portrayed as not yet sullied, soiled, or tainted by sex on these sites is because the underlying offer here is witnessing their loss of innocence. One fan of this genre, writing to Adult DVD Talk, calls this a "knowing innocence," which he defines as "the illusion of innocence giving way to unbridled sexuality. Essentially, this is the old throwback of the Madonna and the Whore. Therein lies the vast majority of my attraction to this genre."[9] This fan, and indeed many others, if their posts are to be believed, makes clear that for him, the pleasure is in watching the (sweet, cute, petite) Madonna being coaxed, encouraged, and manipulated by adult men into revealing the whore that lies beneath the (illusionary) innocence. The pornographers reveal their understanding of the nature of this pleasure when they guarantee that the "girls" the users are watching are "first timers," having their "first sexual experience," which, of course, leads to their "first orgasm ever." The Solo Teen site goes so far as to promise, "Here you will ONLY find the cutest teen girls.... Our girls are fresh and inexperienced and very sexy in an innocent kind of way."[10] It is thus no surprise that most of these sites advertise "fresh girls added each week," since using the same performer twice would cut into the sexual excitement of the viewer. How, after all, does one defile an already defiled girl?

The story of "defilement" told on these sites is formulaic in that it almost always starts with an eager but innocent girl who is gently and playfully coaxed by off-camera adult men into sexually performing for the pleasure of the viewer. This is the narrative informing most of the images on the SoloTeengirls.net site, which has hundreds of movies available to members as well as hundreds of still photographs posted on the site as a teaser for nonmembers. Each woman has five photographs and a written text detailing her supposed first sexual experience. For "Natasha" the story goes as follows: "This lil cutie came in pretending that she couldn't wait to be naked in front of the camera. And...we couldn't wait to see her. As she started to take off her clothes and show off she giggled and smiled but we could tell she was nervous and when she found out that naked meant showing of [sic] her snug little teen pussy she blushed! But showing off her pussy proved to be too much of a turn on and when we encouraged her to play with it she could not resist. This beautiful teen girl really did have her first time on camera and we got to watch her stroke that velvety teen pussy."[11] The message that the written text conveys in this story can be found throughout the Web sites in this category, as it embodies the way the pornographers carefully craft a story of who is really innocent and who is really culpable in the scenario. For all the supposed innocence of the "lil cutie," as evidenced by her nervousness, giggling, smiling, and blushing, it really took only a bit of encouragement to get her to masturbate for the camera, which in Pornland language is another way of saying that it didn't take much for her to reveal her inner slut. It is this culpability on the part of the girl that simultaneously frees the user of his culpability in masturbating to what would be, in reality, a scenario of adult men manipulating a naive girl into masturbating for the pleasure of other adult men and themselves.

The Solo Teen sites are a gentle way to introduce the user to PCP since the absence of adult male performers means that the pornographers can construct a story for the user that avoids talking about heterosexual sex with underage girls and instead talks about a hot girl who, on the cusp of discovering her sexuality, needs just a little gentle verbal encouragement to finally take the plunge. The following classification of sites, those that have actual penetrative sex by a man, construct the male performer as both active and visible, and yet still manage to create a narrative that allows the user to believe he is watching consensual, nonexploitive sex.

Type 4: Penetrative sexual activity between adult(s) and child(ren)

The overriding theme of PCP sites that show nonsadistic sexual activity between a "child" and an adult is her supposed loss of virginity, a loss that the user gets to witness in excruciatingly clear detail. With names such as Bloody Virgins, First Time Sex, Real Virgins, and Defloration, these sites make it clear to the user just what he is getting. I have included these sites in the nonsadistic category not because they don't include images of women in pain—many do—but because the sex acts in and of themselves are not of the body-punishing, abusive type that is standard in the more hard-core sites described in the sadistic category below.

The sex depicted in these sites differs markedly from much of the sex on regular porn sites as the adult male displays affection for the female in the form of kissing and caressing. This is a real departure from most porn sex even in feature movies, where there is some perfunctory kissing and touching, but signs of affection give way quickly to the usual mind-numbing penetration of the female's orifices. In these PCP sites the kissing and touching actually last through much of the movie, and rarely is the woman called a slut or a whore. What is also striking to anyone who is familiar with the codes and conventions of Internet porn is that the male actually keeps asking the female, in a tender way, if the sex feels okay or if he is hurting her.

These differences should not be seen as positive steps toward a less violent type of porn; what they actually represent are techniques aimed at authenticating the supposed consensual loss of virginity. On these sites, there is no mention of coercion or even subtle manipulation; the performer is depicted as eager to lose her virginity. Moreover, as the male performer is clearly older and more mature, were he to behave like most men in porn, he would reveal himself to be a violent and manipulative exploiter of underage girls—an image that would destroy the carefully crafted story of him as a tender teacher, gently leading an innocent yet ripe and ready girl through this major rite of passage. On these sites, any type of text, image, or sex act that remotely suggests coercion would situate the user as a co-conspirator in a scenario that could be read as the rape of a minor, a role that many would likely find uncomfortable and that might prevent them from coming back for more.

One site that seems to be popular, judging from its top billing on many of the teen porn Web portals and its constant pop-up advertisement, which appears on other teen porn sites, is Defloration.com. Claiming to be the "first website about virginity since 1998" and promising the user "real acts of defloration," the home page is dominated by a picture of two hands stretching open a vagina so the user can get a clear view of the internal genitalia, which depicts, the site claims, an "intact hymen." Alongside this picture are four smaller images, one of which shows a doll resting on a woman's thigh and a second that shows a lollipop placed inside a stretched vagina. The text by the side of the picture explains what the hymen is: "A mysterious body part that is lost by young girls when they have sexual intercourse for the first time. Few people have ever seen what this fragile object looks like. A girl who has never had sexual intercourse (a virgin) is supposed to have her hymen intact. In many societies, a girl's virginity until marriage is considered a great virtue. For a girl who possesses such chastity, getting married becomes easy."[12] After the pornographers have eroticized the hymen with its "mysterious" quality and "fragile" state, which is "stretched and ruptured by the erect penis," they explain to the user that the "girl" may experience "discomfort and bleeding" during intercourse. For many porn users this is too good an offer to miss as they anticipate seeing something real unfold before them, rather than a staged performance by a "whore."

For $38 a month, the user can access innumerable images on the site, including pages and pages of young-looking women. One can click on a selection of stills or an actual movie, which is split into two seg-ments: "Hymen Performance" and "Losing of Virginity." In the first, a male masturbates the girl, and then stretches her vagina open so the viewer gets a clear internal shot. The second segment is a long and drawn-out documentation of her being penetrated as she is grimacing and often asking her penetrator to be careful since the act is painful. This continues, sometimes for ten to fifteen minutes, until he withdraws his blood-stained penis. The camera lingers on the penis, showing the user clear evidence of the "defloration" before the male performer takes his penis and smears the blood over the buttocks and thighs of the fe-male, an act that mirrors the usual "money shot" in porn in which semen is rubbed all over the woman's body.

On this site and others of this type, the techniques used to childify the women are not so much childhood clothes or props but the actual behavior of the women during sex. To men accustomed to viewing mainstream adult porn, the women in these sites look inexperienced by comparison. In place of the writhing, oiled, voluptuous women who

look like they know exactly what they are doing, these women resemble younger females who are unsure of how to perform sex for
the camera. Their bodies are not arched enough, their moans not throaty
enough, and their movements are awkward, sometimes to the point of
being clumsy. Given the nature of the porn industry, it is unlikely
that these women are acting the part since they are not top-tier porn
performers—just a few of the many thosands of women who move in and
out of the industry at an alarming rate. It is much more likely that what
is being witnessed is not only their first porn movie ever, but much
worse, the first time they have been penetrated vaginally. Indeed, these
women are having the loss of their virginity documented by the
porn industry, to be circulated over and over again for men's masturbatory pleasure.

No matter how much these girls are grimacing, they say they are
enjoying the sex, and moan intermittently as a way to mimic arousal.
This actually reflects what goes on in real child pornography, according
to retired FBI Special Agent Kenneth Lanning.[13] Much of the illegal
child pornography he has investigated indeed shows the child looking somewhat like a willing accomplice, appearing as if she is eagerly
consenting to the experience. Of course this is a lie but one that, Lanning argues, many perpetrators—and indeed sometimes lawyers, social
workers, and police—believe, since they view the image as the truth
rather than as a carefully constructed representation of reality that is
produced with specific goals in mind. In their research on men convicted of downloading child pornography, researchers Ethel Quayle and
Max Taylor found that these men looked for "superficial clues which
allowed the viewer to believe that the children in the pictures were
consenting and enjoyed being photographed." One such user explained
that he was just looking for "images of girls mainly. Girls actually having sex. And they had to look happy. . . . I mean I wasn't looking for rape
or anything."[14]

In the next type of sites to be discussed, those that can be classed
as sadistic, the girls also look like they are enjoying sex, even though in
this category what we are watching is physical, sexual, and verbal abuse
being perpetrated against them.

Type 5: Sadism

The sites that fit the sadism definition fall within the gonzo genre, I argue, because the acts the women endure are sadistic. These PCP sites dispense with any attempt to project the girls as innocent yet ready to be gently introduced into the world of adult sex. These females, while also depicted as new to sex, are portrayed as wanting it as rough and as hard as all the other women in gonzo porn. The site Teen Dirt Bags, for example, boasts that its "slutty girls are taking cock in their fresh unused pussies" so the viewer can see "the cutest little tramps suck, fuck, swallow and beg for more."[15] Mention is often made of how innocent these girls look, but this is described as a ruse, as just below the surface is a raging slut for whom nothing is too painful, demeaning, debasing, or dehumanizing, as is illustrated in the following description of Keri who, according to the text surrounding the images, is "such a sweet young thing, you'd never believe that she has the mind of a pervert! She looks so innocent and prude but don't let her fool you, this little slut is a dirty little whore! Keri demonstrated that as she spread her ass cheeks apart and begged him to drill her tight little ass! He granted her wish and gave her an anal pounding like she never had before!"[16]

The use of so-called teens in gonzo allows the pornographer to layer yet another level of abuse on the already abusive gonzo genre. The physical and emotional immaturity of teens makes space for a whole range of scenarios that heighten and intensify the violence, since they can be easily manipulated into doing just about anything, no matter how painful and cruel. Moreover, their bodies, not yet fully developed, have more potential to be damaged. Not surprisingly, throughout these sites, constant mention is made of the teen's small vagina and anus, but unlike the solo porn sites, the goal here is not to stress her "innocence" but to highlight the damage that will be done to her body when she is penetrated by an adult male's penis. The men's penises are described as being extra large and thus have the power to "break," "rip," "tear," and "split" her not-yet-mature orifices. On the site I Am Eighteen, the reader is invited to "watch us break her tiny body with some hard, pussy-splitting fucking," while over on the Ass Plundering site, the tag line boasts that "we plunder these tight little virgin asses."[17] The level of cruelty depicted in the movies is made apparent by the accompanying text, which promises all kinds of injuries that the user gets to witness, some so severe that the "bitches wouldn't be able to walk for a week after the utter anal demolishing." The site is littered with pictures of "hot, little, innocent girls" with red, raw anuses. While these are standard images in nonteen gonzo, they have greater authenticity when attached to a "teen" or a "virgin" since her body is less able to deal with such violent penetration.

Many of these sites pair the teen with much older men and highlight the age difference in their names—sites such as Old Farts Young Tarts, Old and Young Gang Bang, Old and Young Porn, Old Men Fucking. These older men, some of them in their sixties and seventies, are depicted as using manipulation and trickery to get the teen, who, shown as naive and unsophisticated, is easily fooled. Not content with just eroticizing the age imbalance between the girl and the man, the pornographers throw in the economic inequality that exists between young and older people as a way to provide the male with even more power over her. On one such popular site, aptly named Teens for Cash, the site banner reads: "They're Young, They're Dumb and They'll do Anything for Money." Here, scenario after scenario depicts teens offering to do odd jobs for extra cash, only to be seduced into prostituting themselves by the promise of real money. A typical scenario reads: "Tatiana arrives to give the guy's house a thorough cleaning. However, housekeeping doesn't pay much, so when Dick and Rod offer her cash to clean her carpet Tatiana is all over them. Once she vacuums the dust off their old pussy punishers, Tatiana is the one left cleaning up the mess!"[18] Surrounding the text are images of "Tatiana" gleefully holding money as she is anally, vaginally, and orally penetrated by men who look to be in their sixties at least.

Another scenario that offers much potential for exploitation by the pornographers is the teen girl as babysitter, since here the females are not only younger, but also in the man's home, and in an employer-employee relationship. Given the multiple power imbalances here, it is no surprise that the teen porn genre is full of sites with titles such as Fuck the Babysitter, Drunk Baby Sitter, Gag the Babysitter, Dirty Babysitter, Babysitter Lust, and Banged Babysitter. While the scenarios may differ at the margins, they are all ultimately the same and tell the similar story of a young hot babysitter who is seduced by an older man.

This desire on the part of users to convince themselves that they are masturbating to images of consensual, thrilling sex explains the narrative found in another popular gonzo PCP subgenre, incest porn. Sites that sexualize and legitimize incest run the gamut of possible incestuous pairings (mother and son, sibling and sibling, extended family, and so on) but without doubt, the most common portrayal is of a father and daughter. While it is clear that any sexual relationship between a father and his minor daughter is rape, the sites go to great lengths to provide the user with an alternative framing of father-daughter incest. This is especially clear on the site YoungDaughter, where the first thing on the home page is the following "explanation": "The disapproval of incest, especially between father and daughter, is a classic example of 'projection.' The alleged reason for diasproval [sic] is that incest is the same as sexual abuse, aggression and violence. These are all rational arguments, but they are used to justify an irrational opinion. In fact, most cases of incest have little to do with violence."[19]

Indeed, if these sites are to be believed, then incest is what happens when a seductive and manipulative "daughter" finally gets her reluctant "father" to succumb to her sexual advances. On the site Daddy's Whore, the reader is invited to watch "sexy naughty girls seducing their own fathers" and on My Sexy Daughter, the female performers are defined as "sweet, irresistible angels teasing and tempting their own daddies."[20] The site First Time with Daddy asks the user to "check out forbidden love stories," where sexually curious daughters are eying their fathers' bodies with lust. A typical story line reads: "I have fancied my father for years. I thought it was a perversion and was afraid to reveal my emotions.... Once I saw him in a wet dream. This was a sign. Still half asleep I went into his room and jumped onto his bed."[21] Of course, it doesn't take much to get the father to acquiesce, and surrounding the text are images of the "daughter" being penetrated orally, anally, and vaginally by the "father."

In those stories where the father is seen as the active seducer, the girls are generally only too happy to oblige. Once the sexual "relationship" begins, it is clear that the sex is better than either one could ever have imagined. Even in those occasional stories where the daughter is somewhat afraid, the end result is orgasmic sex. In one story a "daughter" explains that "my mom died 3 years ago. Since then dad never brought home a woman. Soon I started noticing very strange looks he gave me. I was even a little afraid. One evening dad came to my room. I was sitting on my bed. He approached me and…"[22] A sequence of eight images surrounding the text tell the story of a clothed, anxious girl succumbing to the sexual advances of the father and ending up naked and orgasmic on a bed.

What stands out in this story, and indeed in most of the scenarios in these sites, is the absence of a mother to protect the daughter from the father's abuse. Some of the scenarios, such as the one mentioned above, describe her as dead, but most make no reference to a mother at all, thus creating a family scene where the girl is isolated and at the mercy of the perpetrating father. This lack of a mother is actually not unusual in cases of father-daughter incest. Psychologist Judith Herman found in her study that over half the sexually abused girls she interviewed had mothers who were absent from the daily routine of the family dueto ill health or death. Herman describes the fathers in these families as controlling and patriarchal, noting that "as the family providers, they felt they had the right to be nurtured and served at home, if not by their wives, then by their daughters."[23] For some of these fathers, being "nurtured" extended to being sexually serviced by their daughters, who were turned into surrogate wives, even though they were physically and mentally children. Of course, the real-life consequences of such abuse look nothing like the fairy-tale world of incest porn, since these girls all exhibited numerous symptoms consistent with PTSD.

The reduction of the daughter to an object to be used by the father is most stark on the UseMyDaughter.com site (the banner reads: "Want to Fuck My Daughter?"), which tells the story of a drunken father pimping out his daughter to any man who will pay. The images and the sex in the films are standard gonzo porn, but the stories that contextualize the images tell a tale of economic degradation and poverty, with the way out being the prostituting of a daughter. The text (presented here as posted) introducing the site reads:

> Meet my daughter Janessa, she's 19 years old and like her mom, she is so freakin' hot. And its no fucking secret to the world that she loves to fuck. What a fucking slut! i think she got that from her mom. God damn her womb is so polluted. aaanyways. My daughter fucks some stupid guys anywhere she goes. I was like WTF!? for free? Shit! I didn't raise her to get fucked for free! Well, im a bum old, and im always fucking wasted so fuck that, now i let her fuck any guy she wants as long as the guy pays me some cash bucks.... Aww fuck that, why dont you hit join now!!! Watch this slut take cocks for cash in my pockets.[24]

The "daughter," or slut, as the father constantly refers to her, is depicted as an active and willing player in the scenarios, often leaving her father by the roadside as she speeds off with the latest john. The text makes frequent reference to the father's drinking and poverty as a way to minimize his culpability in turning his daughter into a prostitute and also finds a way to put the blame on the absent mother by mentioning her "polluted" womb.

All the sites discussed so far, even the gonzo ones, depict scenarios where the men do not use overt force to get the girl to comply with their sexual demands but rather seduce, manipulate, and cajole the girl into submission. This picture actually mirrors what goes on in the real world of child molestation where most of the victims are subject to a seasoning process in which the perpetrator first seduces the child with gifts, affection, calculated acts of kindness, and offers of friendship and/or mentoring. Having forged a bond, the perpetrator then manipulates and exploits the emotional connection to erode the child's resistance to sexual activity and to ensure the child's silence. For perpetrators, this is a safer way than overt force since it does not leave visible scars, and because it is an act of breaking the child's will, the victim is more likely to keep the abuse hidden for fear of appearing disloyal to the perpetrator. Moreover, the bond acts as a kind of emotional glue for the child, keeping her connected even when the adult is perpetrating awful acts of sexual violence. Pornographers are well aware of this seasoning process since they do an excellent job of depicting it in their movies by showing a whole range of techniques: from gift giving to strategic acts of kindness, where the perpetrator poses as a kind (sexual) mentor. Always brazen, the pornographers constantly use the word "breaking" to refer to what they are doing to the girls, and one site even calls itself Breaking Them In.

Probably the most detailed, graphic, and violent example of PCP porn that acts as an instructional manual on how to break a girl is the Cherry Poppers series, produced and directed by Max Hardcore. During a scene from *Cherry Poppers*, volume 10, Hardcore, on finding the younger sister of his girlfriend alone in her house, proceeds to show her "what boys like" and warns her not to tell her sister what happened because "she'll get mad."[25]

Hardcore begins by showing the girl how to fondle his penis, instructing her to "give it a little kiss, don't be afraid to suck it. Just like a sucker, just like a lollipop." He continues to instruct her in a soft, gentle voice. She removes her clothes and continues to perform fellatio on him; "Take a deep breath," he tells her, taking his penis out of this mouth at times to let her breathe. He also shows her how to produce enough saliva to make the oral sex pleasurable for him. After Hardcore puts her on the sink and shaves her pubic area, he penetrates her with his fingers before vaginal intercourse, something rapists of girls often find necessary in order to stretch the child's vagina so that it won't be torn or ruptured by an adult penis. He then does the same with her anus. Throughout the sexual activity, Hardcore alternates gentle talk of her being a "good girl" with rougher reminders that she is a cunt. "Say it," he demands, yelling, and she repeats, not looking at him, "I'm a little cunt."[26] This alternating between being gentle and being abusive goes on throughout the film, and is a strategy pedophiles use to terrify, seduce, and confuse the victim. The very last scene is Max Hardcore taking a picture of the naked and semen-covered girl, as she smiles for the camera.

This is a very telling scene, since studies show that in the real world many child molesters take pictures of their victims to document the abuse for several reasons: (1) to use for their own or other men's future masturbation; (2) to blackmail the child into silence as they threaten to show the photos to family and friends if the child reveals the abuse; and (3) to show future victims how to perform sex. Max Hardcore's behavior in Cherry Poppers resembles some of the behaviors discussed by Ken Lanning in his exhaustive study of child molesters, and man watching him may find pointers on how to season a child.

Cherry Poppers, and indeed all the other sites mentioned, is carefully crafted to give the user a sense that the girls depicted are indeed girls and not women. How these images play out in the real world has yet to be researched, since these sites have not been the focus of empirical analysis. What we can explore, however, is how these sites may act as socializing agents for their users by constructing a particular set of ideologies that normalize children as legitimate sexual partners for adult men.

IMAGES AND IDEOLOGY: THE WORLD ACCORDING TO PCP

Once he clicks on these sites, the user is bombarded, through images and words, with an internally consistent ideology that legitimizes, condones, and celebrates a sexual desire for children. The norms and values that circulate in society, which define adult-child sex as deviant and abusive, are wholly absent in PCP, and in their place is the message that sex with children is hot fun for all. As the user clicks on the PCP sites, he enters a virtual community that welcomes him in through constant use of the word "we," rather than the singular "I" or "you." Through the use of "we," it seems to the user that he gets to participate in a ready-made group of like-minded men who actually know him so well they can anticipate his likes and needs, as is shown in the teaser for MySexyDaughter.com: "We know you enjoy rough and bewildering incest action, so we have a very special thing for you."[27]

For those men whose primary sexual interest is children, PCP is an obvious first step into the world of child pornography since it is a relatively safe way to access images that can be used for masturbatory purposes. With their use of uninitiated porn performers who look young, the strategic placing of childhood props, and a written text that highlights and sexualizes the girl's supposed child status, the PCP sites are a workable substitute for those men not yet ready to break the law and open themselves up to possible prison time, not to mention the stigma of being caught with such material. This "community" the user has found by typing into Google a collection of words that speak to his most secret sexual desires plays an important role in validating his feelings and desires, as the sites constantly highlight just how much the object of his lust enjoys the sex.[28] For these men PCP sites can be seen as a kind of low-stakes primer nudging, encouraging, and in a way seducing them into joining the club with promises of community, friendship, and understanding—the very things that a nascent pedophile may lack the most. In a perverse way, the sites are seasoning the would-be user in much the same way a professional predator seasons his prey, since they first find out what the mark lacks and then tease and manipulate him into compliance with the promise of fulfilling these deeply felt needs.

Sometime these sites reel in the user by tossing out a challenge to his masculinity, a sure way to get most porn users to bite. Nowhere is this clearer than on the animated incest site that tells men that incest is "an amazing way of learning about yourself and your dearest people!" But then the site tells the user that if "he is not yet brave enough to try," then the next best thing is "our hand-drawn group incest stories based on totally crazy things real people tried."[29] The implicit question here is: are you man enough to take the first step and masturbate to images that are truly so deviant and transgressive that it takes someone really brave to do the real thing?

While these PCP sites may satisfy the user for a time, desensitization eventually leads to boredom and the need for harder-core and more extreme porn. The obvious next place to go is real child pornography, since here a real child is used and the truly illegal and hence secretive nature of the porn is only going to add an even greater erotic thrill for the, by now, somewhat desensitized user. Quayle and Taylor found in their study of men convicted of downloading child pornography that even the real thing becomes boring after a while, with men seeking out more overtly violent images involving younger and younger children.[30] While this descent into utterly abusive and violent child porn is not a given for PCP users, these sites can only serve to whet their appetite for more images of real child pornography since they will always fall short of delivering on their promise of watching a real child turned into a "whore."

But what about men who are not looking for a substitute to the real thing but rather prefer to have sex with adult women and yet masturbate to the PCP sites? It is clear from the sheer volume of traffic being generated on these sites that such men must be visiting them. Why would they go to these sites rather than the thousands of others devoted to adult on adult sex? The answer is the same for these men as it is for pedophiles: desensitization. Journalist Pamela Paul found that many of the men she interviewed had quickly become desensitized. Many expressed shock at just how rapidly their viewing preferences had turned to increasingly violent and bizarre porn genres—genres that they had previously found distasteful but now actively sought out.[31] Many of these genres featured adult women—in scenes of urinating, bestiality, or heavy bondage—but for some men, children became the object of their sexual desire. David G. Heffler, a psychotherapist who counsels child pornography offenders, was recently quoted as saying that in his clinical work he has had many men who revealed that "after looking at adult porn a long time, they get bored. They want something different. They start looking at children. Then, they can't get enough of it."[32]

This slide from adult to child pornography flies in the face of conventional wisdom, as we tend to think of men who are sexually aroused by children as pedophiles who form a distinct and separate group from other men by virtue of their deviant sexual interests and behavior. However, after a thorough analysis of the empirical literature, feminist sociologists Diana Russell and Natalie J. Purcell argue that the research on pedophiles does not point to a model of two clearly defined groups (pedophiles and nonpedophiles); rather, there is a continuum: some men are clearly situated at either end, but others are scattered at various points. Furthermore, men's position along the continuum is subject to shifts, depending on the particular constellation of their life experiences at any one time.[33] Russell and Purcell note that although in the past, researchers pointed to unusual life experiences, such as the loss of a spouse, substance abuse, and unemployment, as contributory factors, recent studies suggest that ongoing use of pornography is increasingly playing a role in shifting men along the continuum.

In a March 2008 interview I conducted with seven men in a Connecticut prison who were incarcerated for downloading child pornography (and in three cases, for sexually abusing a child), not one of them fitted the definition of a pedophile. All seven told me that they preferred sex with an adult woman, but had become bored with regular pornography. Five of them had looked at PCP sites first and then moved into actual child porn. This backs up Russell and Purcell's claim that for pedophiles and nonpedophiles alike, PCP sites "can serve as a bridge between adult pornography and child pornography."[34] Since there are currently no large-scale empirical studies available on this, it is impossible to point to any findings, but if Russell and Purcell are correct, and the anecdotal evidence suggests that they are, then the continued and increasing popularity of PCP will have devastating implications for child sexual abuse. First, the demand for real child pornography will increase, which will mean a greater number of children being abused for the purpose of production, and second, a greater number of children will be at risk of being sexually abused by men who use the pornography as a stepping-stone to contact sex with a child.

The research on the relationship between consuming pornography and actual contact sex with a child suggests that there are a percentage of men who will act out their desires on real children after viewing child porn. Quayle and Taylor found in their study of convicted child offenders that "for some respondents, pornography was used as a substitute for actual offending, whereas for others, it acted as both blueprint and stimulus for contact offense."[35] While the actual percentage of child porn users who also sexually victimize children varies from study to study, with some putting the number as low as 40 percent, and others as high as 85 percent,[36] the weight of the evidence is that masturbation to images of sexualized children is, for a significant proportion of men, linked to actual child sexual abuse. A government study conducted in 2007 of convicted child pornography offenders found that 85 percent of men convicted of downloading child pornography had committed acts of sexual abuse against minors, from inappropriate touching to rape.[37]

An article detailing the findings was submitted to the *Journal of Family Violence*, and then pulled by the Federal Bureau of Prisons. According to an article in the *New York Times*, many experts in the field are angry that the findings have been suppressed.[38]

In addition to the psychological literature on the effects of child pornography on individual men's behaviors and attitudes, we know from the research conducted within media studies that people construct their notions of reality from the media they consume, and the more consistent and coherent the message, the more people believe it to be true.[39] Thus, the images of girls in PCP do not operate within a social vacuum; rather, they are produced and consumed within a society where the dominant pop culture images are of childified women, adultified children, and hypersexualized youthful female bodies.

Over the years there has been a shift in mainstream society regarding the way girls look. Girls' clothes now mimic sexualized clothes for women to such a degree that communications scholar Mardia Bishop argues that "the majority of clothing available for elementary school girls at the local suburban mall is from the porn industry, which I call 'porn' fashion."[40] Wearing thongs, low-slung jeans, short skirts, and midriff-revealing tops, these girls now appear "hot." Chris, one of the men in the Connecticut prison I interviewed, told me that he had stopped going to the mall because "looking at the girls aroused me and I couldn't stop looking at them." To this Greg added: "I do respond to the sexuality of their dress that they don't even know they're projecting." Both of these men were talking about prepubescent girls.

This cultural shift toward sexualizing girls from an early age is bound to have real social consequences. Not only does it affect the way girls see themselves, it also chips away at the norms that define children as off-limits to male sexual use. The more we undermine such cultural norms, the more we drag girls into the category of "woman," and in a porn-saturated world, to be woman is often to be a sexual object deserving of male contempt, use, and abuse.

Fighting Back

Ironically, pornography has become almost invisible by virtue of its very ubiquity. It seeps into our lives, identities, and relationships. We are so steeped in the pornographic mindset that it is difficult to imagine what a world without porn would look like. It is affecting our girls and boys, as both are growing up with porn encoded into their gender and sexual identities. I opened this book by stating that we are in the midst of a massive social experiment, and nobody really knows how living in Porn-land will shape our culture. What we do know is that we are surrounded by images that degrade and debase women and that for this the entire culture pays a price.

What can we do about the porning of our culture? I wish I had a magic bullet but I don't; we are up against an economic juggernaut. Fighting the porn industry demands that we resist both as individuals and as part of a collective movement. At the moment, most resistance happens at the individual level, and this is a promising start. I meet young women who refuse to date men who are users of porn, parents who teach their children media literacy skills, teachers who develop sophisticated sex-education programs, and men who boycott porn because of the ways it affects their sexuality. Absent a wider social movement, these individual forms of resistance make the most sense.

The pressing question, then, is how to unite these individual acts of resistance into a movement. In 2007, I helped form the group Stop Porn Culture (SPC), whose goal is to educate the public about the nature and effects of porn. SPC consists of activists, academics, teachers, anti-violence experts, parents, and students. The major educational tools we currently use are two slide shows. The first one—*Who Wants to Be a Porn Star?*—I cowrote with Rebecca Whisnant and Robert Jensen. The show comes with a fifty-minute script and over one hundred slides and covers many of the main points made in this book; it introduces people to the concept of a porn culture as well as showing the content of the contemporary porn industry. This show is now being given across the country (as well as in Canada, Scotland, and England) in colleges, anti-violence groups, student groups, and community centers. The slide show is an effective tool for raising people's consciousness and can be obtained free of charge from Stop Porn Culture (stoppornculture@gmail.com).

The second slide show—*Growing Up in a Porn Culture*, written by Rebecca Whisnant—focuses on how the porn culture harms children and youth. Geared toward parents, teachers, and anyone who works with children and youth, this show not only explores the media world of young people, but it also offers advice on how to talk to this age group about the hypersexualized culture we live in. This show can also be obtained free of charge from SPC. On the SPC Web site are links to other feminist anti-porn sites, readings, videos, and resources. Twice a year SPC runs a seminar and training workshop for those who want to learn more about the topic or receive training on how to present the slide show in public venues. Information can be found at http://stop pornculture.org/home.html.

Movements typically begin small, and grassroots education is one way to build an effective vehicle for change. But this movement can't only be about what's wrong with the world. It also needs to offer a mobilizing vision that will excite and entice people to join. We need to offer an alternative way of being, a way to envisage a sexuality that is based on equality, dignity, and respect. Part of this inevitably means organizing against the commodification of human needs and desires. Women and men must throw these industrial images out of our bedrooms and our heads so that we can develop a way of being sexual that does not dictate conformity to the plasticized, generic, and formulaic sex on offer in a porn culture. Such a sexuality cannot be scripted by a movement because it belongs to individuals and reflects who they are and what they want sexually.

A movement that resists the porn culture needs to include men as they, too, are being dehumanized and diminished by the images they consume. Men's refusal to collaborate with the pornographers will not only undermine the legitimacy of the industry, it will also drain it of its profits. For too long women have been the only ones fighting this predatory industry, even though we have long argued that porn also hurts men. What resistance to porn offers men is a sexuality that celebrates connectedness, intimacy, and empathy—a sexuality bathed in equality rather than subordination.

A sexuality based on equality ultimately requires a society that is based on equality. While we fight for a way to define our own sexuality, we must not lose sight of the bigger picture: women still face economic, political, and legal discrimination. Porn is embedded in this wider structure, as nowhere is the practice of inequality so starkly obvious. In porn we are one-dimensional objects who want nothing more than porn sex. What we actually want is equality in all areas of our lives so that we no longer have to fear erasure, poverty, loss of reproductive rights, or men's violence against us. As long as we have porn, we will never be seen as full human beings deserving of all the rights that men have. This is why we need to build a vibrant movement that fights for a world where women have power in and over their lives—because in a just society, there is no room for porn.

ACKNOWLEDGMENTS

This book has been many years in the making and could not have been written without my students. They have generously shared stories, insights, and ideas, helping me to navigate the pop culture world of young adults. Along the way, I have had some great research assistants and would like to give special mention to Amy Beth DiMasi, Dana Bialer, and Megan Byra for their excellent work. Wheelock College, always a place of support, helped to fund this project. Thanks to two great editors, Gayatri Patnaik and Joanna Green, for all their work and skill. Janina Fisher's support throughout the project cannot be measured. I am especially indebted to Diane Levin, Leslie Lebowitz, Jackson Katz, Rebecca Whisnant, Lierre Keith, and, of course, Rhea Becker for offering insights, advice, and, when needed, comfort. My sister Ruth deserves a special mention: she is a true sister in every sense of the word. Researching and writing about porn is not easy, and over the years a number of people have become my support system. For over fifteen years I have had Robert Jensen as a friend and coauthor. His knowledge and understanding of the topic have greatly enriched my thinking and his humor keeps me sane when the porn seems too much. My son, T, makes my world joyful. And to David, the person who has been by my side my entire adult life, thank you for all that you are.

Introduction

1. Quoted in Betsy Schiffman, "Turns Out Porn Isn't Recession-Proof," July 21, 2008, http://blog.wired.com/business/2008/07/turns-out-por-1.html (accessed January 2, 2009).

2. I refer to the user in the masculine since the majority of porn consumers are men. While it is impossible to give an accurate breakdown of male and female consumers, Mark Kernes, senior editor of the pornography trade magazine *Adult Video News*, stated, "Our statistics show that 78% of the people that go into adult stores are men. They may have women with them, but it's men, and 22%, conversely, is women or women with other women or women alone." Mark Kernes, interview with Robert Jensen at the Adult Entertainment Expo in Las Vegas, January 7, 2005. In my January 2008 interviews with porn producers at the Adult Entertainment Expo in Las Vegas, I was told that that the market for gonzo is almost always men.

3. "How Internet Porn Is Changing Teen Sex," *Details*, n.d., http://men.style.com/details/features/full?id=content_10357 (accessed September 12, 2009).

4. I did not look at gay porn as it has its own specific representational codes and conventions.

5. Some of the sites asked for age verification, but all this required was clicking on the "I am over 18" button.

6. http://www.gagmethenfuckme.com/index.htm?id=leonxm (accessed June 12, 2007).

7. http://www.gagfactor.com/videopreview- scarlett.html (accessed May 23, 2007).

8. http://tour.analsuffering.com/home.html?nats=NoAdvert:revs:AS,0,0 ,0,0 (accessed June 12, 2007).

9. http://www.talkingblue.com/DVD/124371D1_Anally_Ripped_Whores _dvd.htm (accessed June 12, 2007).

10. Although there are many parents working hard to protect their children from porn, given its ubiquity, it is almost impossible to avoid. The Internet filters are becoming increasingly sophisticated, but I have heard from parents that their computer-savvy child can easily disable them. More important, parents cannot monitor their children twenty-four hours a day because they use computers at friends' homes and libraries. The much bigger issue here is that to put the responsibility on parents is to ignore the role that culture plays in socializing children.

11. http://internet-filter-review.toptenreviews.com/internet-pornography -statistics.html (accessed April 4, 2008).

12. Robert J. Wosnitzer and Ana J. Bridges, "Aggression and Sexual Behavior in Best-Selling Pornography: A Content Analysis Update" (paper presented at the Fifty-seventh Annual Meeting of the International Communication Association, San Francisco, May 24–28, 2007).

13. Ibid.

14. Holly Randall, "Pushing the Envelope." *XBIZ*, October 25, 2008, http:// www.xbiz.com/articles/100930 (accessed February 9, 2009).

15. The term *gonzo* comes from the type of journalism pioneered by Hunter S. Thompson wherein the journalist actually places him- or herself in the story. According to P. Weasels, "the purest definition of gonzo is filmmaking in which the camerawork is a representation of the cameraman's senses, and in which the camera is an acknowledged participant in the scene; the person behind the camera does not necessarily have to participate in the sex, but often does." Today, the term is used by the industry also to describe the more hard-core porn discussed in this book. See P. Weasels, "The Quick and Dirty Guide to Gonzo," n.d., http:// www.gamelink.com/news.jhtml?news_id=news_nt_101_gonzo (accessed March 2, 2009).

16. "The Directors," *Adult Video News*, August 2005, http://www.avn.com/ video/articles/22629.html (accessed August 23, 2008).

17. Robert J. Stroller and I. S. Levine, *Coming Attractions: The Making of an*

X-Rated Video (New Haven, CT: Yale University Press), quoted in Robert Jensen, *Getting Off: Pornography and the End of Masculinity* (Boston: South End, 2007), 69.

18. This discussion board offers insight into porn fans as they regularly dialogue with each other. Although some posts could well have been planted by the industry to market a specific product, the sheer volume of posts suggests that this is an authentic porn discussion group.

19. Adult DVD Talk, July 12, 2007, http://forum.adultdvdtalk.com/forum/ topic.dlt/topic_id=104388/forum_id=1/cat_id=1/104388.htm (accessed April 10, 2009).

20. Adult DVD Talk, May 22, 2007, http://forum.adultdvdtalk.com/forum/ topic.dlt/topic_id=101587/forum_id=1/cat_id=1/101587.htm (accessed April 10, 2009).

21. Adult DVD Talk, May 23, 2007, http://forum.adultdvdtalk.com/forum/ topic.dlt/topic_id=101587/forum_id=1/cat_id=1/101587.htm (accessed April 10, 2009).

22. Martin Amis, "A Rough Trade," *Guardian*, March 17, 2001, http://www .guardian.co.uk/Archive/Article/0,4273,4153718,00.html (accessed September 8, 2008).

23. Erik Jay, "Gonzo: Taking a Toll," *XBIZ News*, September 10, 2007, http:// xbiz.com/articles/83870 (accessed March 2, 2008).

24. The Adult Industry Medical (AIM) Health Care Foundation, founded in 1998 by Dr. Sharon Mitchell, is, according to its Web site, "a non-profit corporation formed to care for the physical and emotional needs of sex workers and people who work in the adult entertainment industry." The organization provides HIV and STD testing and treatment, counseling services, and support groups. For more information, see http://www.aim-med.org/about/.

One: *Playboy, Penthouse,* and *Hustler*

1. Pornography is defined here as any product that is produced for the primary purpose of facilitating arousal and masturbation. While there may be other uses for the product (for example, *Playboy* as a magazine to teach men how to live a playboy lifestyle), its main selling feature for the producer, distributor, and consumer (whether overtly or covertly) is sexual arousal.

2. Thomas Weyr, *Reaching for Paradise: The Playboy Vision of America* (New York: Times Books, 1978).

3. Michael Kimmel, *Manhood in America: A Cultural History* (New York: Free Press, 1996), 255. Some of the books on the subject are Frank Brady, *Hefner* (New

York: Macmillan, 1974); Russell Miller, *Bunny: The Real Story of Playboy* (London: Michael Joseph, 1984); Barbara Ehrenreich, *Hearts of Men* (New York: Anchor, 1983).

4. Stephanie Coontz, *The Way We Never Were: American Families and the Nostalgia Trap* (New York: Basic Books, 1992); Elaine Taylor May, *Homeward Bound: American Families in the Cold War Era* (New York: Basic Books, 1998); Douglas Miller and Marion Nowak, *The Fifties: The Way We Really Were* (Garden City, NY: Doubleday, 1977).

5. Miller, *Bunny*, 44.

6. Coontz, *The Way We Never Were*, 24.

7. Quoted in Miller and Nowak, *The Fifties*, 154.

8. Ibid.

9. Coontz, *The Way We Never Were*, 33.

10. Ehrenreich, *Hearts of Men*, 30.

11. Kimmel, *Manhood in America*, 240.

12. Ehrenreich, *Hearts of Men*, 36.

13. Miller and Nowak, *The Fifties*, 164–67.

14. Philip Wylie, *Generation of Vipers* (New York: Rinehart, 1942), 99, quoted in Kimmel, *Manhood in America*, 254.

15. *Playboy*, December 1953, 16.

16. Quoted in Ehrenreich, *Hearts of Men*, 47.

17. *Playboy*, September 1958, 78.

18. *Playboy*, September 1963, 92.

19. *Playboy*, June 1954, 38.

20. Weyr, *Reaching for Paradise*, 2.

21. Naomi Barko, "A Woman Looks at Men's Magazines," *Reporter*, July 7, 1953, 29–32.

22. Ibid., 30.

23. Weyr, *Reaching for Paradise*, 5.

24. Ibid., 34.

25. The original name for the magazine was *Stag Party*, but shortly before the publication date, Hefner received a letter from a lawyer representing a field-and-stream magazine called *Stag* saying that there could be possible confusion between the two magazines. Hefner agreed to change the name, and *Playboy* was born. Miller, *Bunny*, 42–44.

26. Ibid., 39.

27. Ibid., 44–45.

28. Quoted in Weyr, *Reaching for Paradise*, 35.

29. Weyr, *Reaching for Paradise*, 43.

30. *Playboy*, December 1953, 41.

31. *Playboy*, January 1954, 4.

32. George Lipsitz, *Time Passages: Collective Memory and American Popular Culture* (Minneapolis: University of Minnesota Press, 1990), 44.

33. Dichter, quoted in ibid., 47.

34. May, *Homeward Bound*, 29–32.

35. Weyr, *Reaching for Paradise*, 55.

36. Brady, *Hefner*, 95.

37. Weyr, *Reaching for Paradise*, 32.

38. *Business Week*, June 28, 1969.

39. Weyr, *Reaching for Paradise*.

40. Quoted in Brady, *Hefner*, 128.

41. Ibid., 129.

42. Miller, *Bunny*, 182.

43. *Newsweek*, March 2, 1970, 71.

44. Miller, *Bunny*, 189.

45. *Forbes*, March 1, 1971, 19; *Business Week*, August 9, 1969, 98; *Time*, November 7, 1969, 88.

46. *Newsweek*, March 2, 1970, 71; *Time*, November 7, 1969, 88.

47. Miller, *Bunny*, 194.

48. Ibid.

49. *Playboy* Advertising Rate Card #44, n.d.

50. *Hustler*, 1984, 7.

51. *Hustler*, 1974, 4.

52. *Hustler*, 1983, 5; *Hustler*, 1988, 5.

53. *Hustler*, July 1988, 7.

54. *Newsweek*, February 16, 1976, 69.

55. Ellen McCracken, *Decoding Women's Magazines: From Mademoiselle to Ms.* (New York: St. Martin's, 1993), 15.

56. *Playboy* Demographic Profile, Fall 1995.

57. *Hustler* Reader Profile, Fall 1995.

58. *Newsweek*, March 20, 1978, 36; *Time*, March 20, 1978, 20.

59. Laura Kipnis, "(Male) Desire and (Female) Disgust: Reading *Hustler*," in *Cultural Studies*, ed. Larry Grossberg, C. Nelson, and P. Treichler (New York: Routledge, 1992), 378.

60. *Hustler* Reader Profile, Fall 1995.

61. *Newsweek*, January 1964, 48; *Saturday Evening Post*, April 28, 1962, 28; *Forbes*, March 3, 1971, 18.

62. *Forbes*, March 3, 1971, 18., 17.

63. *Time*, March 3, 1967, 76; *Newsweek*, January 6, 1964, 48.

64. *Time*, March 20, 1978.

65. *People*, August 2, 1993, 92.

66. *Newsweek*, January 14, 1983, 16; *Time*, March 20, 1978, 20.

67. *People*, July 20, 1987, 32.

68. Dirk Smillie, "Dangerous Curves," *Forbes*, April 7, 2008, http://www
.forbes.com/forbes/2008/0407/056_print.html (accessed October 2, 2008).

69. "Penthouse Owner Sued by Guccione," *South Florida Business Journal*,
February 24, 2006, http://southflorida.bizjournals.com/southflorida/stories/
2006/02/27/story3.html (accessed March 6, 2008).

70. Smillie, "Dangerous Curves."

71. Jennifer Ordoñez, "*Penthouse* Gets Pious," *Newsweek*, May 19, 2008, 47.

72. Ibid.

73. Smillie, "Dangerous Curves."

74. Xeni Jardin, "Life, Liberty, and Pursuit of Porn," February 19, 2004,
http://www.wired.com/politics/security/news/2004/02/62343?currentPage=all
(accessed March 24, 2009).

75. Stuart Miller, "Risqué Business," *Multichannel News*, June 16, 2008,
12–17.

76. Ibid.

77. Steven J. Dubner, "Chris Napolitano on George Bush, the State of Porn,
and Why *Playboy* Is Still Hot," *New York Times*, August 27, 2007, http://freak
onomics.blogs.nytimes.com/2007/08/27/chris-napolitano-on-george-bush-the
-state-of-porn-and-why-playboy-doesnt-suck/?ex=1188878400&en=8e13af140
c83037e&ei=5070&emc=eta1 (accessed March 9, 2009).

78. Izabella St. James, *Bunny Tales* (New York: Running Press, 2008),
158.

Two: Pop Goes the Porn Culture

1. Reed Johnson, "Porn Stars Are the New Crossover Artists," *Los Angeles
Times*, November 3, 2008, http://www.latimes.com/entertainment/news/la-et
-porn3-2008nov03,0,6573308.story (accessed November 6, 2008).

2. This image has recently been somewhat tarnished as Francis is facing a
slew of legal problems ranging from using underage girls to tax evasion. See
Richard Verrier, "Tax Evasion Charges Add to Francis' Legal Woes," *Los Angeles
Times*, April 12, 2007, http://articles.latimes.com/2007/apr/12/business/fi-girls12
(accessed March 5, 2009).

3. Claire Hoffman, "'Baby, Give Me a Kiss'—The Man Behind the 'Girls

Gone Wild' Soft-Porn Empire Lets Claire Hoffman into His World, for Better or Worse," *Los Angeles Times*, August 6, 2006, http://www.latimes.com/features/magazine/west/la-tm-gonewild32aug06,0,2664370.story (accessed October 5, 2007).

4. "*Girls Gone Wild* Helps Shape America," PR Newswire, March 29, 2007, http://www.prnewswire.com/cgi-bin/stories.pl?ACCT=109&STORY=/www/story/03-29-2007/0004556380&EDATE= (accessed June 28, 2007).

5. Gretchen Gallen, "*Girls Gone Wild* Affiliate Program Makes Debut," *XBIZ*, February 2, 2006, http://xbiz.com/news_piece.php?cat=2&id=13236 (accessed June 24, 2007).

6. http://members.girlsgonewild.com/bonus (accessed April 24, 2007).

7. http://www.adultcon.com/indexa.html (accessed April 24, 2007).

8. David Sullivan, "IVD Throws *Girls Gone Wild* Bellagio Bash," *Adult Video News*, n.d., http://www.avn.com/index_cache.php?Primary_Navigation=Articles&Action=View_Article&Content_ID=281697 (accessed June 2, 2007).

9. Gallen, "*Girls Gone Wild* Affiliate Program Makes Debut."

10. Stephen Ochs, "Joe Francis," *XBIZ*, September 1, 2005, http://www.xbiz.com/articles/80073/girls+gone+wild (accessed January 23, 2009).

11. Vicki Mayer has pointed out that, on a televised talk show, the producers call themselves "a documentary film company." Vicki Mayer, "Soft-Core in TV Time: The Political Economy of a 'Cultural Trend,'" *Critical Studies in Media Communication* 22, no. 4 (2005): 302–20.

12. M. Navarro, "The Very Long Legs of 'Girls Gone Wild,'" *New York Times*, April 4, 2004, sec. 9.

13. Ariel Levy, *Female Chauvinist Pigs* (New York: Free Press, 2005), 12.

14. The hip-hop artist Snoop Dog teamed up with Joe Francis in 2002 to make *Girls Gone Wild: Doggy Style*. One year later Snoop Dog cut ties with Francis because of the lack of black women in *GGW*.

15. E. Maticka-Tyndale, E. S. Herold, and D. Mewhinney, "Casual Sex on Spring Break: Intentions and Behaviors of Canadian Students," *Journal of Sex Research* 35, no. 3 (1998): 254–64, quoted in Karen Pitcher, "The Staging of Agency in *Girls Gone Wild*," *Critical Studies in Media Communication* 23, no. 3 (2006): 204.

16. Matthew Miller, "The (Porn) Player," *Forbes*, July 4, 2005, http://www.forbes.com/forbes/2005/0704/124.html (accessed January 24, 2007).

17. "'I Chose the Right Profession': Porn Star's New Book Tells of Rise to Fame," August 27, 2004, http://www.cnn.com/2004/SHOWBIZ/books/08/27/jenna.jameson (accessed March 6, 2009).

18. Jenna Jameson, interview by Judith Regan, n.d., http://www.youtube.com/watch?v=MSzAdntX1As (accessed February 24, 2009).

19. Jenna Jameson, *How to Make Love Like a Porn Star* (New York: Harper Collins), 96–97.

20. Ibid., 67.

21. Ibid., 132.

22. Adult DVD Talk, February 27, 2008, http://forum.adultdvdtalk.com/forum/topic.dlt/whichpage=3/topic_id=114797/forum_id=1/cat_id=1/reply=1270099#post1270099 (accessed March 3, 2009).

23. Adult DVD Talk, September 11, 2008, http://forum.adultdvdtalk.com/forum/topic.dlt/topic_id=125602/forum_id=1/cat_id=1/125602.htm#post0 (accessed March 3, 2009).

24. Adult DVD Talk, January 19, 2007, http://forum.adultdvdtalk.com/forum/topic.dlt/topic_id=115100/forum_id=5/cat_id=1/reply=1206931#post1206931 (accessed March 3, 2009).

25. Adult DVD Talk, January 20, 2008, http://forum.adultdvdtalk.com/forum/topic.dlt/topic_id=115100/forum_id=5/cat_id=1/reply=1206931#post1206931 (accessed March 30, 2009). Chatsworth in Los Angeles is often considered the center of the American porn industry, with companies such as Wicked Pictures, Anabolic Video, and Adult Video News located in the area.

26. According to porn producer and performer Annie Cruz, women make $1,200 for a double penetration scene, $1,300 for multiple penetration by three guys, and $1,500 for double anal. Quoted in *Price of Pleasure: Pornography, Sexuality and Relationships* (Northampton, MA: Media Education Foundation, 2007).

27. Bob Preston, "Sasha Grey Stars in New Ad for American Apparel," *XBIZ*, December 30, 2008, http://www.xbiz.com/news/103170 (accessed March 23, 2009).

28. *Adult Video News*, n.d., http://www.avn.com/performer/companies/830.html (accessed March 4, 2009).

29. Ann Riley Katz, "Family Guy: Steve Hirsch Followed in His Dad's Footsteps by Launching His Own Adult Film Company, Now the Leader in a Very Mainstream Business," *Los Angeles Business Journal*, November 12, 2007, 29.

30. "MSNBC's Rita Cosby Delves into Vivid Valley," *Adult Video News*, December 15, 2005, http://www.avn.com/index.cfm?objectID=70F9F731-B1EE-818D-931BEAF17B36C7C6&articleID=EDA39917-1372-4B41-C477FEEB259C7491 (accessed January 16, 2006).

31. Kathy Brewer, "The Digital Divide," *Adult Video News*, January 3, 2008, http://online.avn.com/articles/1499.html (accessed January 7, 2008).

32. *Dreamworlds 3* (Northampton, MA: Media Education Foundation, 2007).

33. Quoted in Matt Ezzell, "Pornography, Lad Mags, Video Games and Boys: Reviving the Canary in the Cultural Coal Mine," in *The Sexualization of Childhood*, ed. Sharna Olfman (Westport, CT: Praeger, 2009), 16–17.

34. Laramie D. Taylor, "All for Him: Articles about Sex in American Lad Magazines," *Sex Roles* 52, nos. 3–4 (2005): 153–63.

35. Ibid., 162.

36. Ezzell, "Pornography," 18.

37. Thomas Stanton, "*Denver Post* Reports on Mainstreaming of Adult," *Adult Video News*, July 10, 2006, http://www.avn.com/video/articles/27570.html (accessed April 12, 2007).

38. Jackson Katz, *The Macho Paradox* (Naperville, IL: Sourcebooks, 2006), 173.

Three: From the Backstreet to Wall Street

1. http://internet-filter-review.toptenreviews.com/internet-pornography-statistics.html#anchor1 (accessed March 20, 2009).

2. *Brandweek*, October 2000, 41, 1Q48.

3. Jonathan Coopersmith, "Does Your Mother Know What You Really Do? The Changing Nature and Image of Computer-Based Pornography," *History and Technology* 22, no. 1 (2006): 1–25.

4. Sinead Carew, "Porn to Spice Up Cell Phones," January 30, 2008, http://www.reuters.com/article/technologyNews/idUSN3030000720080130 (accessed February 21, 2009).

5. Blaise Cronin and Elisabeth Davenport, "E-rogenous Zones: Positioning Pornography in the Digital Economy," *Information Society* 17 (2001): 41.

6. Coopersmith, "Does Your Mother Know What You Really Do?" 6.

7. Ibid., 7.

8. Amanda Spink and Bernard J. Jansen, *Web Search: Public Searching of the Web* (New York: Springer, 2004), quoted in Coopersmith, "Does Your Mother Know What You Really Do?" 7.

9. Ibid., 8–9.

10. Ibid., 12.

11. Joel Johnson, "Real Touch: Interactive Sex Device Syncs Porn with Belt-Driven USB Orifice (Yay!)," *Boing Boing*, January 12, 2009, http://gadgets.boingboing.net/2009/01/12/real-touch-interacti.html (accessed March 21, 2009).

12. http://www.adultvest.com/index.php (accessed March 23, 2009).

13. Stephen Yagielowicz, "The State of the Industry," *XBIZ*, March 20, 2009, http://www.xbiz.com/articles/106157/ (accessed March 23, 2009).

14. Alex Henderson, "Making Bank," *XBIZ*, April 16, 2007, http://www.xbiz.com/articles/22392/steve+Hirsch (accessed March 20, 2009).

15. Ibid.

16. Ibid.

17. Ibid.

18. Cronin and Davenport, "E-rogenous Zones," 42.

19. "Pink Visual Launches New Mainstream-Friendly Promo Site PVExposed.com," January 20, 2009, http://www.reuters.com/article/pressRelease/id US200142+20-Jan-2009+MW20090120 (accessed April 2, 2009).

20. Coopersmith, "Does Your Mother Know What You Really Do?" 12.

21. Joel Russell, "Brand-New Skin: Publicist Brian Gross Helps Adult Stars, Companies Establish Mainstream Profiles," *Los Angeles Business Journal*, August 18, 2008, http://www.allbusiness.com/entertainment-arts/broadcasting-industry/11581040–1.html (accessed April 1, 2009).

22. Ibid.

23. "Joanna Angel's 'I Am Legend' Cameo," December 20, 2007, http://hotmoviesforher.blogspot.com/2007/12/boys-over-at-hotmovies-blog-have.html (accessed June 3, 2008).

24. Johnson Reed, "Porn Stars Are the New Crossover Artists," *Los Angeles Times*, November 3, 2008, http://www.latimes.com/entertainment/news/la-et-porn3–2008nov03,0,6573308.story (accessed November 29, 2008).

25. "Kevin Smith Talks about *Zack and Miri Make a Porno*," XCritic.com, n.d., http://www.xcritic.com/columns/column.php?columnID=1200 (accessed April 24, 2009).

26. Tod Hunter, "Adam Sandler Prepping Porn-Themed Comedy," *XBIZ*, April 6, 2009, http://www.xbiz.com/news/106797 (accessed April 7, 2009).

27. Anne Winter, "Liberator Gear to Make Appearance in Adam Sandler Romantic Comedy," *XBIZ*, April 23, 2009, http://www.xbiz.com/news/107437 (accessed April 28, 2009).

28. Acme Andersson, "Adult Marketing to the Mainstream," *XBIZ*, April 27, 2009, http://www.xbiz.com/articles/107548 (accessed April 27, 2009).

29. Coopersmith, "Does Your Mother Know What You Really Do?" 13.

30. Free Speech Coalition, http://www.freespeechcoalition.com/FSCview.asp?coid=87 (accessed May 3, 2009).

31. Association of Sites Advocating Child Protection, http://www.asacp.org/page.php (accessed April 5, 2009).

32. Barely Legal, http://barelylegal.com/mansion1/gallery.php?s=4&p=1&w=396250&t=0&c=0&cs=1 (accessed April 6, 2009).

33. Jack Morrison, "The Distracted Porn Consumer: You Never Knew Your Online Customers So Well," *Adult Video News*, June 1, 2004, http://business.avn.com/articles/16315.html (accessed July 20, 2009).

34. Jack Morrison, "Best Marketing Practices," *Adult Video News*, March 1, 2003, http://business.avn.com/articles/16449.html (accessed July 9, 2006).

Four: Grooming for Gonzo

1. Robert Jensen, *Getting Off: Pornography and the End of Masculinity* (Boston: South End, 2007), 26.

2. James Gilligan, *Violence* (New York: Vintage, 1996), 237.

3. For an analysis of masculinity, see Michael Kimmel, *Guyland: The Perilous World Where Boys Become Men* (New York: Harper, 2008).

4. Henry J. Kaiser Foundation, http://www.kff.org/entmedia/upload/Key-Facts-TV-Violence.pdf, 2009 (accessed February 12, 2009).

5. Matt Ezzell, "Pornography, Lad Mags, Video Games and Boys: Reviving the Canary in the Cultural Coal Mine," in *The Sexualization of Childhood*, ed. Sharna Olfman (Westport, CT: Praeger, 2009), 21.

6. For a review of the research on media and violence, see Joanna Cantor, "The Psychological Effect of Media Violence on Children and Adolescents," 2002, http://yourmindonmedia.com/downloads/media_violence_paper.pdf (accessed April 6, 2009).

7. http://assplundering.com/tr/index.php (accessed November 1, 2009).

8. http://www.britishbukkakebabes.com (accessed May 10, 2007).

9. Adult DVD Talk, November 7, 2007, http://forum.adultdvdtalk.com/forum/topic.dlt/topic_id=110848/forum_id=1/cat_id=1/110848.htm (accessed April 7, 2009).

10. I am assuming that most of the contributors to the discussion group are men as they talk in a male voice, often making reference to how "hard" they are or how quickly they ejaculated. They also talk about what they would like to do to women in a way that suggests male subjectivity.

11. Sir Rodney, http://www.sirrodney.com/porn-review/West-Coast-Gang-Bangs.html#commentlist (accessed February 6, 2009).

12. Adult DVD Talk, November 7, 2007, http://forum.adultdvdtalk.com/forum/topic.dlt/topic_id=110848/forum_id=1/cat_id=1/110848.htm (accessed March 4, 2008).

13. Adult DVD Talk, November 8, 2007, http://forum.adultdvdtalk.com/forum/topic.dlt/whichpage=4/topic_id=110374/forum_id=1/cat_id=1/reply=1142120#post1142120 (accessed April 8, 2009).

14. Robert Jensen, "The Cruel Boredom of Pornography," *Last Exit*, September 24, 2008, http://uts.cc.utexas.edu/~rjensen/freelance/boredom.htm (accessed January 2, 2009).

15. Adult DVD Talk, n.d., http://forum.adultdvdtalk.com/forum/topic.dlt/whichpage=13/topic_id=108360/forum_id=1/cat_id=1/reply=1361794#post1361794 (accessed April 7, 2009).

16. A study conducted by the Centers for Disease Control and Prevention in 2002 found that 38.2 percent of men and 32.6 percent of women had engaged in anal sex at least once. "Sexual Behavior and Selected Health Measures: Men and Women 15–44 Years of Age, United States, 2002," http://www.cdc.gov/nchs/data/ad/ad362.pdf (accessed July 24, 2007).

17. Quoted in Jensen, *Getting Off*, 58.

18. Adult DVD Talk, May 8, 2004, http://forum.adultdvdtalk.com/forum/topic.dlt/topic_id=118429/forum_id=1/cat_id=1/reply=1264778#post1264778 (accessed April 7, 2009).

19. "Interview with Legendary Adult Director Max Hardcore," *Foundry Music*, July 20, 2005, http://www.foundrymusic.com/bands/displayinterview.cfm?id=130 (accessed February 18, 2009).

20. *Hardcore*, directed by Steven Walker (2001).

21. Adult DVD Talk, March 25, 2005, http://forum.adultdvdtalk.com/forum/topic.asp?topic_id=57083&forum_id=1&c (accessed March 8, 2009).

22. Ibid.

23. Doll Forum, http://www.dollforum.com/modules.php?name=Forums&file=viewtopic&t=19518&highlight=love (accessed April 23, 2009).

24. Real Doll, http://www.realdoll.com/cgi-bin/snav.rd.

25. Doll Forum, http://www.dollforum.com/ (accessed April 23, 2009).

26. Doll Forum, May 28, 2008, http://www.dollforum.com/modules.php?name=Forums&file=viewtopic&t=19337&highlight=porn (accessed April 24, 2009).

27. Doll Forum, June 10, 2008, http://www.dollforum.com/modules.php?name=Forums&file=viewtopic&t=19504&highlight=waiting (accessed April 24, 2009).

Five: Leaky Images

1. For a fuller discussion of how media images influence consumer behavior, see Jean Kilbourne, *Can't Buy My Love: How Advertising Changes the Way We Think and Feel* (New York: Free Press, 2000).

2. Michael Bader, "Is Pornography Really Harmful?" November 7, 2007, http://www.alternet.org/story/67144/ (accessed November 7, 2007).

3. Daniel Bernardi, "Interracial Joysticks: Pornography's Web of Racist Attractions," in *Pornography: Film and Culture*, ed. Peter Lehman (New Brunswick, NJ: Rutgers University Press, 2006), 221.

4. The idea that images don't simply change viewers' attitudes but rather consolidate their ideas of the world was first developed by George Gerbner and Larry Gross. For an overview of their work, see George Gerbner, Larry Gross, Michael Morgan, and Nancy Signorielli, "Growing Up with Television: The Cultivation Perspective," in *Media Effects: Advances in Theory and Research*, ed. J. Bryant and D. Zillman (Hillsdale, NJ: Erlbaum, 1994), 17–41.

5. Bernardi, "Interracial Joysticks," 240.

6. Psychologists who study the effects of porn conduct *laboratory*-based experiments that involve showing (mostly) men varying degrees and amounts of soft- to hard-core porn to see if there is any shift in the way they think about or behave toward women after being exposed to the images. Some studies expose men to just one porn movie, while others use "massive doses," often defined as less than an hour's exposure each week for six weeks: hardly "massive" given today's levels of use. What is surprising is that even this limited amount of exposure to porn yields consistent findings across a whole slew of studies conducted over three decades. In a review of seventeen studies in which men were shown "massive" amounts of porn, Dolf Zillman, a leading researcher in the field, found that prolonged consumption of pornography

- alters perceptions of sexuality; specifically, it fosters presumptions of popularity for less common sexual practices;
- breeds discontent with the physical appearance and the sexual performance of intimate partners;
- trivializes rape as a criminal offense and also trivializes sexual child abuse as a criminal offense; and
- promotes insensitivity toward victims of sexual violence and promotes men's beliefs that they would be capable of committing rape.

In addition, habitual male consumers of common pornography appear to be at greater risk of becoming sexually callous and sexually violent toward women than occasional users. Dolf Zillman, "Effects of Prolonged Consumption of Pornography," in *Pornography: Research Advances and Policy Considerations*, ed. Dolf Zillman and Jennings Bryant (Hillsdale, NJ: Erlbaum, 1989), 127–58.

7. Pamela Paul, in her book *Pornified*, interviewed men about their porn use and found that they reported desensitization and habituation to porn, boredom with their sex life and their sex partners, and a dependency on porn for both masturbation and staying aroused during sex. In addition, some admitted to pressuring women into doing sex acts that they were uncomfortable with. Pamela Paul, *Pornified: How Pornography Is Transforming Our Lives, Our Relationships, and Our Families* (New York: Time Books, 2005).

8. Stated by a male college student on *20/20*, January 29, 1993.

9. Simon Garfield, "Porn Addicts, Sex Offenders, Rapists, Paedophiles," *Observer*, November 23, 2008, http://www.guardian.co.uk/lifeandstyle/2008/nov/23/health-wellbeing-therapy-society (accessed November 25, 2008).

10. Wendy Maltz and Larry Maltz, *The Porn Trap: The Essential Guide to Overcoming Problems Caused by Pornography* (New York: HarperCollins, 2008), 4.

11. Therapists are finding that there are an increasing number of nonpedophile men who, through boredom and desensitization to adult pornography, are turning to child pornography. See Lou Michel and Dan Herbeck, "The Child Porn Pipeline: Confessions of a Child Porn Addict," *Buffalo News*, updated February 5, 2009, http://www.buffalonews.com/home/story/185614.html (accessed February 21, 2009).

12. Neil Malamuth, Tamara Addison, and Mary Koss, "Pornography and Sexual Aggression: Are There Reliable Effects and Can We Understand Them?" *Annual Review of Sex Research* 11 (2000): 45.

13. Frequent use is not an objective measure since participants were asked to rank their use on a four-point scale (never, seldom, somewhat frequently, and very frequently).

14. Malamuth, Addison, and Koss, "Pornography and Sexual Aggression," 81.

15. These rape myths are taken from the slide show *Who Wants to Be a Porn Star?* The show, written and produced by Gail Dines, Rebecca Whisnant, and Robert Jensen, can be watched at Stoppornculture.org.

16. http://porn.naughtyfiles.net/Reality/naughtybookworms.com/naughtybookworms-lystra (accessed June 8, 2006).

17. http://www.herfirstanalsex.com/anal-porn/?revid=14215 (accessed June 8, 2006).

18. http://porn.naughtyfiles.net/Teen/fasttimesatnau.com/jaclyn_case (accessed June 10, 2006).

19. http://www.hdcreampies.com (accessed June 10, 2006).

20. http://pluginfeeds.com/2.0/index.php?action=updates&product=1142 (accessed June 10, 2006).

Six: Visible or Invisible

1. Betty Friedan, *The Feminine Mystique* (New York: Dell, 1963).

2. Ariel Levy, *Female Chauvinist Pigs* (New York: Free Press, 2005), 32.

3. Angela McRobbie, "Young Women and Consumer Culture," *Cultural Studies* 22, no. 5 (2008): 543.

4. Jennifer Benjamin, "How *Cosmo* Changed the World," *Cosmopolitan*, September 2005, http://www.cosmopolitan.com/about/about-us_how-cosmo-changed-the-world (accessed July 7, 2008).

5. http://www.assocmags.co.za/images/pdfs/Cosmopolitan%20Rate%20Card.pdf (accessed June 6, 2008).

6. Ronnie Koenig, "Thrill Every Inch of Him," *Cosmopolitan*, June 2006, 150.

7. *Cosmopolitan*, http://www.cosmopolitan.com/sex-love/sex/420935 (accessed July 7, 2008).

8. "Cuddle Overkill," *Cosmopolitan*, June 2007, 137.

9. "You Had Sex—Now What?" *Cosmopolitan*, June 2007, 76.

10. Rosalind Gill, "Supersexualize Me! Advertising and the Midriff," in *Mainstreaming Sex: The Sexualization of Western Culture*, ed. Feona Attwood (London: I. B. Tauris, 2009), 106.

11. Ibid., 107.

12. Susan Bordo, *Unbearable Weight: Feminism, Western Culture and the Body* (Berkeley and Los Angeles: University of California Press, 1994).

13. Abra Fortune Chernik, "The Body Politic," in *Women, Images and Reality: A Multicultural Anthology*, 3rd ed., ed. Amy Kesselman, Lily D. McNair, and Nancy Schniedewind (New York: McGraw-Hill, 2003).

14. Neil Postman, *Consuming Images* (PBS Video, 1990).

15. For a fuller discussion of the role of peers in adolescent development, see L. M. Brown and C. Gilligan, *Meeting at the Crossroads: Women's Psychology and Girls' Development* (Cambridge, MA: Harvard University Press, 1992).

16. I would like to thank Meg Lovejoy for generously sharing her work and insights on hookup sex and for providing me with a list of resources.

17. Michael Kimmel, *Guyland: The Perilous World Where Boys Become Men* (New York: Harper, 2008), 195.

18. Kathleen Bogle, *Hooking Up: Sex, Dating and Relationships on Campus* (New York: New York University Press, 2008), 173.

19. Paula England and Reuben J. Thomas, "The Decline of the Date and the

Rise of the College Hook Up," in *Families in Transition*, 14th ed., ed. A. S. Skolnick and J. H. Skolnick (Boston: Allyn & Bacon, 2006).

20. Catherine M. Grello, Deborah P. Welsh, and Melinda S. Harper, "No Strings Attached: The Nature of Casual Sex in College Students," *Journal of Sex Research* 43, no. 3 (2006): 255; Elaine Eshbaugh and Gary Gute, "Hookups and Sexual Regret among College Women," *Journal of Social Psychology* 148, no. 1 (2008): 77–90.

21. Grello, Welsh, and Harper, "No Strings Attached."

22. W. Walter-Bailey and Jesse Goodman, "Exploring the Culture of Slut-hood among Adolescents," in *Contemporary Youth Culture: An International Encyclopedia* (Westport, CT: Greenwood, 2006), 282.

23. Ibid.

24. Marilyn Frye, "Oppression," in *Race, Class and Gender in the United States*, ed. Paula Rothenberg (New York: Worth, 2007), 55.

25. Bogle, *Hooking Up*, 110.

26. William Flack Jr., Kimberly A. Daubman, Marcia L. Caron, Jenica A. Asadorian, Nicole R. D'Aureli, Shannon N. Gigliotti, Anna T. Hall, Sarah Kiser, and Erin R. Stine, "Risk Factors and Consequences of Unwanted Sex among University Students: Hooking Up, Alcohol, and Stress Response," *Journal of Interpersonal Violence* 22 (2007): 139–57.

27. Kimmel, *Guyland*, 209.

28. Bogle, *Hooking Up*, 126.

29. Report of the APA Task Force on the Sexualization of Girls, Executive Summary, http://www.apa.org/pi/wpo/sexualization_report_summary.pdf, 2 (accessed February 5, 2009). The full study can be found at http://www.apa.org/pi/wpo/sexualization.html (accessed February 5, 2009).

30. Bogle, *Hooking Up*, 183.

Seven: Racy Sex, Sexy Racism

1. David Sullivan, "Jeff Mullen: *Long Dong Black Kong* 'Not Racist,'" *Adult Video News*, August 8, 2007, http://business.avn.com/articles/1699.html (accessed August 9, 2008).

2. *Adult Video News*, n.d., http://www.avnonline.com/index.php?Primary_Navigation=Editorial&Action=Print_Article&Content_ID=105809 (accessed December 20, 2005).

3. "Black Video: Forward or Back?" *Adult Video News*, June 1999, http://business.avn.com/articles/13323.html (accessed April 18, 2009).

4. Steven Andrew, "Mr. Marcus," *Adult Video News*, April 4, 2007, http://www.xbiz.com/articles/80453/Mr.+marcus (accessed April 10, 2008).

5. Asian Fever, http://asianfever.com/mansion1/index2.php?s=3&p=1&w=368290&t=0&c=0 (accessed March 23, 2007).

6. Me Fuck You Long Time, http://mefuckyoulongtime.com/tr/index.php (accessed March 23, 2007).

7. http://tour.asianstreethookers.com/ (accessed March 23, 2007).

8. *The Negro Family: The Case for National Action* (Washington, DC: U.S. Department of Labor, Office of Policy Planning and Research, 1965).

9. Lawrence Ross, *Money Shot: Wild Days and Lonely Nights inside the Black Porn Industry* (New York: Thunder's Mouth, 2007), 14.

10. Pimp My Black Teen, http://www.pimpmyblackteen.com/index.phtml?wm_login=warned&warned=y (accessed January 10, 2007).

11. Raw Black Amateurs, http://www.rawblackamateurs.com/ft=ae2171–68af3d38/index.html?cf=0&pp=1 (accessed March 12, 2008).

12. Ross, *Money Shot,* 100.

13. Patricia Hill Collins, *Black Sexual Politics* (New York: Routledge, 2007).

14. Ross, *Money Shot,* 99.

15. Cornel West, *Race Matters* (Boston: Beacon, 1992), 83.

16. Mireille Miller-Young, "Hip-Hop Honeys and Da Hustlaz: Black Sexualities in the New Hip-Hop Pornography," *Meridians: Feminism, Race, Transnationalism* 8, no. 1 (2008): 261–92.

17. Ibid., 270.

18. While the explicit nature of the hip-hop videos has helped to mainstream pornographic images through channels such as MTV and BET, what is even more powerful is the close financial relationship between hip-hop and porn. Increasingly, hip-hop artists are involved in making porn videos to go along with their music, using pornographic imagery and porn stars. According to writer P. Weasels: "Hip hop porn can be divided into two broad categories: porn-centric and music-centric.... In the porn-centric movies, there doesn't tend to be much in the way of new music or original beats; the porn takes center-stage. In the music video-style porn, the artist has taken some time to make new tunes for the film, and generally it will be marketed that way." (P. Weasels, "Porn 101: Hip Hop Porn Primer," *Game Link,* n.d., http://www.gamelink.com/news.jhtml?news_id=news_nt_primer_hip_hop_porn [accessed May 2, 2009]).

AVN's Frank Majors traces the beginning of this relationship back to the 1990s, with artists such as DJ Yella, a founding member of NWA, both directing and acting in porn. But, as Majors argues, the relationship between porn and hip-hop took off in 2001 when superstar rapper Snoop Dog joined with Hustler to make *Doggystyle.* This became the best-selling porn movie of the year and was followed by Snoop Dogg's *Hustlaz: Diary of a Pimp,* which also became a top seller. Following the Snoop videos, other hip-hop artists jumped on the band-wagon and aligned themselves with the porn industry. Majors points out that "soon the market was flooded with the artists such as Mystikal's *Liquid City* (Hustler), Too Short's *Get In Where You Fit In* (Adam and Eve), Lil' Jon & The East Sidaz's *Lil' Jon's American Sex Series* (Video Team), and Ice-T's *Pimpin' 101* (Pleasure Productions)." Frank Majors, "Strange Bedfellows: Rock 'n' Rap Storm Porn, But Where Can It Go From Here?" *Adult Video News*, May 2004, http://www.avn.com/video/articles/15844.htm (accessed January 7, 2009).

Ice-T is especially interesting since he is a one-time pimp turned actor and rapper. According to the director, Tony Diablo, Ice-T's hands-on knowledge of pimping helped to make *Pimpin' 101* more intense as "he broke down every sort of girl and he's sharing his own experiences." "Ice-T's *Pimpin' 101*," *Adult Video News*, n.d., http://www.adultvideonews.com/otset/otso103_02.html (accessed January 7, 2009). This is ironic given that Ice-T plays a caring and empathic police officer who deals with sex crimes against women on *Law and Order SVU*. As an unrepentant pimp and a producer of porn, Ice-T gets to construct an image of himself on television that is greatly at odds with his lived experience.

19. White Dicks in Black Chicks, http://www.whitedicksinblackchics.com/t1/?nats=NjM4Mjo3MjoyOA,0,0,0,0 (accessed March 24, 2009).

20. Ghetto Gaggers, http://www.ghettogaggers.com/tour1/page3.html?nats=MTI3NzoyOjEx,0,0,0,0 (accessed April 5, 2009).

21. Adult DVD Talk, March 19, 2008, http://forum.adultdvdtalk.com/forum/topic.dlt/topic_id=117363/forum_id=1/cat_id=1/reply=1258433#post1258433 (accessed January 5, 2009).

22. http://www.calstate.edu/pa/clips2003/november/3nov/porn.shtml, November 2, 2003 (accessed December 5, 2007).

23. Adult DVD Talk, January 11, 2006, http://forum.adultdvdtalk.com/forum/topic.dlt/whichpage=1/topic_id=74110/forum_id=1/cat_id=1/74110.htm (accessed January 5, 2009).

24. Sir Rodney, December 22, 2006, http://www.sirrodney.com/porn-review/Asian-Man.html (accessed January 5, 2007).

25. Sir Rodney, June 15, 2005, http://www.sirrodney.com/porn-review/Asian-Man.html (accessed January 5, 2007).

26. "Phuck FuMasters Launches, Partners with GigaCash," July 14, 2005, *XBIZ*, http://xbiz.com/news/9519 (accessed October 2006).

27. Oliver Wang, "Asian American Porn," February 2003, http://model

minority.com/modules.php?name=News&file=article&sid=397 (accessed January 5, 2009).

28. Ibid.

29. "Black Humor: The Marketing of Racial Stereotypes in Interracial Porn," *Adult Video News*, February 2009, http://www.mydigitalpublication.com/pub lication/?i=12069 (accessed March 3, 2009).

30. Ibid.

31. White Meat on Black Street, http://tour.whitemeatonblackstreet.com/aa/ index.php (accessed March 4, 2007).

32. Anonymous reviewer submission for "White Meat on Black Street," Sir Rodney, http://www.sirrodney.com/singlereview/White+Meat+On+Black+Stre et#readerreviews (accessed December 13, 2006).

33. Blacks on Blondes, http://blacksonblondes.iwantanewgirlfriend.com (accessed December 16, 2006).

34. For a description of the content of these movies, see Once You Go Black...You Never Go Back movie series, http://www.searchextreme.com/series/ Once_You_Go_Black..._You_Never_Go_Back/97899206841 (accessed December 28, 2006).

35. Gerald Butters, *Black Manhood on the Silent Screen* (Lawrence: University Press of Kansas, 2002), 10.

36. Mel Watkins interview excerpt, n.d., http://www.pbs.org/wgbh/amex/ foster/sfeature/sf_minstrelsy_5.html (accessed December 24, 2006).

Eight: Children

1. There are also gay porn sites with childified men, but for the purpose of this discussion, I am going to focus only on heterosexual pornography since gay pornography has its own distinct visual codes and conventions.

2. Although the female performers are eighteen and over, I am using the term "girls" to refer to them as they are represented as such by the pornographers. The PCP discussed in this article is only that which uses live human beings, rather than computer-generated images.

3. http://www.ultrateenlist.com (accessed December 18, 2007).

4. Internet Pornography Statistics, 2006, http://internet-filter-review.top tenreviews.com/internet-pornography-statistics.html (accessed March 14, 2007).

5. http://www.cbp.gov/hot-new/pressrel/2001/0516–00.htm (accessed February 13, 2008).

6. See especially Diana Russell and Natalie J. Purcell, "Exposure to Pornography as a Cause of Child Sexual Victimization," in *Handbook of Children, Culture and Violence*, ed. Nancy E. Dowd, Dorothy G. Singer, and Robin Fretwell Wilson (Thousand Oaks, CA: Sage, 2006), 59–82.

7. "A Typology of Online Child Pornography Offending," Australian Institute of Criminology, May 16, 2005, http://www.crime-research.org/articles/1236/2 (accessed January 10, 2008).

8. I have not found any PCP sites that include bestiality through the main porn portals, which is not surprising since this is still a taboo in mainstream Internet pornography.

9. Adult DVD Talk, September 11, 2007, http://forum.adultdvdtalk.com/forum/topic.dlt/topic_id=108072/forum_id=1/cat_id=1/108072.htm (accessed January 19, 2008).

10. http://soloteengirls.net/index9.php (accessed February 19, 2008).

11. http://soloteengirls.net/?agent_name=webmaster&account=5586&referer%5B%5D=http%3A%2F%2Fpretty-pussies.com%2FSait1%2Fmain.htm&agent_id=5586&agent_account=5586&idproduct=11 (accessed February 19, 2008).

12. http://www.defloration.tv/eng/hymen.htm (accessed December 17, 2007).

13. Kenneth Lanning, "Child Molesters: A Behavioral Analysis," September 2001, http://www.missingkids.com/en_US/publications/NC70.pdf (accessed December 17, 2007).

14. Ethel Quayle and Max Taylor, "Child Pornography and the Internet: Perpetuating a Cycle of Abuse," *Deviant Behavior* 23, no. 4 (2002): 340.

15. http://www.teendirtbags.com/t2/index.html?site=TDB&pid=1&revid=0&tour=2&popup=1&join=0&lang=en&ref_url=http%3A%2F%2Fwww.google.com%2Fsearch%3Fq%3Dteen%2Bdirt%2Bbags%26ie%3Dutf-8%26oe%3Dutf-8%26aq%3Dt%26rls%3Dorg.mozilla%3Aen-US%3Aofficial%26client%3Dfirefox-a&opt=&track=&a=&prog_id=1 (accessed February 21, 2008).

16. http://tryteens.com/main.php?ref=567&stream= (accessed February 21, 2008).

17. http://www.iameighteen.com/; http://assplundering.com/tr/index.php/?nats=beano33:psu30:ap,0,0,0,0 (accessed February 21, 2008).

18. http://www.teensforcash.com/s1/index.html?page=3&screen=tour&revid=13265&nopop=1 (accessed February 6, 2008).

19. http://youngdaughter.com (accessed February 21, 2008).

20. http://incestpaysites.info (accessed February 21, 2008).

21. http://www.ftwdaddy.com/?advId=4960 (accessed February 25, 2008).

22. http://www.daddyswhores.com/tour-2.php (accessed February 25, 2008).

23. Judith Herman, "Incestuous Fathers and Their Families," in *Feminist Frameworks: Alternative Theoretical Accounts of the Relations between Women and Men*, 3rd ed., ed. Alison Jaggar and Paula Rothenberg (Hightstown, NJ: McGraw-Hill, 1993), 401.

24. http://www.usemydaughter.com/t1/pps2=whaleven/tour1.htm (accessed February 25, 2008).

25. *Cherry Poppers*, vol. 10 (Los Angeles: Zane Productions, 1995).

26. Ibid.

27. http://incestpaysites.org (accessed February 25, 2008).

28. For a discussion of the possible role that Internet communities play in reinforcing illegal sexual behavior, see Keith Durkin, Craig J. Forsyth, and J. F. Quinn, "Pathological Internet Communities: A New Direction for Sexual Deviance Research in a Postmodern Era," *Sociological Spectrum* 26, no. 6 (2006): 595–606.

29. http://www.animatedincest.com/?advId=4775 (accessed February 25, 2008).

30. Quayle and Taylor, "Child Pornography and the Internet," 343.

31. Pamela Paul, *Pornified: How Pornography Is Transforming Our Lives, Our Relationships, and Our Families* (New York: Time Books, 2005).

32. Lou Michel and Dan Herbeck, "The Child Porn Pipeline: Confessions of a Child Porn Addict," *Buffalo News*, updated February 5, 2009, http://www.buffalonews.com/home/story/185614.html (accessed February 21, 2009).

33. Russell and Purcell, "Exposure to Pornography."

34. Ibid.

35. Quayle and Taylor, "Child Pornography and the Internet," 354.

36. Cited on the Web site of the Center for Missing and Exploited Children, http://www.missingkids.com/missingkids/servlet/PageServlet?LanguageCountry=en_US&PageId=150 (accessed March 3, 2008).

37. Julian Sher and Benedict Carey, "Debate on Child Pornography's Link to Molesting," July 19, 2007, http://www.nytimes.com/2007/07/19/us/19sex.html?_r=1&scp=1&sq=child%20pornography%20study&st=cse (accessed April 4, 2008).

38. Ibid.

39. For a discussion of the findings of over thirty years of studies on how

NOTES

190

media shapes the social construction of reality, see George Gerbner, "Cultivation Analysis: An Overview," *Mass Communication and Society* 1, no. 3 (1998): 175–94.

40. Mardia J. Bishop, "The Making of a Pre-pubescent Porn Star: Contemporary Fashion for Elementary School Girls," in *Pop Porn: Pornography in American Culture*, ed. Ann C. Hall and Mardia J. Bishop (Westport, CT: Praeger, 2007), 48.

television, 54–56; mainstreaming of, 47–58; marketing devices for, 49; and media technologies, 48–49; and *Penthouse*, xvii, 1–2, 12–15, 20–23, 49, 95; and pirated or free material on Internet, xvii; and *Playboy*, xvii, xviii, xxix, 1–23, 49, 95; pornographic magazines before *Playboy*, 1, 6; and psychology of consumer behavior, 57–58; public relations for, 53–54; racism of, xxx, 88, 121–40; revenue from, 47, 48, 51, 52; and self-regulation, 56; socially responsible image for, 56–57; statistics on, 47, 48, 51; and video game industry, 49–50; women producers in, xxii. *See also* mainstreaming of porn

pornographic magazines. See *specific magazines*

porn performers: African Americans men as, 67, 122, 133, 135–40; African American women as, xv–xvi, 42, 121, 123–24, 126–30; Arab women as, 131; Asian men as, 131–35; Asian women as, 124–26, 131, 134; awards for, 35, 37; body appearance of, 91, 123; dehumanization of, 63–75; Sasha Grey as, ix, 40–41, 54; Max Hardcore as, 45, 70–75, 99, 157–58; *Hardcore* documentary on, 72; injury and disease risks to, xxvii–xxviii, 35, 38; Jenna Jameson as, ix, 21, 34–40, 123; Latina women as, 131; mainstreaming of, 25, 34–41, 54–55; male fantasy of,

as highly sexual and loving rough sex, 35, 37–38, 63–68, 125; men's difficulty separating girlfriends from, 91–92; of pseudo-child porn (PCP), 147–48, 150–51; recruitment of, 40; salary of, 126; Howard Stern's interviews with, 39, 45, 52, 71, 123; treatment of female performers, 38–39; of Vivid Entertainment, 41–42; women of color as, xv–xvi, 42, 88, 121–31

porn sex: ass-to-mouth sex, xix, 68–69; in black porn, 126–30; boring and predictable nature of, 68–75; "cum swapping" in, xxvi; dehumanization of women in, 63–75; and desensitization to women's pain, 63, 74–75, 93–94, 159–60; and destruction of intimacy, xviii–xxiii, 68; examples of, xviii–xxi; hookup sex as, 114–19; impact of, on female sexuality, xii–xiii, xxx, 67–68, 91–92, 99–119; impact of, on male sexuality, xi–xii, xiii, xvii–xviii, xxii–xxiii, xxix–xxx, 67–68, 74–98; and interracial porn, 122, 129–30, 135–40; and male power, xxv–xxix; "money shot" in, xxvi–xxvii, 59, 67; multiple penetrations in, xviii, xxv–xxviii, 65–66, 137; and negative, dehumanizing terms referring to women, xxii, xxiv, 64, 75, 121; physical and verbal abuse of female performers in, xxii, xxiv, 64; and puke scenes, xviii, xix, 71, 74, 130; racist stereotypes of, xxx, 88, 121–40; research on content